Basketball

FOR

DUMMIES®

3RD EDITION

Basketball
FOR
DUMMIES®
3RD EDITION

by Richard "Digger" Phelps with John Walters and Tim Bourret

WILEY

John Wiley & Sons, Inc.

Basketball For Dummies®, 3rd Edition

Published by
John Wiley & Sons, Inc.
111 River St.
Hoboken, NJ 07030-5774
www.wiley.com

Copyright © 2011 by John Wiley & Sons, Inc., Hoboken, New Jersey

Published by John Wiley & Sons, Inc., Hoboken, New Jersey

Published simultaneously in Canada

For general information on our other products and services, please contact our Customer Care Department within the U.S. at 877-762-2974, outside the U.S. at 317-572-3993, or fax 317-572-4002.

For technical support, please visit www.wiley.com/techsupport.

Wiley also publishes its books in a variety of electronic formats and by print-on-demand. Some content that appears in standard print versions of this book may not be available in other formats. For more information about Wiley products, visit us at www.wiley.com.

Library of Congress Control Number: 2011936923

ISBN 978-1-118-07374-2 (pbk); ISBN 978-1-118-09267-5 (ebk); ISBN 978-1-118-09268-2 (ebk); ISBN 978-1-118-09270-5 (ebk)

Manufactured in the United States of America

10 9 8 7 6 5 4 3 2 1

WILEY

About the Authors

Richard "Digger" Phelps is the renowned basketball coach from Notre Dame, where he won more games than any coach in the school's history. He led Notre Dame to 14 NCAA Tournament appearances, including the school's only Final Four appearance in 1978. He also coached one year at Fordham where he guided the program to a 26-3 record and NCAA appearance in 1970-71. He is still the co-holder of the NCAA record for victories over number one teams with seven. Since 1994 he has been a college basketball analyst for ESPN.

John Walters is a writer at *The Daily,* an iPad-only national publication. He was a reporter and staff writer at *Sports Illustrated* for 14 years and won two Sports Emmys for his work at NBC Sports at both the 2004 and 2008 Summer Olympics. He was nominated for a Sports Emmy in 2006 for his work on "Olympic Ice" at the 2006 Winter Olympics. He is the author of, besides this book, *The Same River Twice* and *Notre Dame Golden Moments.*

Special contributor **Tim Bourret** is the Sports Information Director at Clemson University in South Carolina. In 33 years at the school he has edited over 100 publications that have won national and regional awards, including 15 that deal with basketball. He is also the color commentator on the Clemson Basketball Radio Network. Bourret, a Double Domer (1977 and '78), has followed Digger Phelps's career since 1974, when he was one of the 11,000 Notre Dame fans who stormed the court after the Fighting Irish ended UCLA's 88-game winning streak.

Dedication

To those who have been a part of my basketball life.

—Richard "Digger" Phelps

To my mom and dad who taught me to love sports for all the right reasons.

—Tim Bourret

Thanks to Tim B. and the staff at Starbucks and Cosi for the free WiFi.

—John Walters

Authors' Acknowledgments

From Digger Phelps: To John Walters, Tim Bourret, and Rose Pietrzak, the writing team, as well as Team Wiley, for all your efforts to make this book become a reality. This book is all about teams and how they work together, and our South Bend-Chicago-Indianapolis team proved that the team concept really works!

From John Walters: Thanks to my managing editor Bill Colson, senior editor Dick Friedman, and the rest of the editors at Sports Illustrated for their patience. Also, to the indefatigable Sports Illustrated Library staff, especially Linda Wachtel. To Ted Lovick, the best basketball coach that I ever played for. To my parents, William and Phyllis, the former of whom never backed down from a game of one-on-one. And to my brother, George: You'll beat me one of these days.

From Tim Bourret: To my proofreading parents, Chuck and Irene Bourret. To my good friend (Saint) Rose Pietrzak, who transcribed endless conversations between myself and Digger. Rose is now an expert on Notre Dame basketball of the 1970s and 1980s. To Bob Bradley, my Clemson mentor, who provided many an interesting college basketball anecdote from his over 40 years in college athletics. To Larry Shyatt, Dan Ahearn, Rick Barnes, Dennis Felton, Craig Miller, Steve Nelson, Reno Wilson, and Todd Wright for providing input for various chapters of this book. To Matt Cashore and Bob Waldrop for taking the photos in this book, and Merl Code, Gene Brtalik, R. C. Deer, Justin Dunn, Mike Empey, Chris Hogan, Ben Murphy, Willie MacKey, Stephen Tessier, and Gabe Thompson for being in the photos. To Mike Danch, Mike Enright, and John Heisler for helping to set up the photo shoot at Notre Dame. And to my army of assistants in the Clemson Sports Information Office who spent "off hours" typing and researching: Brett Berg, Sam Blackman, Marsha Byers, Adair Clairy, Brian Hennessey, Jeff Martin, Meredith Merritt, Amy Moore, Will Peeler, Brenda Rabon, Emily Rabon, Brett Sowell, Preston Greene, Philip Sikes, and Heath Bradley.

Publisher's Acknowledgments

We're proud of this book; please send us your comments at http://dummies.custhelp.com. For other comments, please contact our Customer Care Department within the U.S. at 877-762-2974, outside the U.S. at 317-572-3993, or fax 317-572-4002.

Some of the people who helped bring this book to market include the following:

Acquisitions, Editorial, and Media Development

Project Editor: Susan Hobbs

Acquisitions Editor: Lindsay Lefevere

Copy Editor: Susan Hobbs

Assistant Editor: David Lutton

Editorial Program Coordinator: Joe Niesen

Technical Editor: KC Johnson

Editorial Manager: Carmen Krikorian

Editorial Assistant: Rachelle Amick

Art Coordinator: Alicia B. South

Cover Photos: © iStockphoto.com / Mark Herreid

Cartoons: Rich Tennant (www.the5thwave.com)

Composition Services

Project Coordinator: Katherine Crocker

Layout and Graphics: Carl Byers, Shawn Frazier, Joyce Haughey, Lavonne Roberts, Corrie Socolovitch

Proofreader: Nancy Rapoport

Indexer: BIM Indexing & Proofreading Services

Publishing and Editorial for Consumer Dummies

> **Kathleen Nebenhaus,** Vice President and Executive Publisher

> **Kristin Ferguson-Wagstaffe,** Product Development Director

> **Ensley Eikenburg,** Associate Publisher, Travel

> **Kelly Regan,** Editorial Director, Travel

Publishing for Technology Dummies

> **Andy Cummings,** Vice President and Publisher

Composition Services

> **Debbie Stailey,** Director of Composition Services

Contents at a Glance

Table of Contents

Prologue

Digger the Player, to Digger the Coach, to Digger the Fan

· ·

I played college basketball at Rider College in New Jersey. (My roommate was Nick Valvano, brother of the late, widely loved coach of North Carolina State, Jimmy Valvano.) When I graduated in 1963, I had no intention of pursuing the sport any further than recreationally. I had planned to enter the Simmons School of Embalming that summer, because that was the family business (hence my nickname). But I was born to coach the American game. Heck, I was even born on the 4th of July in 1941.

At the time, Tom Winterbottom was a high school coach in Beacon, New York. The previous winter, Tom had taken Beacon High to a 20–0 record, and now he wanted to start a summer league. He knew that I had played for Rider, and he asked me to coach one of his teams. Thus my career in embalming was forever sidetracked.

The Early Years

Obviously, that summer changed my life: I returned to Rider for graduate school and volunteered as an assistant coach. (Today, those positions are more coveted on college campuses than iPads and smartphones.) I knew that I would need a master's degree in education as an entree into coaching.

As a graduate assistant coach at Rider that first year, my job was to scout upcoming opponents. The New York University Violets were a hoops power at the time and an away game for us that season. NYU had not lost a home game since 1938. Perhaps because he sensed that our plight was hopeless, Bob Greenwood, the Rider head coach, allowed me to devise a game plan.

We won 66–63. I thought to myself: I can do this.

I got my start as a head coach, as most people do, at the bottom. St. Gabriel's High School in Hazleton, Pennsylvania, took a chance on me in 1964. The team was winless the year before. In my second year as head coach, however, we won the Class C state title.

Shortly before that season began, one day late in October, I sat down and wrote a presumptuous letter, the type of letter that only a 23-year-old with outlandish dreams can write. Seldom, if ever, do these dreams come true. On that day, I wrote a letter to Ara Parseghian, the head *football* coach at the University of Notre Dame in South Bend, Indiana. In the letter, I explained that my big dream was to coach at Notre Dame. (I assume Ara realized that I was not after *his* job.) Then I affixed my 5-cent postage to the envelope and spent the next six years pursuing that dream.

In those days, I had tunnel vision: I applied for ten assistant coaching jobs at the college level and was turned down ten times. I even wrote a letter to Dean Smith, the head coach at the University of North Carolina. He replied that he was going to hire one of his former players — a guy named Larry Brown. All Larry did was take two different schools — UCLA and Kansas — to the NCAA (National Collegiate Athletic Association) title game in the 1980s, winning once. Today, he coaches the Philadelphia 76ers. Obviously, Dean had no eye for talent.

In 1966, I landed a position as the freshman coach at the University of Pennsylvania, an Ivy League school. One of my duties was to recruit, and I found that a few players did not know the difference between Penn and Penn State, the football powerhouse. "Are you going to a bowl?" they'd ask. Who was I to tell them no?

For two years, we were horrible. In Philadelphia, there are five area Division I colleges — LaSalle, Penn, St. Joe's, Temple, and Villanova — who form an unofficial league known as the Big Five. One night, I noticed a sign hanging in our gym, the Palestra, that read, "The Big Four and Penn."

But I managed to develop as a recruiter. ("Of course we're going to a bowl!") In my third season, the freshman team went undefeated. It was time to move on.

The next stop, in 1970, was Fordham, which is located in the Bronx. We were a small team that pressed and ran and kept the heat on for 40 minutes. At a time when New York City was all abuzz with the Miracle Mets, Joe Namath of the Jets, and the Knicks — a hat trick of pro sports championships within a 16-month period — we took our own bite out of the Big Apple by going 26–3. The highlight of the season was when our little Catholic school from the Bronx stole into Madison Square Garden and defeated mighty Notre Dame. Three weeks earlier, the Fighting Irish had handed eventual national champion UCLA their only loss of the season.

Little did I know at the time that I would be coaching Notre Dame the next season.

Tunnel Vision: Notre Dame

In 1968, I was in Illinois recruiting for Penn when I decided to drive over the state line into Indiana and see Notre Dame for myself. Notre Dame, especially for a Catholic kid raised on its football games via the radio, never seemed to be bound by such a trivial thing as geography. Notre Dame had always seemed to exist more so in my mind, sort of like Oz.

Even though basketball is my passion, when I arrived at Notre Dame that day, I proceeded directly to the football stadium. As I entered the stadium tunnel, with the light from the field gleaming in, I started to cry. This was where I wanted to be.

I understand that many a cynic is eager to dismiss the aura of the school, but I never have questioned the effect that it had on me. Besides, Notre Dame had just built a new basketball arena — the Athletic & Convocation Center (ACC) — and Austin Carr was the National Player of the Year. And, as anyone who ever survived a winter in South Bend will tell you, students need someone to cheer for in January and February, when football begins its hibernation.

To this day, the serendipity of my twenties boggles my mind. I wrote a letter to Ara Parseghian when I was 23, and six years later, my dream came to pass. As Bob Costas once said regarding his own meteoric rise to the top, "I would have been happy to pay my dues, but nobody ever made me."

Building a Program

You don't get tougher by picking fights with your little brother; you toughen up by taking on your *big* brother. (Although it helps if you and your little brother team up against big bro, but now I'm in the realm of child psychology.) So when I arrived at Notre Dame, I resolved to build one of the nation's premier basketball programs. To do so, I believed that we needed to challenge the best.

At that time, the best was spelled U-C-L-A.

We scheduled a home-and-home series with the Bruins so that each year we played them twice (once at Notre Dame, once at UCLA). I'll not deny that Notre Dame's football reputation allowed us to make such a series attractive to UCLA. Besides, I knew that John Wooden, UCLA's coach, grew up in South Bend and would look forward to an annual homecoming. Finally, it never hurt recruiting to have a game in sunny LA on the schedule.

A rivalry blossomed between Wooden, the game's reserved elder statesman, and myself. This rivalry was good for the game and definitely good for our program. The first year (1971) we played UCLA, the Bruins beat us by 58 points. Wooden still had his defense pressing us with four minutes remaining. During the 1973 season, UCLA entered the ACC with an NCAA-record 88-game winning streak. We ended it. That one game did more for our program than any 20-win season could have.

Digger the Fan

After more than 20 years in coaching, I am now simply a fan of basketball. When I left Notre Dame in 1991, I figured that basketball was behind me. I went to work for then-President George Bush, helping to apprise him on issues such as drugs and education in inner cities. Had Bush been reelected the following November, I thought that I might possibly become the Drug Czar. From Notre Dame to the White House. Some alums of that school would consider this a demotion.

My first year away from the game, I doubted that I would become a big fan. I've always enjoyed other interests, such as painting, and believed that I'd devote myself to these pursuits. But then, even in my coaching days, I had moonlighted as a broadcaster. Back in December 1973, UCLA faced Indiana in a dream matchup. I was given the opportunity to be a part of the broadcast. (Of course, Notre Dame was not playing that day.)

Ten years after that game, I shared the microphone with Marv Albert for the National Invitational Tournament (NIT) in New York. Tulsa was playing Syracuse, and I made an innocent observation — which was true, I might add — that probably caused a few beer cans to be tossed at TV sets back in Oklahoma. The game was a tight one. In the final moments, a Tulsa player went to the free throw line to shoot a one-and-one. In a *one-and-one* situation, the player must make the first free throw in order to attempt a second. If the player misses the first shot, the ball is in play. Noting that the Tulsa player's body language suggested a lack of confidence, I said, "He's not going to make the shot." And he didn't. Tulsa fans thought that I was rooting for Syracuse. I wasn't.

In April 1994, Jimmy Valvano, the charismatic former North Carolina State coach who won the 1983 NCAA title and who later worked as an ESPN commentator, died of cancer. I knew Jimmy very well and, like all basketball fans, was saddened by his loss. After Valvano died, ESPN offered me the position that he had held. I've had the job ever since, and I love it. It's a college hoops fan's paradise.

Introduction

As I write this, a German native (Dirk Nowitzki) recently was named Most Valuable Player of the NBA Finals and a Chinese native (Yao Ming) just made news with his retirement from the NBA. Basketball has never been so popular all over the globe,

Basketball is the most popular participatory sport in the United States (more popular even than Angry Birds), too. I've got the numbers and stuff to prove that, but I'll spare you the boring figures. Trust me; you're in with the popular crowd. So, welcome to the third edition of *Basketball For Dummies*. I'm glad to have you on board.

I'm biased, of course, but I believe that basketball is the best sport ever invented. It combines physical prowess, intelligence, grace, and coordination. Although more than 46 million Americans play basketball (okay, so I won't spare you the boring figures), the game is flexible enough to enable each player to develop his or her own style.

I've devoted my entire adult life to basketball. As simple as the game often seems — throw the ball through the hoop — I discover uncharted nuances of the sport each day. I've learned a lot since I first decided to abandon my chosen career path as a mortician (seriously!) to pursue my real love. I'm only too happy to share what I know with you.

Foolish Assumptions

You notice that in basketball, the basket is the same height (10 feet above the ground) for everybody — young and old, tall and short, male and female. I want this book to be that 10-foot basket. No matter who you are and how much or how little you know about the game, this book should provide the information you are looking for.

I am a coach. For more than a quarter of a century, I pursued that career at Catholic schools, so I'm used to preaching to the choir. And isn't that what any author of *Basketball For Dummies* would be doing? The game is more popular than oxygen, or so it seems. But you bought this book for a reason, right?

Maybe you have an unquenchable thirst to find out more about the game. Or you know all there is to know about playing the game, but none of the history. Or vice versa. Perhaps you are completely unfamiliar with basketball and are curious as to what all the fuss is about. Or you want to improve your own game. No matter what you are craving, this book should satisfy.

How to Use This Book

Well, of course, if I were you I would read it. The paper is entirely too small for you to use it to, say, wrap fish in. I mean, if I caught a fish that small, I'd toss it back. Read the book the way you might read *People* magazine's "Most Beautiful People" issue: Pick your favorite spots. There's no need to read the chapters in numerical order.

It might not hurt to have a basketball and a basketball hoop nearby while you're reading. You may happen upon the chapter that talks about shooting and want to put some of my advice to use right away. Go ahead; put the book down and head for the basket. The whole idea of this book is to get you better acquainted with the game, anyway. Feel free to stop and shoot! You won't hurt my feelings.

How This Book Is Organized

This book is divided into sections called, cleverly enough, parts. Here's what you can find in each part.

Part I: Basketball 101

If you have no idea what's going on when you see the players running up and down the court bouncing that round orange thing, this part is a good place to start. First I take some time to explain why basketball is the greatest game on earth (as if I need to tell you that!), and then I talk about what you need to play the game. Chapters 3 and 4 talk about the all-important rules of basketball and explain how to keep and interpret the statistics.

Part II: The Fundamentals of Basketball

Now comes the fun part: picking up a ball and playing the game yourself! The chapters in this part take you through the techniques of shooting, playing offense, playing defense, and rebounding. Chapter 9 talks about setting up special plays and strategies for specific situations.

Part III: The Game

Basketball exists and entertains at all levels: from the playgrounds to the largest arenas. This part talks about understanding every level of the game: high school, college, professional, and international. In Chapter 10, I give you a prompter and the lingo and culture of pickup basketball, from the driveway to the playground to the neighborhood gym. In Chapter 12, I discuss my area of expertise, the college game.

Part IV: And You Don't Have to Pick Up a Ball

Yogi Berra once said, "You can observe a lot by just watching." Even if you don't lace up your sneakers and make those indelible squeaking noises on a hardwood court — the inimitable sound of basketball being played — you can still enjoy the game. In this section I teach you how to watch a game and also how to still be in the running to win your office NCAA tournament pool after the opening weekend.

Part V: The Part of Tens

If you have only a few moments to spare (maybe you're between halves of a game), this is the part for you. Here you can find lists of history-making basketball games and the NBA's all-time best players.

Part VI: Appendixes

At the end of the book, you can find two quick appendixes: a glossary of basketball terms both serious and fun, and a list of drills to use when coaching a kids' team.

Icons Used in This Book

Are you tired of struggling to figure out what Dickie V. and all the other hoops broadcasters are talking about? This icon demystifies those bizarre languages of basketball-speak and sportscaster-ese.

The record books of basketball are full of fascinating stories and fantastic players. This icon points to true stories of basketball stars past and present.

What can I say? Coaches are never at a loss for words. When you see this icon, you can look forward to an anecdote from my coaching career or my opinion on a controversial basketball issue.

This icon steers you toward helpful advice for players of the game.

With 25 years of coaching under my belt, I have plenty of advice for coaches, too. This icon helps you find those words of wisdom.

Watching hoops in person or on TV is much more enjoyable when you know a little bit about what's going on. This icon highlights information that can help you become a more educated viewer of the game.

This icon points out important techniques and truisms that you shouldn't forget.

Where to Go from Here

If you're just getting started in basketball — as a player, as a coach, or as a fan — you may want to start at the beginning of the book to find out about how the game is played. If you're an experienced hoopster, you may want to jump into Part II to work on your fundamentals and pick up a few new tricks, too. Fans may want to head to Part III and Part IV. Coaches, head over to Appendix B.

In this book, I give you timeless information that can help you build a solid foundation of basketball knowledge. If you're interested in finding out more about what's going on in basketball *right now* — whether you're watching the first games of the NCAA season, following March Madness, or watching the NBA or WNBA playoffs — check out the Dummies website, which you can find at www.dummies.com. Click the Sports and Outdoors link at the top right; then click Basketball in the list on the left.

Part I
Basketball 101

In this part . . .

This part gives you an overview of basketball basics. I tell you how the game originated and why basketball is such a great sport — whether you're a player, a coach, or a fan.

Here, you can find out what you need to wear whether you play in your driveway or for the WNBA. You can't play without proper equipment, either, so I give you the scoop on balls, backboards, rims, and nets. I provide some hints on great places to play ball, from a local church parking lot to a playground.

Of course, you can't really play basketball unless you know how. This part answers all your questions about the different elements of the court, rules of the game, fouls, and violations. Finally, I provide a straightforward explanation of the statistics of the game — points scored, assists, rebounds, turnovers, and so on — to help you determine which team outplays another.

Chapter 1

Bare-Bones Basketball

* * *

In This Chapter

▶ Man-eating sharks! (Okay, not really)

▶ This game's for everyone

▶ Whether to play, coach, or cheer?

* * *

*O*utside of death, basketball may be the most non-discriminating exercise known to humanity. The Chicago Bulls team that won an NBA-record 72 games during the 1995–96 season featured among its top six players three black athletes and three white athletes from three different continents: Australia, Europe, and North America.

Twenty-eight of the 30 NBA teams in 2010–11 had at least one foreign-born player, led by the Toronto Raptors with six. Eighty-four of the 436 NBA players on opening day rosters were foreign born, including 59 who never played college basketball in the United States.

What other sport is this accessible? You can always play basketball. You can play indoors or outdoors. By yourself or with a friend (or a few). Half-court or full-court. Winter, spring, summer, or fall.

You need a basket. And a ball. (You're beginning to understand the etymology here, eh?) But that's all you need. No mitt, racquet, shoulder pads, or five-iron required. No ice, no pitcher's mound, and no tee time.

We're Having a Ball

Basketball is an American game — invented by a Canadian (Dr. James Naismith) — that has gained worldwide popularity. Sort of like Levi's. Or *The X-Files*. Why? Because basketball, also known as *hoops, roundball,* and so on, is fun to watch, play, and even — unlike most other sports — practice. When was the last time you witnessed a football offensive lineman working on his blocking technique in the park?

Male-female bonding

Steve Alford, the former All-American guard who led the Indiana University Hoosiers to the 1987 National Collegiate Athletic Association (NCAA) championship, used to love shooting baskets by himself. For hours upon hours, during summer vacations and on weekends, Alford practiced his outside shot. Eventually, Alford's girlfriend, Tanya Frost, realized that if she wanted to spend some quality time with her beau, she'd have to visit the gym.

Frost was the ideal partner for Alford at these shooting sessions. She rebounded for him, and on those occasions when he "hung the net" (meaning that his shot had swished through so cleanly that the bottom of the net had lapped up and become entangled in the rim), as deft shooters often do, Frost located a stepladder and untangled it for Alford. In basketball-mad Indiana, Frost was nothing less than a dream girl.

Alford, now the head coach at the University of New Mexico, realized this. One afternoon in the summer of 1986, he arrived at the gym early and hung the net. When Frost appeared, Alford behaved as if he had just hung the net moments earlier. Without a word, she grabbed a ladder and began climbing — and then noticed a tiny box perched on the back of the rim.

Inside the box? An engagement ring. (She said yes.) Twenty-five years later they have three children and are enjoying life in Albuquerque.

You can practice alone: just you, the ball, and the basket. Or you can grab a friend. Shooting hoops is one of the most fail-safe means of bonding (male or female) around — see the sidebar titled "Male-female bonding" if you don't believe me. Nothing beats just standing around a basket with a pal, shooting the ball and the breeze, and getting to know one another better as you work on your jump shot. Such scenes often appear on the hit television show *ER*: A back-alley basketball hoop sits just outside the emergency room — not more than a bounce pass away from the defibrillators and operating tables.

The game evolves like so: You shoot alone long enough, and eventually someone ambles over and asks if she can shoot with you. You say yes — having someone rebound your misses saves energy. Competitive juices soon begin to flow, and the two of you find yourselves playing one-on-one. The game attracts a crowd, and now you have enough players (ideally six) to stage a half-court contest, in which both teams shoot at one basket. Such spirited action attracts more interest, and now you have a bona fide full-court, two-basket game. Just add uniforms, referees, 18,000-seat arenas, and two dozen 7-foot centers and — voilà! — you have the National Basketball Association (NBA).

The Object of the Game, Simplified

Basketball is a simple game, although not everyone may see it that way. At an interview session with the United States' Dream Team II before the 1996 Olympics, a Finnish journalist timidly approached NBA forward Karl Malone and said, "Excuse me, I'm not very familiar with this game. Why do you get *two* points for a basket?"

Malone laughed, but the question was a good one. I answer that and similar questions — like, what's that white square on the backboard for? — later, in Chapter 3. For now, I can tell you the simple object of the game: *to put the ball in your basket and try to prevent your opponents from putting the ball in theirs.*

Digger's Ten Reasons to Like Basketball

Like basketball? Maybe I should say love. This section lists a few reasons why I love this game — and why I think you should, too.

Basketball is ballet

The 94-x-50-foot stage (or 91'10" x 49'2.6" in international basketball) holds ten performers (the players), two maestros (the coaches) and three judges (officials). Seeing the grace and finesse of the performers reminds me of watching the ballet Swan Lake. The performers run, leap, and even pirouette in the air to perform a dunk. Take a look at Figure 1-1; Kobe, Carl, Lamar, and Shane are like poetry in motion! And while he is no Mikhail Baryshnikov, Nate Robinson showed some artistic ability when the 5'9" guard won the 2010 NBA Slam Dunk Championship, his third win at the event in four years. The NBA's clever marketing arm often sets promotional highlights to classical pieces of music.

Basketball is a simple game

As I said earlier in this chapter: Put the ball in the basket. Keep your opponent from doing the same. Do I need to review?

Okay, coaches can make the game sound complicated. You may hear nonsense like, "Double down on the center in the low post after he puts the ball on the floor, and watch the skip pass to the three man beyond the arc." But making baskets and keeping your opponent from scoring is the gist of it.

Figure 1-1: Like poetry in motion, Kobe Bryant (#24) and Lamar Odom (#7) of the Los Angeles Lakers reach for a loose ball against Carl Landry (#14) and Shane Battier (#31) of the Houston Rockets in Game One of the 2009 Western Conference Semifinals.

Basketball requires very little equipment

What are you wearing right now? Chances are you can play basketball in it. Shorts, a shirt, and sneakers make up the only outfit you need to play the game. And if you're playing a pickup game (see Chapter 12), one side is probably skins anyway, so if you're a man (or a very adventurous woman) you may not even need the shirt. True, you wear less in surfing, but then not everyone lives near an ocean or owns a board.

Not everyone owns a basket, either, but you can find a court in practically every gym or playground. If you can't find a court, you can improvise by using a milk crate with the bottom punched out, which is basically what founder James Naismith used. If a peach basket was good enough for him, it's good enough for anyone.

You don't even need a net to play hoops; you can get by with just the rim and a backboard. Many an outdoor court at a school or playground is net-free, which is a shame. If I were elected president, one of my first initiatives would be "No rims without nets." Every good shooter lives for the satisfying swish of a net.

You don't need anyone else to play

One of my neighbors in South Bend, Indiana, has had a hoop over his garage for 20 years. Just about every weekend or after school, kids shoot jump shots in the family driveway.

You can play basketball by yourself, like my neighbor, or you can play the game with any number of players. If you have an even number, divide by two and play a half-court or full-court game, depending on the number. (If you're in good shape, four-on-four makes for a good full-court run.) If you have 15 people, split up into three five-person teams and play a revolving format, with the loser going out each game. If you have 637 people, I'd suggest ordering out for a couple hundred pizzas instead.

You're watching people, not uniforms

Whether you attend a game in person or view one on TV, basketball is intimate theater. You can see the faces of the players because no caps or helmets hide them. Plus, the dimensions of the court allow less distance between the fan and the athlete. As a result, you experience the emotion up close. You see the players' emotions when they go up for a rebound or dive after a loose ball. By the time you're done watching a game, you feel as if you've glimpsed the character of at least a few players.

One of the reasons that NBA stars Kobe Bryant and LeBron James are so marketable is that everyone can see their expressions on the court. James is well known for throwing powder into the air prior to the tip-off. (The powder supposedly gives him a better feel for the ball.) The powder reaches the nearby patrons within the first five rows of the stands. It is a ritual that fans in Cleveland . . . check that . . . Miami, look forward to prior to every game.

You're home by supper

You don't need all day to play hoops. You set your own time limit, by virtue of how many points you play to in a pickup game. If you have time to play to 21 baskets, do it. If the sun is going down, or if Mom said that you had to be home for dinner (tonight is lasagna night), shorten the game to 15 points. You still play the same game.

Watching hoops can be another story, however. College games usually take about two hours, and pro games last slightly longer. But coaches — and I was as guilty of this as anyone — milk the clock at all levels. Coaches seem to possess an endless reserve of time-outs at the end of a game. (Don't you hate that?) I tried to save all my time-outs for the end of the game to help set up the defense after a scored basket in case my team was behind. I'm sure that many of my cohorts can make the same argument. (If you were late for Saturday night mass or a date because of all those time-outs, I'm sorry.) Ironically, in the greatest comeback Notre Dame ever made (versus UCLA in 1974), we made up an 11-point deficit in the final 3 minutes and 22 seconds without taking a time-out. Hmm.

One rule that has been added since I last coached cuts down on hoarding time-outs for the end of a game. In 1993–94, a rule was added to the college game that stops the clock after a made basket inside the last minute of each half and the last minute of overtime. The clock does not restart until the ball is in-bounded.

The game flows

Basketball brings constant action. As an experiment, I invite you to videotape a baseball game, a basketball game, and a football game. Now break down each tape into the amount of minutes of live action, and divide this number by the total length of the game. You'll find that basketball is your best action-per-game deal around.

The momentum of hoops is one of its greatest entertainment assets. When a football player runs back a punt for a touchdown in the Super Bowl, the stadium is jumping. But by the time the extra point is kicked, the network goes to three minutes of commercials, and then the ball is kicked off . . . well, do you even remember how I began this sentence? Exactly my point.

Basketball, however, moves a lot faster. In the 2010 NCAA Championship game between Duke and Butler, Duke's Lance Thomas made an outside jumper off a sharp pass from Kyle Singler. Before Jim Nantz had a chance to describe the play to his CBS audience, Butler's Ronald Nored drove the length of the court for a layup. How can you top that?

Weather or not, you can play

Rain, sleet, or snow — it's not just the mail that will go. Your scheduled basketball game will go on because you can play inside.

A baseball game can be rained out. A football game can't, but at times, excessive heat or cold may make you wish that you'd taken up bowling instead.

Unlike baseball or football, you can play hoops just as easily indoors as outdoors. If on a beautiful summer day you want to hoop it up outside, you can bask in the sun. On a snowy New Year's Day, you can still play; just move the game indoors.

Basketball's all-season accessibility may explain why the college and pro seasons usually run from November to April or later, but Olympic teams and the WNBA play it in the summer.

NBA outdoor games

On October 12, 2008, the NBA held an outdoor exhibition game at the Indian Wells Tennis Garden in Indian Wells, California. The game featured the Phoenix Suns against the Denver Nuggets, the first outdoor NBA game of any kind since 1972, when an exhibition game involving the Milwaukee Bucks and all-time greats Kareem Abdul Jabbar and Oscar Robertson, played on a court placed on top of a baseball field in San Juan, Puerto Rico.

The conditions are always an issue when it comes to outdoor basketball, as it was this night in 2008. Temperatures dipped into the low 60s, and more important, there were 15 mph winds that affected shots in the second half.

The Nuggets made just 18-38 free throws and shot 36 percent from the field. The Suns shot just 31.6 percent from the field, as players were not used to taking the wind into account on their three-point shots. The two teams combined to make just 3-27 three-pointers.

The 2008 experience did not damper the NBA's enthusiasm, and they have continued to play one outdoor exhibition game each year during the exhibition season in this same facility. The last two years, the weather has cooperated. Both teams reached the century mark in the second meeting, which was played in 90-degree temperatures and no wind.

Don Nelson, the winningest coach in NBA history who has since retired, coached in the second indoor game for the Golden State Warriors against the Suns. Nelson once commented, "It's kind of fun to play outside. I didn't even think about it much, but once in a while I would look up and there was a big hole in the sky."

March Madness

Upsets. Cinderella stories. Miracle buzzer-beater shots. Sixty-eight teams, 67 games. Nothing in sports matches the 21-day spectacle that is the NCAA men's basketball tournament. The distaff version, which is staged at the same time and employs a 64-team single-elimination format, is gaining on the men's tournament in popularity. In both tourneys, everyone has a chance for an upset. Unlike the NBA playoffs, you have to be sharp every game, or it's *hasta la vista*.

Above all, the single-elimination format of the tournament makes everything so dramatic. During the second round of the 2010 NCAA Tournament in Oklahoma City, the number-one seed Kansas Jayhawks were riding high with a 33-2 record, including a sparkling 15-1 ledger in the competitive Big 12. But, they lost to upstart Northern Iowa, 69–67. It was a shocking two-point loss for Kansas, who many had selected to win the NCAA title.

Since 1977, 21 teams have entered the men's NCAA tournament with zero or one loss and not one of them has won it. Five times a team has entered with two losses and won the NCAA tournament since 1977. Go figure.

Only three times since 1983 (Duke in 1992, UCLA in 1995, and Duke in 2001) has the number-one ranked team entering the tourney gone on to win the NCAA title.

Fun for boys and girls everywhere

Although basketball is not the only team sport that offers men and women opportunities to play professionally (volleyball comes to mind), it is the most visible. The WNBA, the distaff version of the NBA, which began play in the summer of 1997, has 12 teams and has been growing in popularity each year thanks to the support of the NBA. Pro leagues for both sexes also exist overseas. Someday — who knows when — a female will have the goods to play in the NBA.

Facing the master

"It takes ten hands to make a basket."

That was one of the many great axioms of basketball John Wooden professed on his famous Pyramid of Success.

That team-first approach is one of the reasons Wooden was the master, winning 10 NCAA championships in 12 years, an accomplishment that will never be duplicated.

When Coach Wooden passed away in the summer of 2010, I was asked for my thoughts on his career because we became linked when we were fortunate enough to end UCLA's 88-game winning streak in 1974.

John Wooden was successful for many reasons, but three things stand out and they are basics that young coaches can use as their career progresses.

First, keep it simple. Wooden had some basic principles that featured a full-court trapping defense that moved to a man-to-man that put a priority of guarding the interior when the opposing team broke the press. Offensively, he featured a high-post-based offense that put a high priority on having balance between scoring from the post and the perimeter. Work on these basics and become proficient in each area.

Second, be disciplined in working on the fundamentals. He taught all his players to use the square behind the basket. They all became proficient at banking the ball in the basket, whether it was Bill Walton under the basket, or Keith Wilkes from the outside.

Finally, he was honest with his players from the day he recruited them to the day they graduated. A team will reflect a coach's personality, and if you have that basic trust you can go a long way.

Coaching a Team

In my mind, basketball is the best team sport to coach. Every player must play both offense and defense (unlike football) and must switch from one to the other at any moment (unlike baseball). If you enjoy teaching, these qualities provide two huge plusses — the former because any lesson you teach applies to all your students, and the latter because you must teach those students to make split-second decisions on their own.

Soccer is similar to basketball in this respect, but soccer games last more than twice as long — and soccer fans have been known, on occasion, to kill one another. That puts a little undue pressure on a coach. Intimacy is another attractive facet of coaching basketball. A basketball court is tiny compared to a football field or a baseball diamond, and you have fewer athletes to manage. When you conduct a basketball practice, you don't feel as if you're Louis Gossett, Jr., in *An Officer and a Gentleman;* you feel as if you're Professor Kingsfield in *The Paper Chase* . . . although you may bark like Louis Gossett, Jr.: "I am a basketball coach. The court is my classroom. Class is never canceled on account of lightning."

Another thrill that a basketball coach has is proximity to the opposing team's coach. Unlike football, for example, you share the same sideline, and you are usually no more than 40 feet apart — almost within spitting distance and, yes, definitely within shouting distance. (That is unless you are coaching at Vanderbilt where the benches are in the end zones.)

Coaches are competitive, after all. Being that close to your nemesis is much more exhilarating. See the sidebar "Facing the master" for one of my favorite coaching run-in tales.

Don't Become a Tunnel-Vision Fan

Unlike many other sports, basketball can be as fun to watch as it is to play. As a fan, you need not concentrate solely on the player who has the ball. Try watching the game that occurs away from the ball, something you can more easily do when you attend a game in person. Observe how UCONN star guard Maya Moore works without the ball to get open. The same can be said at the NBA level for Kevin Durrant of the Oklahoma City Thunder.

 After you read this book, you should be able to spot a double down on defense or a pick and roll on offense. But to understand the game fully, you'll need to take that last step: Play. You can memorize notes and chords, but unless you pick up a guitar and strum, you don't really understand music. The same rule applies here.

So grab a ball and shoot. It'll make you a better player *and* a better fan. Making two free throws in a row isn't as easy as it looks on TV, is it?

Chapter 2

The Wear and Where of Basketball

Abig advantage of hoops is that it requires very little equipment. This chapter tells you exactly what you need to be able to play — and how to find a game after you're all geared up.

The Wear of Basketball

No shoes, no shorts, no game. That's the etiquette of basketball, pure and simple. Whereas most dining establishments insist that you wear a shirt (although their "No shoes, no shirt, no service" signs make no mention of pants), basketball doesn't even require that much — if you're male. All you need are some rubber-soled shoes, cotton socks, and a pair of gym shorts or sweats. I recommend a shirt, too.

Sneakers

The sneaker craze all started in the 1950s. The Chuck Taylor Converse All-Star was the first shoe that anyone really bothered to market. It was a simple canvas shoe with a rubber sole and — for the high-top version — a round patch on the ankle that bore the sneaker's name. The white Chuck Taylor, the most popular color, had All-American red and blue stripes along the side of the sole.

Clyde: The first sneaker contract

The first pro basketball player to be paid to wear a certain type of basketball shoe was Walt Frazier of the New York Knicks. Frazier, far and away the most stylish player of his era (he played from 1967–1980), even earned his nickname, "Clyde," because of his flair for fashion. Folks thought that he dressed like a gangster, as in "Bonnie and Clyde."

Frazier, who also happened to be a future Hall of Famer who helped the Knicks win two championships, was paid $5,000 by Puma to wear a low-cut suede sneaker, known as "the Clyde," in the 1970s. At the time, other NBA players were receiving free shoes, but nobody was being paid to wear them.

If you keep something long enough, it eventually comes back in style. (Just look at my ties. And for those who follow me on ESPN, you know that I have added the highlighter since we last updated this book!) The Chuck Taylor went out of style in the mid 1970s as players switched to leather shoes that offer far more ankle support. But today, you can see that hoops icon Michael Jordan still promotes his line of Air Jordans. He has been retired as a player since 2003.

High or low

In the early years of sneakerdom, all players wore high-tops. Then John Havlicek of the Boston Celtics began wearing low-cuts in the 1960s because he felt that a lighter shoe made him quicker. When you're as gifted a player as "Hondo," people begin to imitate you — low-tops became a fad. Soon, players who didn't even rely on their quickness were wearing them. Havlicek's Hall of Fame partner on the Celtics, center Bill Russell, wore them, too.

DIGGER SAYS

If you play forward or center and are thus less reliant on speed than a guard, I suggest that you wear a high-top sneaker or at least the three-quarter-cut shoe that is out on the market today. This type of shoe extends to cover the ankle but doesn't go as high as a normal high-top. I advise the three-quarter-cut for guards as well. It's a very popular style in college and pro hoops.

Purchasing a sneaker

A good fit is critical for basketball shoes — you can acquire some serious blisters if your feet slide around inside your shoes. Do the following when you're shopping for sneakers to make sure that you get the best fit:

✔ Shop late in the day when your feet are swollen because your feet swell while you're playing hoops, too.

✔ Measure your feet before you buy, even if you're an adult.

✔ When trying on a pair of sneakers, wear socks of the same thickness, and the same number of pairs, that you'll be wearing when you play.

✔ Don't be satisfied with the first pair you put on, no matter how good they look or how comfy they feel. Try a few different brands.

✔ Walk around in the shoes. Jog in the store. Make quick starts and stops. Just don't ask the salesperson if you can dunk on the store's hoop.

✔ Lace up the sneakers tightly (as if you were playing) to make sure that they get snug everywhere.

✔ Check out the big toe of each foot. Is your big toe separated from the toe of the shoe by about the length of your thumbnail? It should be.

✔ Sizes can vary according to brand and product line. Always try on the shoe that you're considering buying.

✔ Pick up the shoe and try to bend it in half. If it flexes at the arch, you don't want it. If it bends at the ball of the foot, it deserves consideration.

Socks

Socks have been the subject of a lot of fads in recent years. As shorts have gotten longer, socks have grown shorter. Ankle socks, like those worn by tennis players, are in vogue today. A few years ago, Michael Jordan began wearing *black* socks and NBA players and high school kids alike copied that fashion statement. When you're wearing black sneakers, as Jordan did, the black sock is a good look.

Some players feel comfortable wearing two pairs of socks. Others prefer one thick pair of cotton socks. Listen to your feet and choose what works for you.

A mouthpiece

Many players wear a mouthpiece during games. If your position has you crashing the boards for rebounds quite often, then a mouthpiece — available at most sporting goods stores — is a good idea. Elbows have a way of displacing teeth from gums. Getting used to breathing while wearing a mouthpiece takes a little time. But getting used to root canal surgery takes longer. Wear your 'piece.

A new type of jewelry problem

My co-author, John Walters, coaches a girls' high school basketball team in New York City. One of his players was going for a breakaway layup when she was fouled from behind fairly hard. She stayed on the floor for a brief period, so John rushed over to see if she was okay. "Are you hurt?" he asked. "No, coach," she answered. Lifting up her jersey slightly, she said, "She knocked out my navel ring and I can't find it."

Uniforms

The basic uniform resembles a men's underwear ad: shorts and a tank top. Of course, you can pay as much as $150 for an official NBA team jersey — *sans* shorts — which is about the same price as a year's supply of undergarments for some people. But if you're just looking to play in a pickup game and the weather is nice, here's all you need:

- ✔ A loose-fitting pair of gym shorts
- ✔ A T-shirt or tank top

Remember these hoops fashion don'ts:

- ✔ *Don't* play hoops in blue jeans, cycling shorts, or a bathing suit. (You need to be as comfortable as you can to really get into the game, so avoid tight clothing.)
- ✔ *Don't* play hoops in shirts that have buttons. (Other players may get caught on your buttons or the openings between them and hurt themselves — or your shirt.)
- ✔ *Don't* wear your watch. (It will inevitably scrape someone.)
- ✔ *Don't* wear a baseball cap. (The bill of a baseball cap may injure someone, and it will definitely impair your vision.) However, a *'do rag* — a bandana wrapped around your head — is acceptable in pickup games.

Of all the equipment used in basketball, uniforms change the most. In the old days of basketball, uniforms were made of wool. Players wore tape on their chests because the jerseys irritated that part of their body. Later, the switch to cotton was made, and the game moved forward in a rash-free manner.

The most noticeable change in uniform style in the last 20 years has been the universal switch to baggy shorts, spearheaded by Michael Jordan. He wore them first, after he entered the NBA. Then the University of Michigan's Fab Five (including Juwan Howard, Jalen Rose, and Chris Webber, who started together and advanced to the NCAA championship game as freshmen in 1992) took the hem to even lower levels. The latest fashion accessory has been the addition of a long elbow sleeve on one arm. Allen Iverson authored this look in the late 1990s when he had an elbow injury. "AI" continued to wear it even after his elbow healed. Nowadays John Wall of the Washington Wizards, whose game is similar to Iverson's, sports the single-arm sleeve look.

But unlike so many fashion revolutions, the baggy trunk has a practical purpose. When players are tired, they've always found that a good way to catch their breath is to bend over while another player is shooting free throws. But where would they rest their hands — on their thighs? Their thighs were sweaty, and their hands would slip. Baggy trunks allow players to grab the hem of their shorts, and make bending over much more comfortable.

Equipment

Any Generation Xer is familiar with the mantra: "Mom always says, 'Don't play ball in the house.'" This piece of sage advice was delivered on an episode of *The Brady Bunch* after Peter, the middle boy, broke a vase with a basketball. Peter had been playing hoops in his bedroom when his ill-advised (not to mention ill-fated) toss missed its target — a trash can — and flew into the hallway, hit a wall, bounced down the stairs, and crushed said pottery. Sadly, thanks to syndication, this may be one of the most recognized shots in television history.

Although no bats (baseball), blades (hockey), or teeth (boxing) are used in basketball, hoops equipment is not intended for domestic use. Play outside or at a gym. Mom knows what she's talking about.

The ball

As far as game equipment, all you need are a basketball and a basket, complete with rim and net. The ball part isn't too complicated: A basketball is spherical and orange and has eight panels. The old American Basketball Association (ABA) used a red, white, and blue ball (the colors alternated on each panel), and the Women's NBA (WNBA) uses a ball with orange and white alternating panels.

A regulation men's basketball is 29.5 inches in circumference, 9.39 inches in diameter, and 20 to 22 ounces in weight. A slightly smaller ball (28.5 inches in circumference, 9.07 inches diameter and 17.5 to 19.5 ounces) is available for women; women's teams at most levels play with this ball.

If you often play outdoors on concrete or blacktop, invest in an outdoor ball. An outdoor ball is made of rubber as opposed to leather, which is the material used for indoor balls. You'll play outdoors 80 percent of the time, and outdoor balls can be used indoors, too. If you do own a leather ball, *never* use it outdoors. Concrete or blacktop will scuff it, and rain will ruin it.

Which ball is it?

One of the differences between the men's college game and the women's college game is the size of the ball. The men's ball, known as a Size 7 ball, is an inch larger in circumference and two ounces heavier.

It would seem that men, if allowed to play with a women's ball, would make a higher percentage of their shots. First, because their hands would exercise more control of the ball and second, because it's easier to fit a smaller object through a hoop.

On December 8, 2010, that assumption fell flat. Oakland University visited Illinois for a game at the Illini's arena, Assembly Hall. A women's game had taken place on the same court earlier and somehow the game ball from that contest was mixed into the rack of possible game balls for the men's game.

When an official selected the game ball, he grabbed the smaller women's ball. For the first seven minutes of the contest, the men unknowingly played with the smaller women's ball. Oakland took a surprising 15-6 lead, but neither team shot the ball well. The Illini shot just 3-13 with the women's ball, while Oakland made 7-16. And these were two teams that would later make that season's NCAA tournament.

During the game's first timeout, Illinois' star guard Demetri McCamey complained to his coach, Bruce Weber, that the ball didn't feel right.

"You guys are just missing shots," Weber replied. "Shut up and play."

Finally, during a second timeout, Illinois center Mike Tisdale brought the ball to the referees. The officials examined the ball by comparing it to another one and, sure enough, it was a women's ball.

McCamey went on to score 30 points and lead Illinois to the 74–63 victory.

The backboard

The backboard is a rectangular mount upon which a rim is hung. Regulation backboards measure 6 feet x 3½ feet and are made of transparent Plexiglas. Backboards have been known to shatter due to the excessive force of some dunks, which cause the rim to shake. The resulting tremor shatters the Plexiglas. A shattered backboard requires a good half-hour to replace. The thrill of witnessing a backboard-breaking slam is not worth the wait, believe me.

Just ask fans and television viewers of the 1996 NCAA Tournament when Darvin Ham of Texas Tech shattered a backboard in a game against North Carolina. It led to a 20-minute delay. It proved to be a good thing for Texas Tech, however, because the play changed the momentum of the game and the Red Raiders went on to pull off the upset and advanced to the Sweet 16 for the first time in their history.

Make sure that the backboard is perpendicular to the ground. If it is not, you will be unable to shoot a true bank shot. The angles will be askew.

The rim

The rim is attached to the backboard and is suspended 10 feet above the floor. That's the way the rim was 100 years ago, and that's the way the rim is today, even though humans on average are much taller today. (NBA center Yao Ming of the Houston Rockets, who stands 7'6", can touch the rim with his middle finger when he stands on his tiptoes.) The inside of the rim is 18 inches in diameter, almost twice the diameter of a men's basketball.

The net

The net, which is composed of nylon mesh cord, hangs down from the rim approximately 15 to 18 inches. The net hooks onto the rim at eight different rungs located around the rim's bottom. The net's primary function is to slow the path of the ball as it passes through the basket and help you tell whether the ball actually went through the hoop. However, it also serves a secondary function by providing depth perception for the shooter. (See the sidebar "The net effect.")

The net effect

Nets can have a significant impact on a game. For example, when John Wooden coached at UCLA, his teams employed an effective full-court zone trap press. The key to the press's success was having the defenders in position as soon as the other team in-bounded the ball.

One way to ensure that the Bruins always had enough time to set up a press was to make the nets tight. The best way to "tighten the net" is to make it shorter; a shorter net "catches" the ball, while a long net allows the ball to pass through more swiftly. When the net was tight, the ball was momentarily trapped inside it. The net was never so tight that it restricted the ball's passage, but rather just tight enough to slow the ball's momentum. After UCLA made a shot, therefore, you'd have to wait for the ball to drop from the net as if a hen were laying an egg. By the time you were set to in-bound the ball, the Bruins were already in their press positions.

Coach Paul Westhead's Loyola Marymount teams of the late '80s used the exact opposite tactic. Westhead wanted to accelerate the action, to run until the opponent was gasping for air. So Westhead put loose nets on his rims. Loose nets, which let the ball pass through the cylinder with negligible loss of speed, allowed the Lions to retrieve the ball quicker and charge up court before the opponent was able to catch its breath.

Too bad Wooden and Westhead, whose schools are located not far from one another in Los Angeles, coached in different eras. I would have liked to see their teams play one another to see what the "net" effect would have been.

The Where of Basketball

Although astronauts don't play basketball on the moon — the low force of gravity there *would* make for a fun game — hoops is played almost everywhere else. In prison yards. On ships (watch the Veteran's Day 2011 game between Michigan State and North Carolina onboard the USS Carl Vinson). Chevy Chase's Fletch character in the movie *Fletch* — ignoring the wisdom of *The Brady Bunch* — used his living room as a court. You really need little more than a flat surface roughly the size of a classroom and at least 20 feet of vertical space.

Your own driveway

The fact that basketball and the automobile were invented within 15 years of one another is indeed serendipitous. The advent of the auto meant the arrival of the driveway, which can serve a dual role as a basketball court. And the garage has long been an ideal place upon which to mount a backboard and rim.

Putting up a hoop in the driveway or backyard

Installing your own basketball hoop in or near your driveway can cost anywhere from $50 to $250, the high-end hoops being mobile units mounted upon dollies that require nearly no assembly. Before you decide to install a court at your home, first determine whether your driveway or other concrete or asphalt surface is level. If it's relatively level, the next step is to choose whether to purchase a pole that you will plant in the ground, and upon which you will mount the backboard and rim, or to simply mount the backboard and rim on or above a preexisting structure, such as a garage, sloped roof, or barn. (A common taunt when your shot is off is, "You couldn't hit the broad side of a barn!" Well, now you can.)

Neither option is better than the other. Simply assess your own property. If you select a pole, be sure to plant it at least 24 to 36 inches in the ground and support it by fixing it into the ground in a bed of cement. Allow the cement to set for 48 hours before mounting the backboard on the pole.

Mounting a hoop on the garage

From a cost point of view, the less expensive approach is a universal mounting bracket, which costs about $55. This bracket allows you to mount the backboard to a garage wall with the hoop at the desired level. The advantage of a universal bracket is that you can mount it on a sloping roof, a side wall, or a pole. To that, you attach the backboard, which should already have a rim attached. You can buy a quality backboard and attached rim for about $130.

School yards or playgrounds

School yard and playground hoops offer full-court game possibilities and so much more. It's where you meet new people — hopefully upstanding types (the only junkies I ever want to see at a school yard are basketball junkies). You also face better levels of competition. (The driveway court is fun, but face it: Uncle Leo can't go to his left.)

The school yard is also where children learn to be grownups in a positive sense. They learn how to fit in with a group, settle disputes ("Call the foul before the shot misses the basket!"), and stand up for themselves.

Youngsters should always be accompanied — if not by an adult, then at least by an older sibling — when going to shoot at a school yard. Also, no matter how badly you get beaten on the court, don't ever take your basketball and go home as a retort. Crybabies are not welcome at the school yard. See Chapter 12 for more information about pickup basketball.

Basketball Hotbeds: Where the Best Players Come From

When I was recruiting during the 1960s at Penn and in the 1970s and 1980s at Notre Dame, basketball was a city game. My best players in the 1970s were from the New York and Washington, D.C., areas. When Notre Dame defeated UCLA in 1971, the only loss the Bruins suffered that year, three of the Fighting Irish starters were natives of Washington, D.C. When we ended UCLA's 88-game winning streak three years later, my most-effective five included three New York metro players and a D.C. player.

Adrian Dantley was that player from Washington, D.C., and in 1973–74 he helped us to a 26–3 season and number-three final ranking. He played at DeMatha High School for the legendary Morgan Wootten, and went on to play 15 years in the NBA. He was still in the top 25 in NBA history in scoring entering 2011 and was inducted into the Naismith Hall of Fame in 2008. He is my only former player enshrined in Springfield.

Why did it seem as if the best hoopsters were from cities? Because that's where the game was most popular. In the suburbs, kids were into other sports and activities (and this was even before Nintendo!).

New York was the hoops hotbed then. Chicago, D.C., Detroit, and Los Angeles were not far behind. Today, that situation has changed; you find outstanding players not only all over the country but also all over the world. (See Chapter 16 for more information about international basketball.)

Consider for a moment some of the NBA MVPs (most valuable players) in history. Sure, Kareem Abdul-Jabbar was a native New Yorker, but look further. Larry Bird (see Figure 2-1)? From French Lick, Indiana. Michael Jordan? From Wilmington, North Carolina. Karl Malone of the Utah Jazz? From Summerfield, Louisiana. True, LeBron James is from Akron, Ohio, but it is very close to the big city of Cleveland.

For many years, however, New York was the epicenter of basketball talent. Table 2-1 shows the top ten states of high schools attended by McDonald's All-Americans between 1977 and 2010. California leads with 81; New York is second with 63.

It is interesting to look at Table 2-1 and see the importance of recruiting. Kentucky, North Carolina, and Kansas are the top three programs in college basketball in terms of victories, yet none of these states are ranked in the top 10 in producing the most McDonald's High School All-Americans. North Carolina is 13th with 23, Kentucky is 19th with 13, and Kansas is way down the line with just seven total McDonald's All-Americans since 1977.

This shows you how important it is to recruit when it comes to a job description for a college head coach.

How important is it to get the great players? Since 1977, only one NCAA champion has had a roster without at least one McDonald's All-American. That was Gary Williams' 2002 Maryland team that beat Indiana in the National Championship game. Another reason why Williams should be in the basketball Hall of Fame, but we address that in a later chapter.

Table 2-1	State of High School Attended by McDonald's All-Americans (1977–2010)				
Rank	**State**	**Number of Players**	**Rank**	**State**	**Number of Players**
1.	California	81	6.	Maryland	37
2.	New York	63	7.	Michigan	36
3.	Illinois	58	8.	Indiana	35
4.	Virginia	58	9.	New Jersey	32
5.	Texas	38	10.	Georgia	31

Check out Table 2-2 for a list of the NBA's 50 greatest players by home state or country. Home state is where the player played high school basketball.

Figure 2-1:
One of the game's greatest players, Larry Bird came from the small southern Indiana town of French Lick.

Table 2-2   The NBA's 50 Greatest Players by Home State/Country

Home State/Country	Number	Players
New York	7	Kareem Abdul-Jabbar, Nate Archibald, Bob Cousy, Billy Cunningham, Julius Erving, Dolph Schayes, Lenny Wilkins
North Carolina	5	Sam Jones, Michael Jordan, Earl Monroe, James Worthy, Pete Maravich
Louisiana	5	Robert Parrish, Bob Pettit, Willis Reed, Karl Malone, Elvin Hayes
Ohio	3	John Havlicek, Jerry Lucas, Nate Thurmond
California	3	Bill Russell, Bill Sharman, Bill Walton
Michigan	3	Dave DeBusschere, George Gervin, Magic Johnson
Pennsylvania	2	Paul Arizin, Wilt Chamberlain
Washington, D.C.	2	Elgin Baylor, Dave Bing
Indiana	2	Larry Bird, Oscar Robertson
Illinois	2	Isiah Thomas, George Mikan
West Virginia	2	Hal Greer, Jerry West
Virginia	2	Moses Malone, David Robinson
Kentucky	2	Wes Unseld, Dave Cowens
Texas	2	Clyde Drexler, Shaquille O'Neal
Alabama	1	Charles Barkley
Arkansas	1	Scottie Pippen
Georgia	1	Walt Frazier
Massachusetts	1	Patrick Ewing
Minnesota	1	Kevin McHale
Washington	1	John Stockton
New Jersey	1	Rick Barry
Nigeria	1	Hakeem Olajuwon

Chapter 3

The Rules

*I*n December of 1891, James Naismith introduced his gymnastics class at the Springfield (Massachusetts) YMCA to his yet-unnamed invention. Naismith, a physical education teacher, nailed peach baskets to the lower rail of the balcony at both ends of the gym and grabbed a soccer ball. He tacked a list of 13 rules, which would govern this new game, to a bulletin board. Soon after the first game was played, the rules were stolen. (I guess "Do not steal the rules" was not one of the original 13.)

A few days later, one of Naismith's students, Frank Mahon, 'fessed up to the crime. "I took them," Mahon said. "I knew that this game would be a success, and I took them as a souvenir. But I *think* now that you should have them."

Mahon later atoned for his crime by suggesting a name for the infant sport. Having had his first idea (*Naismith Ball,* no kidding) rejected by Naismith himself, Mahon asked, "How about *basketball*?" "We have a basket and a ball," said Naismith. "It seems to me that would be a good name for it."

Naismith never could have dreamed that the document he wrote in 1891 would have value 119 years later. His original document was put up for auction by the Naismith International Basketball Foundation and sold for $4.3 million in December of 2010. The document was purchased by an alumnus of the University of Kansas, the school where Naismith became the first head coach in 1898.

Naismith coached the Jayhawks for nine years and finished with a losing record, the only coach in the history of University of Kansas basketball with a losing record.

Naismith's Original 13 Rules

In less than one hour, sitting at a desk in his office at the YMCA, James Naismith framed the 13 rules that would govern basketball. (Compare that to today, when rules committees take months to make a decision about a single rule.) The father of basketball envisioned the game with the following rules:

1. The ball may be thrown in any direction with one or both hands.

2. The ball may be batted in any direction with one or both hands (but never with a fist).

3. A player cannot run with the ball. The player must throw it from the spot on which he catches it; allowance to be made for a man who catches the ball when running at a good speed.

4. The ball must be held in or between the hands; the arms or body must not be used for holding it.

5. No shouldering, holding, pushing, tripping, or striking in any way the person of an opponent shall be allowed. The first infringement of this rule by any person shall count as a foul; the second shall disqualify him until the next goal is made, or, if there was evident intent to injure the person, for the whole of the game, no substitute allowed.

6. A foul is striking at the ball with the fist, violation of Rules 3, 4, and such as described in Rule 5.

7. If either side makes three consecutive fouls, it shall count as a goal for the opponents. (*Consecutive* means without the opponent in the meantime making a foul.)

8. A goal shall be made when the ball is thrown or batted from the grounds into the basket and stays there, providing that those defending the goal do not touch or disturb the goal. If the ball rests on the edge and the opponent moves the basket, it shall count as a goal.

9. When the ball goes out of bounds, it shall be thrown into the field and played by the person first touching it. In case of a dispute, the umpire shall throw it straight into the field. The thrower-in is allowed five seconds. If he holds it longer, it shall go to the opponent. If any side persists in delaying the game, the umpire shall call a foul on them.

10. The umpire shall be the judge of the men and shall note the fouls and notify the referee when three consecutive fouls have been made. He shall have power to disqualify men according to Rule 5.

11. The referee shall be judge of the ball and decide when the ball is in play, in bounds, and to which side it belongs, and shall keep the time. He shall decide when a goal has been made, and keep account of the goals, with any other duties that are usually performed by a referee.

12. The time shall be two 15-minute halves, with 5 minutes rest between.

13. The side making the most goals in that time shall be declared the winners. In case of a draw, the game may, by agreement of the captains, be continued until another goal is made.

You may notice a few discrepancies between Naismith's rules and those adhered to today. For starters, the rules are shorter — the NBA's illegal defense rule alone is more verbose than Naismith's entire set of rules. Another difference: The game, as originally conceived, doesn't account for dribbling.

The Court

A basketball court has symmetry; one half of the court is a mirror image of the other. The entire court (see Figure 3-1) is 94 x 50 feet (84 x 50 in high school). On each half-court, painted lines show the *free throw lane* and *circle,* as well as the *three-point arc,* whose distance from the basket varies based on the level of hoops being played.

Indoor basketball courts are almost always made of hardwood. Outdoor courts are most commonly composed of asphalt.

The borders of the court have their own commonsense names:

✔ Along the length of the court, the borders are the *sidelines.*

✔ Along the ends, the borders are the *endlines,* or *baselines.*

✔ Separating both halves of the court is a *half-court line.*

✔ In the very center of the midcourt line is the *center circle* (12 feet in diameter), where the *center toss* takes place to begin the game. (See the section "To begin" later in this chapter for more information about the center toss — also known as a *jump ball* or *tipoff.*)

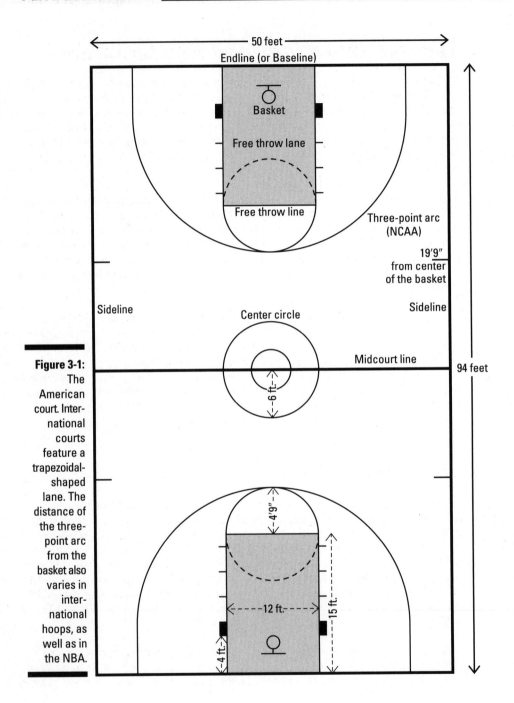

Figure 3-1:
The American court. International courts feature a trapezoidal-shaped lane. The distance of the three-point arc from the basket also varies in international hoops, as well as in the NBA.

The free throw lane and free throw line

The *free throw lane* is the hub of the action in each half-court. This rectangle is 12 feet wide — 16 feet at the men's pro level. Its length, as measured from the basket to the *free throw line,* is 15 feet at all levels. An offensive player may not stand inside the lane for more than three seconds unless he or one of his teammates is shooting the ball. After a shot is taken, the count starts over again. A defensive player may remain inside the lane for as long as he desires.

A player fouled by another player (see the "Fouls" section later in this chapter) sometimes receives *free throws,* also known as *foul shots.* She takes these shots (they aren't really "throws") from the free throw line at the end of the lane — 15 feet from the basket. The shots are "free" because a defender does not guard the shooter while she's shooting. When a player shoots a free throw, her feet may not cross the free throw line until the ball hits the rim, or the shot is nullified.

The remaining players line up alongside the free throw lane (or behind the shooter) and cannot interfere with the shot. They line up in order, on either side of the lane, of defense-offense-defense-offense. (Up to three players may stand on one side of the lane.) If a player opts not to take a spot (say, for example, the second defensive spot), then a player from the opposing team is permitted to step into that spot. The fans behind the basket usually scream, jump up and down, and wave their hands to try to distract an opposing team's shooter during free throws.

The three-point arc

The *three-point arc* is the other important marked feature of the court. The arc extends around the basket in a near semicircle, and its distance from the basket differs according to the level of play. Even at one level, the distance can change as rules committees grapple with the best distance for the good of the sport. The NBA has changed the three-point distance on two different occasions since first adopting the trey, as the three-point shot is called, in the 1979–80 season. The three-point distance was moved back to its original 23'9" for the 1997–98 season. The college distance is 20'9" (an increase from 19'9" in 2008–09), while the international distance is 20'6".

Any shot made from beyond this arc — even a desperation half-court shot at the buzzer — is worth three points. A three-point shooter must have both feet behind the arc as he launches this shot, but either foot is allowed to land on the other side of the arc.

That's three! No, two! Or is it three?

Perhaps the most unusual application of the three-point rule took place on January 27, 1997, when Villanova freshman Tim Thomas, who went on to play 13 years with seven NBA teams, attempted a pass over a Georgetown defender. The Hoya defender deflected the ball while his own feet were outside the three-point line. The ball caromed high in the air and banked into the basket. The officials huddled and awarded three points to Thomas.

After the season, the officials at the NCAA huddled again and changed the rule. Now, if the offensive player does not intend to shoot a three-point shot, he is only credited with two points if that unusual situation occurs.

This rule goes against the rule on a missed lob pass that goes into the basket. In that case, even though the outside player attempts a pass and not a shot, the basket still counts as three points. Figure that out!

The back court and front court

Thinking of the entire court as two half-courts, divide it into front court and back court. The *front court* is the half of the court where the offense's basket is located. The *back court* is the other half. Thus one team's back court is the other team's front court.

The Players

At every level of organized basketball, five players per team are on the court at one time. The usual division of players by position is two *guards,* two *forwards,* and one *center.* Many teams play a three-guard offense today due to the importance of the three-point goal and being able to score from behind that arc. And many teams use a point guard, two wing players, and two post players.

(See Chapter 6 for information about each position.)

Most basketball teams consist of 12 players; NBA rules, for example, call for 12 players per team, plus three roster players who are considered inactive on game day. So they have 15 players at practice, but just 12 who are in uniform on game days. High school and college teams may have a few more or less. Each player wears a uniform that, in most cases, consists of trunks and a tank top.

One player may be substituted for another only during a stoppage in play. The player or players intending to enter the game approach the *scorer's table,* which is located at midcourt along one sideline. The game's official scorer and timer sit at the scorer's table. When play stops for whatever reason, the referee acknowledges the player's presence at the table — although the referee doesn't shake her hand or hug her or anything that friendly — and waves her into the game. At that time, the player being replaced leaves the game.

The Game

The objective in basketball is simple: score more points than your opponent. You accomplish this goal by making baskets on *offense* (when your team has the ball) and preventing your opponent from scoring baskets while you're playing *defense* (when your opponent has the ball).

In basketball (unlike football), the same players remain in the game to play both offense and defense. In rhythm and in the roles of its players, basketball resembles soccer or hockey, where the transition from offense to defense can occur in the blink of an eye. You can find out much more about what the offense and defense specifically do in Chapters 6 and 7, respectively.

To begin

Each game begins with a *tipoff,* or *center toss,* at the center circle. The referee stands in the center of the circle and tosses the basketball directly upward. Each team's center then leaps and attempts to tap the ball to one of her teammates, who must position themselves outside the 12-foot-diameter circle. (***Note:*** The center is not allowed to grab the ball during a tipoff; she can only tap it.) Any player may be involved in the tipoff, but the center — usually the tallest player — almost always does the honors. (Height is very helpful in this case.)

Time-in, time-out

Think of the game in two parts: time-in, when the clock moves and action takes place; and time-out, when play (and therefore the clock) stops. How long does a game last? The length varies from level to level:

- ✔ An NBA contest has four 12-minute quarters.

- ✔ WNBA (Women's NBA, a women's pro league), international, and college basketball games consist of two 20-minute halves.

- ✔ High school basketball games have four 8-minute quarters or two 16-minute halves.

The shot clock

The offense must shoot the basketball within a certain amount of time, monitored by the shot clock, or forfeit the ball to the defense. The shot clock rule provides the game with more offense and rewards the defense for a job well done. In the NBA, the shot clock is 24 seconds. In men's college hoops, the shot clock is 35 seconds, and in women's pro and college, 30 seconds is the agreed-upon time.

Danny Biasone, a bowling alley proprietor and owner of the Syracuse Nationals (an original NBA franchise), invented the shot clock in 1954. The shot clock may have saved the pro game. The college game, which has featured games with scores as low as 1–0, did not adopt the shot clock as a national rule until 1985–86. Biasone's idea was held in such high esteem that he was inducted into the Naismith Hall of Fame as a special contributor in 2000.

Ten seconds

After a team makes a basket, the opposing team takes the ball out of bounds under the basket at which the points were just scored. The team with the ball must *in-bound* it (throw it into play) within five seconds of touching it. The team must then advance the ball toward its own basket, passing the midcourt line within ten seconds of in-bounding the ball. (***Note:*** Entering the 2011–12 season, this rule does not apply in women's college basketball.) Failure to either in-bound or advance towards the basket within the time restrictions results in a loss of the ball.

If a player advances the ball toward half court and a defensive player knocks the ball out of bounds, a new ten second count begins. An offensive team can also escape the ten second violation by calling a time-out. After the time-out, you have another ten seconds to get the ball over half court. After the offensive team advances the ball past midcourt, the ball — or the player possessing it — may not retreat behind the center line (to his team's back court). However, an offensive player not in possession of the ball may stand in the back court. Obviously, however, an offensive player in the back court is of no help to his team.

If a team has the ball under its scoring basket, a team may inbound the ball into the back court, but the ball must go into the back court before it is touched by an offensive player.

The game that brought the shot clock to college basketball

Although the shot clock has been a part of the NBA since the 1954–55 season, the college game did not have a shot clock until the 1985–86 season when a 45-second clock was adopted. The time was reduced to 35 seconds in 1993–94.

College basketball purists felt they wanted their game to be unique, and they wanted to refrain from becoming just like the NBA game. That feeling changed during the 1981–82 season when coaches coveted every possession, and offenses seemed to grind to a halt. The shot clock controversy came to an apex at the 1982 ACC Tournament in Greensboro. That year the average score of the seven tournament games was 56–44. The first round game between NC State and Maryland was 40–28. The championship game featured North Carolina, led by Michael Jordan and James Worthy, against a Virginia team led by National Player of the Year Ralph Sampson. The contest was televised nationally by NBC and had great ratings, but all the fans saw was a lot of standing around by the three future NBA stars.

North Carolina won 47–45. The low score was not due to bad offense. Virginia shot 66.7 percent from the field (22–33) and lost. The two teams scored a combined 27 points and 25 field goal attempts in the second half. North Carolina did not score a basket the last 8:44 of the game and went into a spread offense for a 7:06 time period late in the game. My co-author, Tim Bourret, the long-time Clemson sports information director, attended the game. Tim said, "It was comparable to going to the Miss Universe contest and watching the contestants wear only baggy sweat suits."

The following spring, the ACC adopted a 30-second clock and a 17' 9" three-point goal distance. That was a little extravagant, but the excitement of the up-tempo ACC season of 1982–83 led to the national adoption of the shot clock just two years later.

One other note on that 1982 ACC Tournament: The only game that was not low scoring was Wake Forest's 88–53 win over Duke. The Duke coach who lost that game by 35 points was Mike Krzyzewski, who 30 years later was on the verge of becoming the winningest coach in college basketball history.

Time-out

Time stands still for no one — except a referee. The game clock in basketball can stop for the following reasons:

- A coach or player on either team calls a time-out to discuss matters with her players.
- The referee blows his whistle to signal a violation.
- The ball goes out of bounds.
- A quarter or period ends.
- A player makes a basket inside the last minute of a college game or within the last two minutes of an NBA game.

A coach or player may call time-out only during a stoppage in play or if her team has the ball. In other words, a defensive player may never request a time-out while the clock is running. Each team receives a specific number of time-outs per half in the pros and per game in college. If a team exceeds that number, the referee penalizes it with a technical foul.

Overtime

A basketball game cannot end in a tie, but there have been some exceptions (see the sidebar "A tie in basketball."). When a regulation game ends with the score tied, the teams play an extra period, five minutes in length in both the pros and college. (In high school, the overtime period is three minutes long.) Each player retains his personal fouls during overtime; you often see one or more players foul out during this extra session. No matter how large a lead one team builds during overtime, the game doesn't end until the teams play all five minutes. If the score is still tied at the end of the five-minute overtime, the game goes into another overtime period — ad nauseum, until one team comes out victorious.

A tie in basketball?

Notre Dame finished the 1935–36 season with a 22–2–1 record and the Helms Foundation National Championship (no NCAA Tournament in those days). Yes, 22–2–1, a tie in basketball, the only tie in Notre Dame history, which dates back to 1898. The tie came about because of an error by the official scorer.

It all happened on New Year's Eve 1935 in Evanston, Illinois. The game was a defensive struggle, even for those days. With just seconds left, Notre Dame's Johnny Moir, the national player of the year that season, made a free throw to give the Irish a 21–20 victory.

"While we showered in the locker room, the official scorer, Wilfred Smith of the Chicago Tribune, ran into the dressing room and told Coach George Keogan that he had made an error during the game," recalled then Notre Dame assistant Moose Krause, who later became my boss as athletic director.

He had inadvertently given Notre Dame an extra point in the running score, but properly recorded a free throw attempt as a miss in the individual scoring area. When he put the final box score together he discovered the mistake because Notre Dame's individual totals added to 20.

Moose went on to explain, "Coach Keogan told us to put our uniforms on and go back to the court for overtime. But Northwestern coach Dutch Lonborg refused to send his players back because he said the officials had declared the game over. The official scorebook was final."

Notre Dame had beaten Northwestern earlier in the season 40–29, and Lonborg must have felt he was lucky to get out of there with a tie. For some reason, the game officials did not force the issue. After many minutes of shouting back and forth, the teams left the arena with a 20–20 deadlock, the only tie in either school's history.

Dealing with officials

Gary Muncy, one of the most respected officials during my era as a coach, was working our game with Lafayette during the 1978–79 season. We had been to the Final Four the previous year and were ranked number one in the nation for the first time since ending UCLA's 88-game winning streak in 1974.

We had just beaten an 11th-ranked Marquette team on the road, and we were flying high. But in the first half, Lafayette was giving us all we could handle, and the crowd was not into the game. A couple of minutes into the second half Orlando Woolridge was injured and time was called. We needed some kind of spark.

So I went on the court to Gary and started acting like I was mad at him. I got right in his face and said with tremendous expression, "Gary, I am coming to talk to you so our fans will think I am getting on your case. We need our fans to get into this game." Then I pointed at his face and said with a stern grimace, "Gary, you guys are doing a great job, keep it up."

The crowd went crazy and they could not hear what I said to him. Neither did our players, but everyone was fired up. We ran off 20 straight points and won, 91–66.

The longest NBA game lasted through six overtimes. The Indianapolis Olympians defeated the Rochester Royals 75–73 on January 6, 1951. The longest men's college game went seven overtimes when Cincinnati defeated Bradley, 75–73 on December 21, 1981.

The officials

Officials have the responsibility to enforce the rules and maintain the order of the game. This is a very difficult job at all levels because you have ten players in constant movement in various degrees of physical contact.

Three referees work in each basketball game in college and the professional ranks. In the college game, the referee is the one who throws the ball into the air at the center jump to start the game; the other two referees are called *umpires*. In the NBA, the crew chief throws the ball in the air; the other two referees are called *officials*. All three officials have equal right to make calls during the game. If there is a disagreement between two of the three officials, usually the referee or the crew chief has the final say.

You often hear announcers say that referees are calling a game either *close* or *loose*. If they call it close, that means even minor contact results in a foul call. A loosely called game, or "letting the players play," resembles a playground or pickup game — the referees allow more physical contact.

Fouls

A *personal foul* is a violation that occurs when an official determines that a player engages in illegal contact with an opponent. Both defensive and offensive players can commit fouls, although defensive fouls are much more common. (You can read about the more common fouls later in this chapter.) Though a certain amount of contact in the game is both permissible and inevitable, you can think of a foul as physical contact that disrupts the normal flow of a game. If not called a foul, the contact would create an advantage for the team committing it.

Offensive fouls

The three most commonly called offensive fouls are

- ✔ **Charging:** The player with the ball moves into a defender who has already established his stationary defensive position.

- ✔ **Moving pick or screen:** The player setting a *pick* (see Chapter 6) for his teammate moves to block the path of the defender.

- ✔ **Over the back:** An offensive player who is *boxed out* while attempting to grab a rebound tries to jump over the defender and makes excessive contact with the defender. (See Chapter 8 for a description of boxing out.)

An offensive foul, like a defensive foul, counts as one personal foul against the player who committed it.

Technical fouls

Technical fouls (which someday may be redubbed "Rodmans," after the former NBA rebounding great who set records for getting technical fouls) may be whistled against either a coach or a player. In the most common technical foul, a referee whistles a technical foul against someone who has either spoken or behaved in an extremely unsportsmanlike fashion. Rodman, whose dossier includes kicking a courtside photographer and headbutting a referee, was called for one technical foul in each of the Chicago Bulls' first 11 playoff games in 1997. Two technical fouls during one game result in automatic ejection.

A technical foul does not count toward a player's personal foul limit in the pros, but some do in college. Thus if an NBA player had five personal fouls and the referee whistled for a technical foul, he would remain in the game. But if a college player received her fourth foul, complained about it, and received a technical foul, she would be disqualified because the technical foul counts as her fifth personal foul.

Nonfoul Violations

Because referees whistle most nonfoul violations against the offensive team, I discuss the defensive nonfoul violations first:

- ✔ **Goaltending:** A referee calls goaltending when a defensive player illegally interferes with a shot. If the defensive player touches the ball as it makes its downward path to the basket, touches the ball while it is on the rim, or touches the rim or net itself as the ball is being shot, the offensive team receives the basket.

- ✔ **Kicking:** A defensive player may not kick the ball as a means of deflecting a pass. On any kicked ball violation in pro ball, the offense retains possession of the ball, but the shot clock continues running. In college, the shot clock is reset to 15 seconds if the clock was under 15 seconds at the time of the violation. It is reset to 14 seconds at the professional level. Most coaches encourage this defensive tactic even though it violates the rules because it forces the opponent to reset its offense.

Offensive nonfoul violations result in a loss of possession. Such violations are listed as *turnovers,* and almost all result from the player mishandling the ball. For that reason, most coaches put a premium on having a reliable point guard who commits as few of these violations as possible. The team that turns over the ball the most usually loses. Mistakes such as these cause coaches' hair to turn gray. A few of the more grating violations include:

- ✔ **Traveling:** Any time a player possessing the ball is not dribbling, he must keep one foot (known as his *pivot foot*) planted on the floor. He may move the other foot in any direction and as many times as he desires. After a player establishes a pivot foot, he may not move it, or the referee whistles him for traveling.

- ✔ **Double dribbling:** A double dribble occurs when a player either dribbles the ball with two hands at the same time or dribbles the ball, stops, and then resumes his dribble (known as *picking up his dribble*).

- ✔ **Carrying** or **palming:** A player dribbling the ball may not bring her palm under the ball when it reaches its apex off the dribble. Always keep your palms facing the floor when dribbling the ball. Palming became an area of emphasis with the NBA in the late 1990s. Former NBA guards such as Allen Iverson of the Philadelphia 76ers and Stephon Marbury of the New Jersey Nets would freeze their defenders by palming the ball in the middle of a dribble. The move was almost like being able to stop your dribble and then restart it. In the 1999–2000 season, referees became much more vigilant about whistling this violation. (Now if they would only call traveling violations.)

✔ **Three seconds:** No part of an offensive player may remain in the free throw lane for more than three consecutive seconds unless the ball is being shot. If the shot hits the rim, the player standing in the lane gets a new three seconds. Thus if you happen to be camping out in the lane for two seconds and the shot hits the rim, you may remain in the lane for another three seconds.

After a player steps out of the lane, the count resets, and she can re-enter the lane for another three seconds. A player can go in and out of the lane as often as she likes.

For your own sake, treat the three-second lane as if you were swimming in the ocean: If you suspect you have ventured too far offshore, you probably have. Swim back to shore. (That is, jump out of the lane — quick!)

✔ **Lane violation:** This rule applies to both offense and defense. When a player attempts a free throw, none of the players lined up along the free throw lane may enter the lane until the ball leaves the shooter's hands. If a defensive player jumps into the lane early, the shooter receives another shot if his shot misses. An offensive player entering the lane too early nullifies the shot if it is made.

Finally, not a violation but a good rule to know:

✔ **Out of bounds:** When the ball touches the floor outside the borders of the court (or on the borders themselves), the referee awards the ball to the team that did *not* touch the ball last. The plane of the borders (sidelines and endlines) does not constitute out of bounds, but rather the ground itself does. Thus if the ball is flying out of bounds and a player jumps from inbounds and tosses it back inbounds before any part of his body touches the out-of-bounds floor, the ball is still alive.

As Dennis Rodman learned by sailing into a photographer, be careful where you hurdle yourself. The landing is not always soft.

Every League for Itself

Yep, things have definitely changed since Naismith's day. The rules of the game are more complex, and some aspects of the game change depending on the league and level of play. Tables 3-1 and 3-2 give you all the basics — the details of the game as played by NBA, WNBA, and college men and women's teams.

Table 3-1	NBA and College Men's Hoops	
Rule	*NBA*	*NCAA*
Game duration	Four 12-minute periods	Two 20-minute halves
Overtime duration	5 minutes	5 minutes
Halftime length	15 minutes	15 minutes
Court dimensions	94′ × 50′	94′ × 50′
Free throw lane	16′ × 15′	12′ × 15′
3-point FG distance	23′9″	20′9″
Shot clock	24 seconds	35 seconds
Shot clock reset	FG attempt hits rim	FG attempt hits rim
Game clock stops after made FG	Last 2 minutes of fourth	Last minute of game
Player foul limit	6	5
Bonus free throw	Fifth foul per period	Seventh foul per half (1 and 1); tenth foul per half (2)
Time-outs per televised game	Seven full and two 20-second	Four 30-second and one 60-second
Time-outs per non-televised game	Same as above	Four 30- and two 60-second
Jump ball	Yes	Alternate possession
Referees	3	3

Table 3-2	WNBA and College Women's Hoops	
Rule	*WNBA*	*NCAA*
Game duration	2 20-minute halves	2 20-minute halves
Overtime duration	5 minutes	5 minutes
Halftime length	15 minutes	15 minutes
Court dimensions	94' × 50'	94' × 50'
Free throw lane	12' × 15'	12' × 15'
3-point FG distance	19'9"	19'9"
Shot clock	30 seconds	30 seconds
Shot clock reset	FG attempt hits rim or backboard	FG attempt hits rim
Game clock stops	Last 2 minutes of fourth	Last minute of game; last after FG
Player foul limit	6	5
Bonus free throw	Seventh foul per half	Seventh foul per half (1 and 1); tenth foul per half (2)
Time-outs per televised game	1 full and 2 20-second per half	4 30-second and 1 20-second
Time-outs per non-televised game	1 full and 2 20-second per half	4 30 second and 2 60-second
Jump ball	Yes	Alternate possession
Referees	3	3

Chapter 4

Statistics

*I*f the outcome of a basketball game were decided in court like a legal trial, then statistics would be the evidence that each side would use to make its case. The number of points scored is the single most important piece of evidence, but other statistics (or *stats*), such as assists, rebounds, and turnovers, usually offer convincing proof as to which team outplays the other — and wins the game.

During halftime of pro, college, and often even high school games, you may spot coaches studying the stat sheet before addressing their respective teams. The stat sheet provides all the incriminating evidence that the coach needs to see who's being outplayed, who's got the hot hand from three-point range, and so on. Stats quantify the game. They never tell the *whole* story, but they don't lie, either.

Scoring: King of Stats

You may win every other statistical battle in the game, but if you fail to out-score your opponent, then you've lost the war. If you score more points than your opponent, you win; assists and all other such self-gratifying stats don't matter. It's that simple.

Of course, all other stats are simply tributaries feeding this big river called Scoring. For example, if you grab more offensive rebounds, you take more shots and hopefully score more points. That's why stats mean so much.

Scoring: One, two, three

Each free throw that a player *converts* (shoots successfully) is worth one point. Field goals converted from within the three-point line, or with at least one foot touching that line when the shooter takes the shot, are worth two points. Field goals made from beyond the three-point arc are worth three points.

Scoring was not always this way. Before 1896, all shots — field goals and free throws alike — were worth three points. Prior to the 1979–80 NBA season, the three-point line did not exist, so all field goal attempts were worth two points. The college game did not adopt the "trey" (three-point goal) until the 1986–87 season. Keep all that in mind when evaluating individual players' scoring averages over different eras. Table 4-1 lists scoring records for college men, college women, and the NBA, respectively.

Table 4-1	Single Game Individual Scoring Records			
NCAA Men				
Points	**Name**	**Team**	**Opponent**	**Date**
113	Clarence "Bevo" Francis	Rio Grande	Hillsdale	2/2/54
100	Frank Selvy	Furman	Newberry	2/13/54
85	Paul Arizin	Villanova	Philadelphia NAMC	2/12/49
81	Freeman Williams	Portland State	Rocky Mountain	2/3/78
72	Kevin Bradshaw	U.S. International	Loyola Marymount	1/5/91
69	Pete Maravich	Louisiana State	Alabama State	2/7/70
68	Calvin Murphy	Niagara	Syracuse	2/7/68
NCAA Women				
Points	**Name**	**Team**	**Opponent**	**Date**
67	Jackie Givens	Fort Valley	Knoxville	2/22/91
64	Kim Brewington	Johnson Smith	Livingston	1/6/90

NCAA Women

Points	Name	Team	Opponent	Date
63	Jackie Givens	Fort Valley	LeMoyne-Owen	2/2/91
61	Ann Gilbert	Oberlin	Allegheny	2/6/91
60	Cindy Brown	Long Beach State	San Jose State	2/16/87

NBA

Points	Name	Team	Opponent	Date
100	Wilt Chamberlain	Philadelphia	New York Knicks	3/2/62
81	Kobe Bryant	Los Angeles	Toronto Raptors	1/22/06
78	Wilt Chamberlain	Philadelphia	Los Angeles Lakers (3 overtimes)	12/8/61
73	Wilt Chamberlain	Philadelphia	Chicago Bulls	1/13/62
73	Wilt Chamberlain	San Francisco	New York Knicks	11/16/62
73	David Thompson	Denver	Detroit Pistons	4/9/78
72	Wilt Chamberlain	San Francisco	Los Angeles Lakers	11/3/62
71	Elgin Baylor	Los Angeles	New York Knicks	11/15/60
71	David Robinson	San Antonio	Los Angeles Clippers	4/24/94

Free throws

Any time a player is fouled while in the act of shooting, no matter how poorly she shoots the ball or how unlikely it is to drop in for a basket, referees award that player free throws. (The shot attempt does not count against her FGA, or *field goal attempts,* total.) If she is fouled on an attempt from inside the three-point arc, she gets two free throws. If she is fouled while attempting a three-point shot, she gets three free throws. (And the player who fouled her usually gets a hurricane of verbal abuse from her coach.)

Jason McElwain

The best shooting performance I have seen in the last ten years was not turned in by Kobe Bryant or Ray Allen in an NBA game, by Carmelo Anthony at Syracuse or J.J. Redick at Duke, or even LeBron James when he was in his final year of high school. The best shooting performance I have seen in the last ten years was performed by a high school kid in the only game he ever played.

Jason McElwain, who is autistic and did not speak until he was five years old, was the manager of his Greece Athena High School team near Rochester, NY. He had a pure love of basketball, but at 5'6" he was considered too small to even make the junior varsity team. But he was an inspiration to the team, so for Greece Athena's Senior Night game with Spencerport High on February 15, 2006, head coach Jim Johnson decided to dress McElwain. There were no guarantees he would get in because this was a game that would decide the division title.

With four minutes left, Greece Athena was up by double digits, and Johnson summoned McElwain to the scorer's table. Everyone in the sold out gym knew his story and hoped for just an opportunity, perhaps a layup to get him in the scoring column. McElwain missed his first two shots, one a three-pointer and one a layup. But those would be his last miscues of the night. He proceeded to make six consecutive three-pointers and a two-pointer in the last three and a half minutes to finish the night with 20 points in Greece Athena's 79–43 victory. It was truly a remarkable feat.

As soon as the final horn sounded, the fans rushed the floor and carried McElwain in celebration. The next day, a local television station in Rochester showed video of Jason's performance and soon it was a YouTube sensation (with over 2.5 million views entering 2011). *The Today Show*, *Good Morning America*, and even Oprah followed with features and interviews.

At the end of the year, McElwain was honored with an ESPY (Excellence in Sports Performance Yearly) award, for providing the best sports moment of 2006. Among the performances he beat out that year was Kobe Bryant's 81-point scoring performance against Toronto in an NBA game just two months prior.

Charles Barkley, who retired after the 1999–2000 season, was one of the wiliest players ever to bounce a ball. "Sir Charles" perfected the art of throwing the ball toward the hoop the moment he heard a whistle. Often Barkley had no intention of taking a shot but was fouled while moving, so he heaved up a prayer at the shrill of the whistle, hoping to be awarded two free throws. Barkley was so talented, however, that his heaves often went in. Kobe Bryant of the Los Angeles Lakers continues this practice today.

You cannot shoot a free throw unless another player fouls you. But not every foul results in free throws. Each level of basketball allows a defensive team a certain number of nonshooting, or *common* fouls, before that team shoots free throws. (See Chapter 3 for more information.)

Why do people love free throw stats? Because free throw shooting is the lone statistic that can be compared across all levels; it's the only aspect of the game that remains static regardless of the level of competition. Every player — man or woman, NBA, college, or high school — shoots the ball from 15 feet away at a basket that's 10 feet above the floor. You can compare, say, Steve Nash's free percentage for the Phoenix Suns with your son's at the junior high level.

Although I cover free throw shooting in-depth in Chapter 5, I want to stress the importance of free throw shooting in this chapter, too. The free throw is the highest-percentage shot available to a team (meaning that it's the easiest shot to make). A good squad converts at least 70 percent of its free throws. Compare that with field goal percentages, which seldom eclipse 50 percent.

Field goals

You can score field goals from anywhere on the court. They are worth two or three points, depending on the point of departure of the shooting player's feet when he releases the shot. (See "Scoring: One, two, three" earlier in this chapter.)

A field goal attempt must come from within the boundaries of the court. Referees disallow any inbound pass that happens to go in the basket without being touched first by a player in bounds, and the shot results in a turnover.

The three-pointer

In the 1967–68 season, the now-defunct American Basketball Association (ABA) introduced three-point goals, which have revolutionized basketball by affecting offensive positioning and, ergo, defensive positioning.

Before the 1975–76 season, the NBA, wise to the cult-like popularity of the ABA and covetous of its cache of offensive showstoppers (open-floor artists such as Julius Erving, George Gervin, and David Thompson), offered a merger. Four ABA teams — the Denver Nuggets, Indiana Pacers, New Jersey Nets, and San Antonio Spurs — joined the fold, and the remainder of the league went under.

Maybe the establishment league was too proud to admit that some facets of the ABA, such as the three-pointer (which nowadays might be termed "intellectual property" of the ABA), would improve the NBA. That may explain why the NBA dragged its feet before adopting the rule four years later — to overwhelming support, even from traditionalists.

To foul or not to foul?

The three-point shot has created another dilemma for coaches: to foul or not to foul. Here's the scenario: Your team leads by three with little time remaining — say, less than ten seconds. The opposition is on offense. Do you foul them before they can attempt a three, thereby putting one of their shooters on the free throw line to shoot just two free throws? Or, in hopes that your opponent misses the three, do you adopt the more traditional, pre-three-point era strategy of playing tough defense?

As a coach in this situation, you must compare your team's ability to defend the three-point goal versus its prowess in rebounding a missed foul shot. It's a potential darned-if-you-do, darned-if-you-don't situation. Play straight-up D and you'll be second-guessed. Foul someone and you can be sure that the opposition will intentionally miss the second free throw (provided that they make the first), resulting in chaos under the hoop and possibly an offensive rebound or a careless foul by your defense.

Most coaches choose not to force the action — they attempt to defend the three-point shooter. If you spread out your defense and get a defender's hand in the face of the shooter, the three-point shot is difficult to make. The worst that can happen is that your defender allows the three-pointer and fouls the shooter: You were up three a second ago, and now you lose by one, assuming that the shooter makes the free throw.

Suddenly, the guard, who had been forgotten in the late '70s while giants such as Kareem Abdul-Jabbar and Bill Walton terrorized the league, was a threat again. Nowadays, the trey is so much more than a gimmick, especially in the college game (where I believe it is too simple a shot). Today, 33 percent of all shots in college and 35 percent of all shots in the NBA are three-point shots.

For a shot to count for three points, both of the shooter's feet must be entirely behind the arc as the ball leaves his hands. The player can land on the line or over the line, but when his feet leave the floor no part of his feet can be on that line. Officials may tell you that this judgment call is most difficult when a player's sneakers are the same color as the painted line.

Three versus two

The three-pointer has transformed coaches into mathematicians and probability specialists. Smart coaches (not an oxymoron, I swear) understand that a 33 percent shooter from three-point range can score as many points as a 50 percent shooter from two-point range.

At the college level in 2009–10, the national average for three-point goals was just 34.33 percent. The national average for two-point field goal shooting was 48 percent. Ask yourself, "Would I prefer a 34-percent three-point shooter or a 48 percent two-point shooter?" Of course, you take other factors into account when rating a player, but in terms of pure shooting, you can examine the products.

The formula is simple. Say that Maya Moore of UCONN makes 34 of 100 shots from three-point land. How many points does she score? The answer is 102 (34×3). If her Huskies teammate, Tiffany Hayes, makes 48 of 100 two-point attempts, how many points does she score? 96 (48×2). There's no contest; Maya wins, 102–96.

A more realistic means of evaluating the production of a three-point shooter is to convert her three-point performance on a two-point basis. Here's the formula:

1. **Take the total of a player's three-point conversions and multiply that number by 3.**

   For example, if Maya makes 34 treys, multiply by 3. The answer is 102.

2. **Divide that number by 2.**

   $102 \div 2 = 51$.

3. **Divide that quotient by the number of field goals the player attempted.**

   Sticking with Maya, who has 100 attempts, the figure is .51. That figure is the three-point shooter's *effective yield* (in this case, 51 percent).

This statistic puts things in perspective. Folks have a tendency to think that a skilled college three-point shooter converts roughly 40 percent of her shots. But even if she is only a 34 percent shooter from outside the arc, that's equivalent to being a 51 percent shooter from two-point range. Hoopsters, as you've no doubt discovered, are skilled in their multiplication tables. (See Table 4-2.)

Finding a 50 percent three-point shooter is like uncovering a 75 percent marksman from inside the arc: No starter at any level has ever shot 75 percent from the field in the college or pro game for a season. But there have been some 50 percent three-point shooters over the years.

The NCAA men's record for three-point shooting in a season (given a minimum of 100 made three-pointers) is .573 by Steve Kerr of Arizona in 1987–88. That equates to an 86 percent two-point shooting yield. No wonder Michael Jordan wanted him on his Chicago Bulls Championship teams.

Table 4-2	Three-Point Shooting Yield Chart		
Three-Point Shooting	*Percentage*	*Points*	*Two-Point Percentage Shooting Field Goal*
1-10	.100	3	.150
2-10	.200	6	.300
3-10	.300	9	.450
4-10	.400	12	.600
5-10	.500	15	.750
6-10	.600	18	.900
7-10	.700	21	1.050
8-10	.800	24	1.250
9-10	.900	27	1.400
10-10	1.000	30	1.500

Three- and four-point plays

A *three-point play* occurs when a player scores a two-point field goal and a defender fouls her in the act of shooting. If she converts the free throw, her team accumulates a total of three points.

The *four-point play,* like polyester, does not occur naturally. The four-point play (*the quad?*), the rarest of scores, occurs when a player makes a three-point goal and a defender fouls him in the process. Some players, usually poorer shooters, attempt to draw this foul by intentionally taking a dive after minimal contact with a defender. This action is akin to a punter in football summoning his thespian skills to draw a penalty for roughing the kicker.

The official scorer

The duties of the *official scorer* in a game make air-traffic control work seem like a cinch. This person is responsible for tabulating field goals made, free throws made and missed, and a running summary of the points scored as well. In addition, the scorer must record the personal and technical fouls whistled against each player and must notify the official immediately when a player fouls out (which happens when a player gets five fouls in a college game, six in the NBA and WNBA).

The scorer also records time-outs taken by each team and keeps track of the possession arrow in high school and college hoops, which alternates with each held-ball situation. The scorebook of the home team is the official book. If discrepancies arise between the home team's book and that of the visitor, the home book assumes priority.

Official rules obligate each team's scorer to enter the complete roster in the scorebook before the game, matching numbers with the players' names. If this is not done, the referee assesses a technical foul.

Statistical genius: The box score

The ultimate statistician keeps all the elements of the *box score*. In addition to field goals, free throws, points, and fouls, an official box score contains assists, turnovers, blocked shots, steals, field goal attempts, three-point goals and attempts, and playing time. In all college and pro games, an official statistician (different from the official scorer) keeps tabs on the items listed in Figure 4-1 for each player in the box score.

The duties of the official scorer (the person in the striped shirt) are to keep track of:

- ✔ Field goals made
- ✔ Three-point field goals made
- ✔ Free throws made and attempted
- ✔ Personal fouls
- ✔ Team fouls

A stat crew keeps the other items in the box score, such as turnovers, blocked shots, and steals. This used to be done by hand when I was coaching, but today all the data is entered into a computer program.

For one person to monitor all these items is nearly impossible. *Do not try this at home,* especially because you are unable to see the clock in order to monitor each player's minutes played. Keeping every stat may be possible if you are watching a slow-tempo team, such as Princeton. But doing so while watching an up-tempo team, such as the Los Angeles Lakers, is out of the question unless you've been doing so for years.

Official Basketball Box Score -- Game Totals -- Final Statistics
BUTLER vs UCONN
4-4-11 8:23PM at RELIANT STADIUM, HOUSTON, TX

BUTLER 41 • 28-10

##	Player		Total FG-FGA	3-Ptr FG-FGA	FT-FTA	Rebounds Off	Def	Tot	PF	TP	A	TO	Blk	Stl	Min
54	HOWARD, Matt	f	1-13	1-6	4-4	2	4	6	2	7	0	0	0	1	37
44	SMITH, Andrew	c	2-9	0-0	1-2	6	3	9	3	5	1	1	1	1	29
01	MACK, Shelvin	g	4-15	4-11	1-2	4	5	9	1	13	1	3	1	0	36
02	VANZANT, Shawn	g	2-10	1-5	0-0	2	6	8	1	5	2	2	0	3	36
33	STIGALL, Chase	g	3-11	3-9	0-0	1	1	2	1	9	1	0	0	1	16
03	HAHN, Zach		0-2	0-1	0-0	0	0	0	2	0	0	0	0	0	7
05	NORED, Ronald		0-2	0-1	2-4	3	1	4	4	2	0	0	0	2	26
20	HOPKINS, Chrishawn		0-0	0-0	0-0	0	0	0	1	0	0	0	0	0	4
23	MARSHALL, Khyle		0-2	0-0	0-2	1	1	2	2	0	0	0	0	0	8
32	BUTCHER, Garrett		0-0	0-0	0-0	0	0	0	0	0	0	0	0	0	1
	Team					1	0	1							
	Totals		12-64	9-33	8-14	20	21	41	17	41	5	6	2	8	200

FG % 1st Half: 6-27   22.2% 2nd half: 6-37   16.2% Game: 12-64 18.8%
3FG % 1st Half: 5-14   35.7% 2nd half: 4-19   21.1% Game: 9-33 27.3%
FT % 1st Half: 5-8   62.5% 2nd half: 3-6   50.0% Game: 8-14 57.1%

Deadball Rebounds 2

UCONN 53 • 32-9

##	Player		Total FG-FGA	3-Ptr FG-FGA	FT-FTA	Rebounds Off	Def	Tot	PF	TP	A	TO	Blk	Stl	Min
10	OLANDER, Tyler	f	1-3	0-0	0-0	2	1	3	1	2	1	0	0	0	7
22	SMITH, Roscoe	f	0-2	0-1	0-0	1	3	4	4	0	0	2	4	0	22
34	ORIAKHI, Alex	c	5-6	0-0	1-1	2	9	11	2	11	0	0	4	0	25
03	LAMB, Jeremy	g	4-8	1-2	3-4	1	6	7	2	12	2	1	1	1	31
15	WALKER, Kemba	g	5-19	0-4	6-7	1	8	9	2	16	0	2	0	1	37
02	BEVERLY, Donnell		1-2	0-0	0-0	0	0	0	0	2	1	1	0	0	8
04	COOMBS-MCDANIEL, J		0-3	0-1	0-0	1	1	2	0	0	0	0	0	0	6
05	GIFFEY, Niels		1-3	0-1	2-2	3	3	6	1	4	0	2	0	0	24
13	NAPIER, Shabazz		1-6	0-2	2-2	0	4	4	1	4	2	3	0	2	27
35	OKWANDU, Charles		1-3	0-0	0-0	4	1	5	2	2	0	0	1	0	13
	Team					2	0	2							
	Totals		19-55	1-11	14-16	17	36	53	15	53	6	11	10	4	200

FG % 1st Half: 9-31   29.0% 2nd half: 10-24 41.7% Game: 19-55 34.5%
3FG % 1st Half: 0-5   0.0% 2nd half: 1-6   16.7% Game: 1-11 9.1%
FT % 1st Half: 1-1   100.0 2nd half: 13-15 86.7% Game: 14-16 87.5%

Deadball Rebounds 0

Officials: John Cahill, Verne Harris, Doug Shows
Technical fouls: BUTLER-None. UCONN-None.
Attendance: 70376
2011 NCAA Championshiop National Title Game

Figure 4-1:
An example of an official box score.

Score by periods	1st	2nd	Total
BUTLER	22	19	41
UCONN	19	34	53

Points	In Paint	Off T/O	2nd Chance	Fast Break	Bench
BU	2	13	20	0	2
UCONN	26	2	13	4	12

Last FG - BU 2nd-0:41, UCONN 2nd-05.05.
Largest lead - BU by 6 2nd-19:40, UCONN by 14 2nd-05:49.

Score tied - 4 times.
Lead changed - 8 times.

The more stats you try to keep, the less accurate you're going to be. Start out slowly when it comes to keeping stats. Keep a few items like scoring and fouls first, and master the process before you move on to more challenging stat-keeping figures, such as field goal attempts or offensive rebounds.

Other Statistics Worth Watching

Some ratio stats that you won't find in the box score have tremendous appeal to both coaches and fans. Again, the more you understand about the game, the greater meaning these stats have. They reveal why one team consistently plays better (or worse) than its foes.

Assists

An *assist* is a pass that leads directly to a basket. And I do mean directly. Assists are not credited when a player receives a pass, dribbles the ball many times, double-pumps, and then scores. Perhaps the best way to think of an assist is as a pass without which the receiver would not have been able to score.

The assist is the most discretionary of all stats. The definition reads that an assist may be credited when a player, "in the judgment of the statistician," makes the principal pass contributing directly to a field goal. The distance of the pass and the distance from where the player who receives the pass shoots are irrelevant. Two examples are:

✔ **March 28, 1992:** Duke trails Kentucky 103–102 in the East Regional final of the NCAA tourney. Only two seconds remain, and the Blue Devils must in-bound the ball from their own baseline. Grant Hill tosses a 60-foot pass to teammate Christian Laettner, who fakes to his right, dribbles, and then spins left to shoot. Assist to Hill? You can argue that Hill's pass led directly to Laettner's field goal — and what a superb pass it was. Then again, you can argue that Laettner was not in a scoring position when he received the pass and that he could never have made the shot without faking to his right and then spinning. For the record, Hill received credit for the assist.

✔ **May 26, 1987:** Detroit is playing Boston at Boston during Game Five of the NBA Eastern Conference Finals. The Pistons lead the Celtics 107–106 in the waning seconds when the Celtics' Larry Bird steals the ball in Detroit's backcourt. Bird dishes to teammate Dennis Johnson, who catches it to the left of the free throw lane, dribbles once, and then scores the winning lay-up. Assist? Yes. Although "DJ" did not score from the point at which he caught the ball, Bird's pass led directly to his basket.

I feel that two aspects of the assist should be changed. First, I have always felt that you should be able to give two assists — like in hockey — on one play. Many times, a point guard gives a great pass, and another player makes a pass that leads to the basket. That first pass should get some credit because it can be more important than the second pass.

Second, at present, a great pass that leads to the shooter being fouled is not credited as an assist, and it should be. How many times have you seen a player on a fast break make the extra pass to a teammate, leaving the defender no choice but to either foul the receiver of that pass or surrender an easy deuce? Shouldn't the player who made that pass be rewarded with an assist if his teammate makes both — or even one — of the subsequent free throws? As the rule reads now, you may only give an assist on a made field goal.

Turnovers (not the cherry kind)

A *turnover* occurs when the offense loses possession of the ball by a means other than a missed shot. An offense, or offensive player, that's prone to turnovers is usually considered sloppy, not very smart, poorly coached, or all of the above. Defenses that force a lot of turnovers usually win. After all, an opponent can't score if it doesn't shoot or have possession of the ball.

Turnovers are far more important in football, where fewer possessions occur per game. However, in hoops, turnovers can be huge in terms of building or losing momentum. And just because a team is skilled at forcing turnovers does not mean that it knows how to avoid turnovers on offense. During the 1995–96 NBA season, for example, Seattle SuperSonics guard Gary Payton led the league in forcing turnovers (231), but his then-teammate, forward Shawn Kemp, was second in the NBA in committing turnovers (315).

Following are the common causes of turnovers:

- ✔ **Violations:** Offensive violations that result in loss of possession include traveling, double dribbling, palming, standing in the free throw lane for more than three seconds, stepping out of bounds while in possession of the ball, and offensive goaltending.

- ✔ **Offensive fouls:** When your team has possession of the ball and you are called for a *charging foul* (you have the ball, and you initiate contact with the defender) or an *illegal screen* (a teammate has the ball, and you block off a defender illegally), you lose possession of the ball and are thus charged with a turnover. An offensive foul called during a rebounding situation is not considered a turnover as long as the shot was attempted before the referee whistled the foul.

- ✔ **Steals:** A steal is a stat in itself (see "Steals" later in this chapter), but it is also a turnover. When a defender intercepts a pass or simply takes possession of the ball away from the offensive player controlling it, the statistician charges a turnover against the last offensive player who had possession of the ball before the steal.

- ✔ **Technical fouls:** If your team is in possession of the ball and you mouth off at the referee or perform an equally reckless act (such as kicking an opponent), the referee calls a technical foul. Your team loses possession of the ball, and you are charged with a turnover.

✔ **Special situations:** All kinds of special examples exist when discussing the turnover statistics. For example, what happens when a defender forces an offensive player into a *held-ball* (a.k.a. *jump ball*) situation? If you have possession of the ball and a held-ball situation arises, you establish the next possession in two ways. In the NBA, the two players involved participate in a jump ball: The ref tosses up the ball, and the players attempt to tap it to their teammates. In college, players use an alternating possession arrow.

Stat rule: If your team loses possession of the ball as the result of a held ball, the statistician must charge a turnover. The turnover is charged to the person who last had possession of the ball. That could be the person involved in the tug of war, but not always. If Player A has the ball knocked loose by Player B, for example, and Players C and D are involved in a held-ball situation, the statistician charges the turnover to Player A, not Player C or D. Player A made the mistake that led to the held ball. Similarly, if Player A happens to be simply holding the ball and Player B (a defender) grabs it, resulting in a jump ball, then Player A receives the turnover charge.

Blocked shots

Only defensive players get credit for blocked shots. When, in the opinion of the head statistician, a defender alters the shot by making contact with the ball and the shot fails to go in, she credits a blocked shot to that player.

According to the NCAA rule book, under blocked shots, the ball "must leave the shooter's hand" in order for a defender to get credit for blocking the shot. I think that phrase has to go — quite frankly, most statisticians don't pay any attention to it. Tim Duncan of the San Antonio Spurs, for example, is a maestro at stuffing a shot before it even left the shooter's hand. Why should he wait?

No other stat in hoops is so closely associated with a player's height as blocked shots. Taller players not only stand above their opponents, but they almost always have longer arms, too. More often than not, leading shot blockers are 7-footers (for women, players who are taller than 6'5"). Baylor's Brittney Griner led the nation in blocked shots in both 2009–10 and 2010–11 with nearly five per game. She is 6'8" tall.

The best shot blockers are those who understand that swatting a shot is only half the job. Swatting it to another defensive player, or at least keeping it in bounds so that a teammate may grab it, is the ice cream with your cake. Check out some old films of former Celtics great Bill Russell. He was a master at blocking a shot and keeping the ball in play.

Steals

A player receives credit for a *steal* when she makes a positive, aggressive action that causes the opponent to turn over the ball. A player may accomplish a steal by

- ✔ Taking the ball away from an opponent who had control.

- ✔ Instigating a held-ball situation, leading to the defender's team gaining possession. If the defender's team does not gain possession, it is not a steal.

- ✔ Batting a ball off an opponent to a defensive teammate, who then gains possession.

- ✔ Batting a ball off an opponent out of bounds, leading to the defense gaining possession.

- ✔ Intercepting an opponent's pass.

In case you're wondering, the first and the last items in the preceding list are the most common types of steals, as well as the biggest crowd-pleasers. Players who lead the NBA in steals, such as Chris Paul of the New Orleans Hornets and Rajon Rondo of the Boston Celtics, are generally quick, smart players who are able to anticipate an offensive player's actions.

Minutes

Playing time is the easiest of all statistics with which a player may receive credit — all he has to do is just get into the game.

Statistically, playing time is kept to the nearest minute. If a player sees action for 27 minutes and 15 seconds, his playing time appears in the box score, under MIN, as "27." If he plays for 27 minutes and 35 seconds, it appears as "28."

A player can appear in a game — and even score a basket — yet have a playing time figure of 0. This occurs when a player participates for less than 30 seconds. On the stat sheet, her minutes figure is recorded as "0+☐." Conversely, say that a player starts and plays the entire game. With less than 30 seconds remaining in the game, the coach takes her out of the game. In college it is recorded as "40-" (40 minutes being the length of a college game).

Playing time is an important statistic because it allows you to compile ratios from raw data. With these ratios, you can compare the performances of players whose length of participation varies dramatically.

Ratios

Ratios measure the relationship between two pieces of data. Speed, for example, is a ratio of distance to time. Hoops junkies use ratios to measure the relationship between two related statistical units (such as offensive rebounds and second-shot baskets) or two units that directly contradict each other (such as assists and turnovers).

These ratios enable hoops junkies to measure a player's worth. (Fear not: None of the following information is on the final exam.)

Assist/turnover ratio

Being a great point guard requires more than just assists. If a point guard averages ten assists per game but just as many turnovers, her coach may want to advise her to play more conservatively.

An assist/turnover ratio, which most often applies to comparing point guards, measures a player's effectiveness as a passer. It is a more revealing stat than assists alone because each pass stolen from a player negates an assist that player might have made.

For example, in 2009–10, Allison Lacey of Iowa State had 187 assists and 63 turnovers for a 2.97 assist/turnover ratio. Andrea Riley, who played at Oklahoma State, the same Big 12 Conference as Lacey, had more assists with 220, but she committed 147 turnovers. That is an assist/turnover ratio of 1.5. Most coaches would take the higher assist/turnover ratio over the higher assist total.

A good assist/turnover ratio is 2 to 1 or better at the college level and 3 to 1 or better at the NBA level. Why the difference? The NBA is more liberal with assists; in addition, each team has more possessions in an NBA game, leading to more scoring and more opportunities for an assist.

Per-minute statistics

You can have only five players on the floor at one time, which invariably leads to some players seeing more action than others. As a coach or fan, how can you measure the contributions of players who play less than the starters and thus have fewer points, rebounds, and so on?

Use the per-minute stat to measure a player's value in terms of any other raw data stat. Say that WNBA 2010 MVP Lauren Jackson of the Seattle Storm scores eight points in a game. However, Jackson plays only eight minutes. Her per-minute scoring average is one point per minute, which, extrapolated to a 40-minute game, would be 40 points per game. Nobody in the WNBA — or the NBA, for that matter — averages 40 points per game. Suddenly, Jackson's eight points look more impressive.

Although coaches find the per-minute stat helpful in evaluating players, and this stat makes for great arguments among fans, it has its limitations. Imagine that Jackson had buried a three-pointer in her first minute of play and then sat out the rest of the game due to injury. Does anyone truly believe that she would've scored 120 points (3×40 minutes) in that game had she played its entirety?

Per-game statistics

Per-minute statistics tend to be used by coaches more than fans or the media. Per-minute stats often seem a little too technical because the raw numbers don't look meaningful. Comparing 0.5 points per minute to 0.67 points per minute just doesn't have a ring to it.

On the other hand, when you see scoring averages of 12.5 or 16.0 per game, these are meaningful to people other than coaches. Per-game statistics enable fans to make comparisons between players, especially when comparing a player who's been injured and missed a few games to someone who's been healthy all year.

Per-game stats are also used to determine which player receives the title of league leader in a statistical category. Consider this hypothetical example. Say Kevin Garnett of the Boston Celtics plays only 70 games in a season and scores 2,100 points, and Tim Duncan of the San Antonio Spurs plays all 82 games and scores 2,378 points. Garnett receives recognition for being the league scoring leader for having a higher per-game average (30 points per game to Duncan's 29 points per game).

Here's where the per-game stat becomes even kookier. Imagine that Garnett plays 40 minutes per game, whereas Duncan plays 30. (**Remember:** None of this is on the final. Relax.) Multiply each player's total games played by his average minutes per game to find his total minutes (Garnett 2,800, Duncan 2,460). Now divide total points by total minutes to find each player's points per minute. Garnett's average would be .75 points per minute, and Duncan's average would be .96.

Hence Duncan could score more total points *and* average more points per minute (the more valid stat), but based on points per game, Garnett still wins the scoring title. Who says life is fair?

Bench scoring

To calculate bench scoring, you add up the points scored by players who did not start the contest.

What's so important about bench scoring? A team that consistently receives a lot of scoring from its bench is able to substitute more freely, hence all the players are fresher at game's end. Also, the impact of a starter fouling out is less.

This stat has more relevance at the college level. Most players who advance to the NBA are capable of scoring 20 points a game at least once a season. However, many a winning college team gets exposed in the NCAA for its lack of depth. In the 1996 championship game, for example, Kentucky's bench outscored Syracuse's 26–0. Not surprisingly, in the final ten minutes, Kentucky pulled away from the valiant Orangemen, who by that time were out of juice.

This is not always the case however. In 2010, Duke won the NCAA Championship with a victory over Butler, and UCONN won the women's title against Stanford. Neither Duke nor UCONN had a single point off their bench in their respective championship games. The two championship teams were outscored by a combined 26–0 in bench scoring.

Second-chance points

Second-chance points are points scored on offensive rebounds. In the 1995 NCAA championship game between UCLA and Arkansas, for example, UCLA got 21 offensive rebounds and scored 27 points off those offensive rebounds — or second-chance points.

Note: Getting an offensive rebound by itself is not enough; you have to score off the offensive rebound to be awarded second-chance points.

Points off turnovers

Points off turnovers are very similar to second-chance points. Forcing turnovers is great, but you have to score points when you get those extra chances.

This is a very important stat for teams that press a lot. The University of Maryland has used a full court press for many years and its ability to force a turnover and turn it into a quick score is important to what they do. If Maryland is not winning this stat, they probably aren't winning the game.

Triple doubles

Triple double may sound like a figure skating term, or perhaps two very productive at-bats in baseball. But in fact, former Los Angeles Lakers public relations director Bruce Joelsch coined this basketball term in the early '80s.

Joelsch, ever the dedicated PR flak, was in search of a pithy way to describe the all-around contributions of Laker point guard Earvin "Magic" Johnson.

Magic was, above all other things, a master passer — arguably the best that the game has ever seen. At 6'9", however, he was also a point guard who could use his height advantage to outscore and outrebound opponents. Magic rarely led the NBA in those other two categories, however, so Joelsch invented the triple double. Every time Magic reached double digits (that is, at least ten) in assists, points, and rebounds, Joelsch credited him with a triple double. Joelsch's gimmick stuck; it's now recognized, although not in the box score, as a legitimate stat.

A triple double may be any troika of positive double-digit stats. Points-assists-rebounds are the most conventional means of achieving a triple double, but a point guard may achieve a points-assists-steals triple double, or a center may achieve a points-rebounds-blocked shots triple double.

You can travel back in time to record triple doubles for players who retired prior to the stat's creation, but you cannot always use the blocked shot statistic as one-third of the triple double. The NBA did not introduce the blocked shot stat into its games until the 1973–74 season. By then, noted sultans of swat, such as Bill Russell, had retired. Wilt Chamberlain actually led the NBA in assists (8.6) in 1967–68, in addition to leading the league in rebounding (23.8) and finishing third in scoring (24.3). I'm sure that he had many triple doubles, and probably a few quadruple doubles, that season if you factor in blocked shots.

Oscar Robertson's legend grew ten years after he retired when this statistic was introduced. Researchers found that Robertson averaged a triple double per game over the course of the 1961–62 season, still the only player to do that over the course of an NBA season. He had 181 triple doubles for his 14-year career, still the all-time record in NBA history and 43 more than Johnson accumulated in his career.

Quadruple doubles

A *quadruple double* is the same as a triple double, except that it involves one more category of ten or better. Only four quadruple doubles have occurred in NBA history, with the last recorded by David Robinson of the San Antonio Spurs on February 17, 1994. He had 34 points, 10 rebounds, 10 assists, and 10 blocks, and is the only player to have at least 30 points in a quadruple double.

Figure 4-2:
Tamika
Catchings.

The only Division I men's college basketball quadruple double took place on November 13, 2007 when Lester Hudson of UT-Martin had one against Central Baptist.

The women are not left out of this. Ann Meyers, who is in the Naismith Hall of Fame, had 20 points, 14 rebounds, 10 assists, and 10 steals against Stephen F. Austin on February 18, 1978.

There has been just one quintuple double in history at any level of basketball. Tamika Catchings (see Figure 4-2), now with the Indiana Fever of the WNBA and a star at Tennessee under Pat Summitt, had 25 points, 18 rebounds, 11 assists, 10 blocked shots, and 10 steals in a high school game for Duncanville High School in Texas in 1997. What makes it even more eye catching was that it was accomplished in a 32-minute high school game.

Part II
The Fundamentals of Basketball

The 5th Wave   By Rich Tennant

In this part . . .

Chock-full of information, this part gives you the low-down on basketball fundamentals like shooting, playing offense and defense, rebounding, and setting up plays. For your added reading pleasure, I sprinkle in my personal anecdotes from my coaching career to help illustrate my points.

Whether you are a coach, a fan, or a player, you can't help but benefit from the information here. One chapter is devoted to each fundamental element, so just read whichever chapters interest you (or read about the element you need help with!).

Chapter 5

Shooting

. . . .

In This Chapter

▶ Perfecting the mechanics of shooting

▶ Developing free throw skills

▶ Utilizing the five sweet spots on the floor

▶ Practicing dunking, three-pointers, and other fancy stuff

▶ Running shooting drills

. . . .

This chapter talks about that all-important aspect of basketball, shooting. Simply put, *shooting* is the act of tossing the ball toward the basket in an attempt to *score,* which happens when the ball goes through the basket. Every player in the game may shoot. If you don't shoot, you don't score. And if you don't score, you can't win.

Becoming a Good Shooter

Odd as it sounds, being a great *shooter* is not the same as being a great *scorer.* Wilt Chamberlain is tied with Michael Jordan as the most prolific scorer in NBA history. Both players averaged 30.1 points per game. In 1962, while playing for the Philadelphia Warriors, Chamberlain scored 100 points against the New York Knicks (during which one could hear some of his Philadelphia Warriors teammates utter, "Hey, Wilt, I'm open!").

Chamberlain's record for points in a game still stands. The nearest anyone has come is LA Laker Kobe Bryant, who scored 81 points in a game against the Toronto Raptors in 2006. Still, no one ever thinks of The Big Dipper, which was one of Chamberlain's pseudonyms, as one of basketball's great shooters.

That's because Chamberlain scored so many of his points within ten feet of the basket. His scoring aptitude had more to do with his physical dominance than his shooting touch. Chamberlain's subpar free throw shooting percentage, which hovered just above 50 percent during his career, underscores that fact.

A player is either a shooter or he isn't. You may improve a player's form — and hence his shooting percentage — but some players simply do not have the touch.

Why not? Nonshooters lack the proper mechanics and, more importantly, they lack confidence. Being a shooter is like being a gunslinger: You can buy Clint Eastwood in the role, but not Adam Sandler. Two of the NBA's current more prolific scorers, Kevin Durant and Dwyane Wade, are the last guys you'd ever find reading *I'm OK, You're OK*.

Putting a 9-inch ball through an 18-inch hoop

The first step in building your confidence is to recognize how vast that gaping hole 10 feet above you really is. I once visited UCLA and worked with Bruins forward Kris Johnson, whose dad, Marques, had been a scoring machine for 11 NBA seasons. That afternoon I grabbed two basketballs, which are a little over 9 inches in diameter, and showed Kris that both balls are basically able to fit simultaneously within the 18-inch diameter rim. (See Figure 5-1.) Kris was shocked. "I never thought of it that way," he said.

The reason why making a shot at one of those booths at a county fair is so difficult? It isn't only because you're trying too hard to impress your date — the rim diameter is much smaller than a regulation basketball hoop's.

Developing a soft touch

Shooting is an anagram of *soothing,* which is how a shot should feel: soft, with a light touch. Play word-association for a moment. Former Los Angeles Laker forward Jamaal Wilkes, a deadly shooter who was inducted into the Basketball Hall of Fame, was nicknamed "Silk." The onomatopoetic term *swish,* which describes the feathery sound of a basketball sailing through the net without hitting the rim, conjures images of softness. On the other hand, poorly shot balls are commonly known as *bricks,* and players who shoot them, bricklayers. Not very soothing.

If you have a soft touch, you can make the shot you might have otherwise missed. Don Nelson had that kind of soft touch when he played for the Boston Celtics. In 1969 "Nellie" stepped to the free throw line with a championship at stake. Nelson's shot hit the back iron of the rim, bounced five feet straight up in the air above the basket, and then fell through the hoop for the clinching point. Not a pretty shot, but Nelson's soft touch kept it within the cylinder.

Figure 5-1:
Shooting
seems much
easier when
you keep
in mind
that two
basketballs
fit through
the hoop at
once.

Proper mechanics allow you to take advantage of the rim's diameter — commentators refer to this as "getting the kind bounce" — so even if you don't shoot the ball with a marksman's precision, the ball has a chance to fall through the basket.

Digger's Five Keys to Shooting

Former Seattle Supersonics forward Chuck Person was known as "The Rifleman." The comparison between shooting a basketball and shooting a rifle is worth making. You've heard, "Ready. Aim. Fire!" Before you fire that bullet, you need to be ready and take aim. Pulling the trigger is just the final step in the process.

This section talks about the five main points that you should concentrate on when working on your shooting form.

Balance yourself

Once I was advising a college player as he was practicing free throws. After one of his attempts, I pushed one finger on his chest and he teetered off balance. "That's your problem," I told him.

His body was not balanced. So we worked on having him balance his body as he came out of a shot. "Spread your feet the width of your shoulders," I said. He did so and then shot again. This time, when I nudged him with my finger, he was firm as an oak tree. (See Figure 5-2.)

Figure 5-2: At left, the shooter's feet are too close, resulting in no balance after the shot. At right, the shooter's feet are spread to shoulder width to give him balance.

 Your body should be balanced after every shot, even when you follow the shot (in case it misses) and prepare for a rebound. (See Chapter 8 for more on offensive rebounding.) You can become a better shooter if you're in balance with both your lower and upper body. But having your upper body in balance and square to the target (facing the basket) is even more important than balancing your lower body.

Shoot with your legs

Your knees and associated leg muscles needed are the booster rockets for the body. Your legs, not your arms, provide the power needed to propel the basketball. Some of the most accurate three-point shooters in NBA history, such as 6'3" Steve Kerr and 6'4" Tim Legler (whose nickname, oddly enough, was "Legs"!), were neither very tall nor spectacularly muscular. Kerr and Legs bent their knees and relied on leg strength to heave the ball up from 23 feet away. And they did so with far greater accuracy than players who were half a foot taller.

Your legs are much stronger than your arms. You involve your arms, all the way down to the tips of your fingers, in aiming the ball toward the rim. The less power your arms exert, the more precision you get.

Think of it this way. Below your waist is all about power. Above your waist is all about precision.

By bending your knees and thrusting upward, you provide all the thrust that the ball needs to reach the basket. Let your arms be the guidance system.

Grab the rim

The majority of missed shots are neither too short nor too long, but rather off a little to the right or left. These misses happen when you fail to extend your arm straight. You turn your wrist, and that is how you miss half the shots. If you shoot it straight and are a little short or long, the ball still has a chance to go in the bucket.

Remember Kris Johnson? When Kris and I analyzed his shot with the rim at eye level, I had him stand close enough to the rim so that he could grab it with his fingertips on the follow-through. When he grabbed the rim, his hand didn't turn. It was straight and parallel to the ground. If you visualize grabbing the rim straight on as you shoot, you are in balance and have a better follow-through. (See Figure 5-3.)

During a game, of course, the rim is never at eye level (if it is, I'd like to be your agent). Still, visualize grabbing it. Doing so accomplishes two goals:

- ✔ It lines up the shot as straight as it can be.
- ✔ It gives the ball a backward rotation, the result being the softest shot possible.

Figure 5-3:
Visualize grabbing the rim when you shoot a free throw.

Watch any good shooter and you notice that his arm looks like the neck of a swan on his follow-through. Observe that the ball has a noticeable backspin as it sails toward the hoop. Watch a good shooter swish a jump shot. Notice how the twine of the net often jumps up onto the rim. I'm no physicist, but I do know that the backward rotation of the ball is responsible for that. A net entangled in the rim is the sign of a shooter who "grabs the rim."

Control the ball with your fingertips

Quarterbacks grip a football by the seams for control. You should do the same when shooting a basketball. The best shooters give their shots a high arc, which starts with having good fingertip control on the seams. Try this one-hand shooting drill:

Lay down on your back. Now, lay the ball in the palm of your hand. Grab the seams with your fingertips and pretend that you're going to shoot, only shoot the ball straight up in the air, just a few feet above your head. Concentrate on your fingertips giving the ball backspin by using the seams to initiate the spin.

Only your middle three fingers are on the seams. The middle finger should rest a little bit higher on the seam, and your ring and index fingers rest in the seam. The thumb plays more of a support role, and the pinkie, as in so many situations, does best by just staying out of the way.

Arch your shot

Remember that you are aiming above the rim, not at it. The best shots soar in a parabolic arc toward the basket, as opposed to a line drive. Keep an eye on the kid on your team, or an opposing team, who always seems to score the most points. Chances are that his shots seem to hang in the air longer. That's a product of the previous two keys — grabbing the rim and fingertips — but it is important to remind yourself to arch that shot. Put a little air under it.

Perfecting the Free Throw

The *free throw* is the most important shot in basketball. Shoot it poorly, and it becomes an Achilles heel that defenses will exploit. Shoot it well, and it becomes the most potent weapon in your offensive arsenal. (See Chapter 3 for more information about free throw situations.) It should also be the easiest shot. You stand 15 feet from the rim, perpendicular to the backboard, and, most important, nobody guards you. You even have plenty of time — ten seconds — to relax. Your only opposition when you attempt a free throw is yourself.

The free throw is the shooter's shot because it's all about proper mechanics and mental discipline. The free throw is the great leveler in basketball because you don't need to soar like Blake Griffin or drive like Rajon Rondo to be deft at it.

The man who owns the world record for consecutive free throw shooting, Tom Amberry of Rossmoor, California, is a retired podiatrist. In 1993, Amberry made 2,750 free throws in a row. It is worth mentioning that Amberry was 71 years old at the time.

Amberry's secret? "Focus and concentration," he says on his website, www. freethrow.com. "When I'm shooting a free throw, I don't think of anything else. I am 100 percent positive I will make the basket. Never have a negative thought on the free throw line."

"It is important to have the right mechanics," Amberry says. "Once you have that, the rest is mental."

 The mechanics explained above are the same for all types of shooting. If I can get you shooting foul shots at 75 percent like the pros do (which is about 30 percentage points higher than for shots attempted during live action, known as *field goals*), then I can get you to shoot a 12-foot jumper.

Actually, you shouldn't be satisfied with 75-percent success on free throws. Don't be satisfied to give up 25 percent of your scoring ability. Why let that rim beat you 25 percent of the time?

Taking the pressure shot

You have your feet in balance, at shoulder width and parallel to each other. You know that your knees are going to provide the thrust and that you grab the rim after you shoot, and you're visualizing how big that hoop is: twice as wide around as the ball. You can add your own routine at the beginning: dribble one, two, or three times, talk to the ball, anything.

Adrian Dantley, who was an All-American while playing for me at Notre Dame, had a distinct pre-shot ritual. Massaging the ball close to his chest, Adrian would repeat the following mantra: "Over the rim, backspin, follow through." That little reminder helped Dantley shoot 81.8 percent from the line for his 15 years in the NBA.

Before each free throw, Steve Nash of the Phoenix Suns, who is currently the most accurate free throw shooter in NBA history (90.4 percent), pantomimes his follow through. He "shoots" the ball before the referee tosses the ball to remind himself of what his form should be. No matter what your ritual, take a deep breath before a free throw. Suck air in and let it out. This relaxes your body. You may not have 20,000 lunatics screaming at you as you attempt the shot, but in any game pressure is a companion at the charity stripe (as the free throw line is also known).

If you relax your shooting arm, you have a better chance of making the shot. If you shoot like a stiff board, you're going to catapult the shot, not shoot it.

Now simply aim for the top of the front of the rim. *Just get it over the rim —* that's what you should be thinking. You don't necessarily look at the square on the backboard, although doing so helps you keep your arm straight and to have that all-important accuracy. But look over the rim; get it on top of the rim.

The ball rests loosely in your hand. Your palm does not touch it; your fingertips control the shot. Hold the ball at waist level with both hands, take your deep breath, and then lift it up, aim, and shoot.

Drilling home free throw mechanics

During a game, you usually shoot two free throws during one visit to the foul line. Do the same when you practice: Shoot two straight and then step off the line. Too many young players can make nine of ten without moving their feet from the same spot because their body gets into a rhythm. This instills a false sense of accomplishment. Back off and reset after every two free throws.

To keep free throw practice fun, I try to make it competitive. The following games add a little pressure to free throw practice, which only makes sense. After all, making your shots depends a great deal on nerves.

Seventy percent . . . or you run

Shoot ten free throws. Remember, step off the line after each set of two. You must make seven of your ten free throws. If you don't, sprint to the opposite baseline and back to the foul line and start again. And, if you miss four of your first six, you still must shoot the other four fouls shots before you do your sprint.

Ten straight one-and-ones

The *one-and-one* situation, in which the shooter must convert his first free throw attempt in order to receive a second, exists in high school and college play. A coach must have invented it because it directly rewards good free throw shooting and punishes bad. As if free throws weren't stressful enough.

A good drill to simulate the one-and-one situation is vital. At the end of practice, have the team line up on the baseline. Then randomly call on players to step to the foul line to shoot both ends (you hope) of a one-and-one. If the player misses her first shot, call another player. Oh, but first have the team sprint down to the other baseline and back. The drill ends only after three players in a row make both ends of the one-and-one.

Free throw practice and conditioning are two of the less popular aspects of practice. You may as well combine them.

Situations in a scrimmage

Be realistic. When one player fouls another during a scrimmage, stop play and have the fouled player shoot free throws. However, make every free throw situation a one-and-one. I cannot overemphasize the importance of one-and-ones. These are bonus points that you're giving away when you miss.

Don't psyche out a tyke

If you're teaching your 7-year-old to shoot free throws, do not have him shoot from the regulation free throw line with a regulation-sized ball on a 10-foot basket. He'll have to fling it slingshot-style just to reach the rim. He'll soon become bored because the sport seems too difficult, and will want to take up another sport — such as stock car racing.

Instead, use a 7-foot basket if you can find one. Have the child shoot from 8 feet away, not 15. If you have a smaller basketball, such as a women's ball, use that. Then go over the five keys to shooting, beginning with nudging your child in the chest to show the importance of balance.

The Five Shooting Areas

Now that you know how to shoot, from where do you shoot? Trigger-happy shooters such as Monta Ellis of the Golden State Warriors might answer, "From wherever you're open." For us mortals, this section talks about five sweet spots on the floor. Jump back to Chapter 3 if you need a refresher on the areas of the court.

Under the basket (the layup or dunk)

Layups and dunks are easy shots if no defenders are nearby. Use the square on the backboard instead of aiming for the top of the rim. But if defenders are nearby, expect to extract one or two of them from your tonsils; defenses don't surrender the layup — or dunk, for that matter — gladly.

If you're tall or springy enough to dunk the ball, be my guest. In a bygone era, the dunk was seen as a showboat play. Now coaches and players see it for what it is: the game's highest-percentage shot.

The square is your friend

Behind every missed layup is a tale of the square neglected. When shooting a layup, you need not even look at the rim. Focus on the square painted on the backboard. Lay the ball there — softly, no matter how speedily you race down the court to beat your defender.

Use the correct foot

Layups start at the bottom; that is, at your feet. Beginners must learn to shoot layups off the proper foot. A right-handed layup requires your left foot as the spring (the right foot is in the air first). The left-handed layup uses the right foot.

If you can learn to shoot layups with either hand, you will have a tremendous advantage over your peers. You'd be surprised how many pro basketball players — men and women — cannot comfortably shoot a layup with their weak hand.

Layups from the right side of the bucket should always be shot with the right hand, and those from the left with the left hand. Why? A righty who shoots a layup from the left side with her right hand is going to discover that the rim (and the defense) blocks a lot of her shots.

It is never too early to learn to be ambidextrous when it comes to layups.

Footstep drill

Player A receives the ball at half-court and takes it in for a layup as if it is a fast break. Player B begins from 5 feet behind and acts as a chasing defender. Will the offensive player blow the layup because he hears footsteps?

Player A should not look behind him or take his eyes off the square on the backboard. What he should be thinking about is:

- ✔ Beating the defender down court
- ✔ Jumping off the correct foot
- ✔ Putting the ball in the square

Beyond the arc

The three-point arc is a line painted on the court that runs in roughly a semicircle around the basket. In college, the radius of the three-point arc is 20'9" inches from the basket whereas in the NBA the distance is 23'9". In high school and in lower grades the radius is 19'9". Some players love to shoot a three-pointer from the top of the key — directly behind the free throw line — whereas others prefer the corner. If you are not yet high school age, do not devote too much time to this shot.

The elbows

Elbow is a term for the two spots on the floor that mark the intersection of the foul line extended and the lane line.

The right or left wing

Tim Duncan of the San Antonio Spurs is a low-post player, but he loves to position himself between the elbow and the baseline. Here, at the wing, is the ideal spot on the court for players who prefer shooting bank shots, as Duncan does. A bank shot is one in which you aim for the white square on the backboard, as opposed to shooting the ball over the front of the rim.

The right or left corner

So you want to make it a little tough on yourself, eh? From the corner (taking what's known as a *baseline shot*), the backboard cannot be your ally. It's not in your sight line to provide depth perception, nor is the square visible. You shoot most of your blush-inducing airballs from here.

That said, many a pure shooter, especially those who love the feel of a swished shot, swear by the corner shot.

Shooting for Variety

While every shot requires a special touch, the following three truly test the hoops marksman. The first demands that you actually aim at the backboard — not at the basket — while the other two are studies in the contrast of power that you must apply to the shot.

The bank shot

The bank shot — any shot that uses the backboard — is one of the lost arts of basketball. When you know the angle, the target is easy to hit. Legendary UCLA coach John Wooden, who directed the Bruins to ten NCAA titles in the 1960s and '70s, had his teams practice this shot all day. Currently in the NBA, only Spurs center Tim Duncan "visits the bank" regularly.

A good exercise is to play an entire pickup game, or a game of H-O-R-S-E (see Chapter 10), shooting nothing but bank shots.

Use the square as your target on the bank shot, although you learn via practice that from different spots on the court you have to aim for different areas of the square. Why is the bankshot so successful? One reason: It compels you to give your shot a higher arc to hit the square, and high-arcing shots always necessitate proper mechanics.

The baby jumper

Who says that you have to shoot from far outside or directly under the hoop? Give me the guy who can shoot the 8- to 12-foot jump shot, the *baby jumper*. I can teach him how to pivot with his back to the basket to create room for himself.

The skills required to shoot the baby jumper are the same as those needed to make free throws. The big difference between the two is that with the baby jumper, you often are shooting off-balance because your body is twisting in midair. But remember this: Only your lower body is off-balance. The upper body is square to the rim. Watch any pure shooter and note this. (Kobe Bryant is your best example.) No matter how he twists, wriggles, or soars to give himself an opening, by the time he shoots his upper body is facing the basket and in control. His elbow is inside his hip to act as the barrel of the rifle.

Always look for the location of your defender's hands. Does the player guarding you have his hands down at his sides? If so, you're golden. Shoot, baby!

Baby Jumper Drill: Place your player, with his back to the basket, about 12 feet from the bucket. Pass the ball to him — the bounce pass or high lob are the two most likely passes in a real game — and have him square up and shoot. Do so repeatedly for 30 seconds and keep track of how many he makes. Do this every day, and when his improvement begins to plateau, place a defender on him — just to stand there as an obstruction — to give him a new challenge.

Believe it or not, you catch the ball with your eyes, not your hands. Look the ball into your hands before you try to do anything else with it. What else do you have to look at?

The three-point shot

The three-point shot, accepted into the NBA in 1979–1980 and in college ball seven years later, has provided the biggest revolution in the game since the shot clock. The NBA actually stole this idea from the now-defunct American Basketball Association (ABA) with the intent to open up the floor offensively.

The distance of the NBA and the NCAA men's three-point arc has changed throughout the years. Currently, here are the distances within the different levels of basketball.

NBA	23 feet, 9 inches
NCAA Men and Women	20 feet, 9 inches
WNBA	20 feet, 6.25 inches
International	22 feet, .08 inches

The 40-50-90

When the NBA introduced the three-point shot in 1979–80, it also unwittingly created a new gold standard of shooting: the 40-50-90. The numbers refer to a shooter who is able to make at least 40 percent of his three-point shots, 50 percent of his field goals, and 90 percent of his free throws.

At the time of publication, there have only been six different NBA players who have put together a 40-50-90 season. Steve Kerr, Reggie Miller, Dirk Nowitzki, and Mark Price each did it once. Legendary Larry Bird did it twice. And Steve Nash of the Phoenix Suns, who is better known as an assists leader, has done it an astounding five times. In another season, Nash fell one missed free throw shy of doing it a sixth time.

Shoot with your legs

Leg strength is the most important thing when shooting the three. You still follow the basic mechanics, but you must have the natural strength to get the ball to the hoop with your legs. Always start in close and then move out to three-point land.

Shooting Drills

Scientists have yet to find a basketball player who prefers defense drills to shooting drills. You'll never have a problem motivating your players for this phase of practice. Still, shooting drills should have a purpose: Relate the exercise to actual game conditions so that it has meaning for the players, and they'll derive more from it.

Drills without a defender

The following drills are great for improving your or your players' shooting skills. (If only real games were this simple.)

Thirty-second spot shooting

Three players participate in this drill: One shoots, and the second rebounds and passes the ball to the third, who then passes to the shooter. Use two balls to keep the drill fast-paced. After 30 seconds, all three rotate roles so that, after 90 seconds, everyone has had a turn as the shooter.

Work different spots on the floor during each 90-second rotation. Start, for example, at the left corner, and then the left wing, left elbow, top of the key, right elbow, and so on.

Chart the number of shots each player attempts and makes in this drill. Players need something to shoot for — besides the hoop — and charting your progress on a daily basis accomplishes this. Make each shot a good shot. Shooting as quickly as you possibly can does not simulate actual game conditions.

Benefits: The shooter gets needed repetition of shots and takes shots off a pass, which is how she will take most game shots.

Come off a chair

In this drill, the chair acts as your teammate setting a screen for you. (Student managers espouse the traditional folding chair as opposed to, say, a Barca-lounger.)

Catch the ball coming around the chair just as if your teammate is setting a screen for you. Plant your lead foot, catch the ball (with your eyes), and face up to the hoop. Come around the chair, catch, turn, and face up. Your trail foot can help you square up and balance before you shoot. You want to catch and turn off the lead foot simultaneously. (See Figure 5-4.)

Figure 5-4:
The "come off a chair" drill.

You can run this drill on multiple baskets at the same time. Just pair up two players so that while one player practices a shooting drill, her partner actually works on her passing. Sneaky, eh?

Benefits: This drill emphasizes shooting after working to get yourself open. The game moves quickly, and this drill echoes that pace.

Seven out

This drill, more like a game, is best done with two or three players. The first player shoots from a spot. If he makes it, the second player must also make it from the same spot. And the third, until someone misses. The first player to miss gets a number of points equal to the number of made shots in that round. As soon as a player hits seven points, he's out.

This game is a lot like H-O-R-S-E, but it's fun because the more people make a shot from the same spot, the higher the stakes for that shot.

Benefits: Repetition builds confidence. Competition keeps it interesting.

Free-throw golf

Former NBA player Tim Legler, a career 84 percent free throw shooter, taught me this one. As many players as want to play are welcome. Each player takes 18 free throws, as in 18 holes of golf, but one at a time. Everyone shoots one free throw before anyone attempts a second.

Scoring is as follows: A miss equals a bogie, or a +1. A made shot that hits the backboard or rim equals par, or zero. A made free throw that only touches the net is a birdie, or minus-one. Low score wins.

Fast-break shooting drill

Form three lines at the baseline, with your guards (1) in the middle. One guard penetrates up the middle of the court with a player on either side (2 and 3) filling the fast-break lanes. By the time the guard reaches the far free throw line, he should either pass the ball to one of his wings, who pulls up for a jumper, or take the jumper himself (making him a somewhat unpopular guy with his teammates).

When the point guard gets to the spot where she's going to either pass or shoot, she needs to correct her forward momentum and get under control. She should jump stop (plant both feet) so that she doesn't draw a charging foul if a defender is standing right in front of her. Now she can pass or shoot.

Variation: As the three players race up court, have the player in the middle alternate passes from one wing to the other — no dribbling allowed until the middle player receives the ball beyond mid court.

Benefits: This drill helps hone conditioning and teamwork, and it effectively simulates game situations. If you can, chart each player's percentage from each wing to find out who's stronger from which side.

Knockout drill

My co-author — who used to coach a girls high school team in New York City — found that his players loved to end practice with this game. The rules for this drill are quite simple. Players line up in a straight line, the first one in line standing at the free throw line prepared to shoot. The first two players in line have a basketball (the number of players that may participate is unlimited). The first player shoots. If she makes her shot, she retrieves the ball, passes it to the third person in line, and goes to the end of the line. If she misses, she retrieves the ball and tries to make a basket as quickly as she can.

Player 2 (the second one in line) can shoot from the free throw line immediately after Player 1 launches her initial shot. If Player 1 misses and Player 2 makes her shot before Player 1 is able to rebound the ball and make a shot, then Player 1 is eliminated. And so on down the line. Player 2 must make her shot before Player 3, Player 3 before Player 4, and so forth. Keep playing until only one player remains.

Benefits: This drill simulates free throw shooting and forces you to perform under pressure. It's also a good conditioning drill. Players love to compete against one another, and this is as pure and manic as a shooting game gets.

Drills with a defender

To turn up the heat during practice, try the following drills, which simulate game conditions by adding the element of defense.

Fly at the shooter

This drill uses two balls and three players. Player 1 shoots the ball while Player 2 *flies,* or lunges, at him from a few feet away, as a defender would do in a zone defense. Player 1 follows his shot and rebounds the ball. Player 2 turns and becomes Player 1; that is, he becomes the shooter. Player 3, who has the second ball, passes the ball to Player 2 and lunges at him. Player 2 rebounds, Player 3 becomes Player 2, and 1 becomes 3. Player 1 then flies at 3 as he attempts his shot. Lather, rinse, repeat; you get the idea. Have the shooter stand at different spots on the floor for this drill.

With the advent of the trey, this drill takes on even greater importance. Division I college teams attempt on average 18 to 20 three-point shots per game. When the defense plays a zone, that number is even greater. Often, defenders find themselves in the middle of the floor playing a helping-style defense (see Chapter 7) and have no chance to block a three-point attempt. Instead, they charge at the shooter in an attempt to distract him.

Benefits: The shooter learns to focus on the shot, not the defense. The drill also provides good three-point practice and mild conditioning.

The defender in this drill may clap his hands together, yell, or sing if he feels the urge — anything to distract the shooter, who should use this drill as a means to hone his focus. As you're shooting, remember that the defender isn't going to run into you — that's football — so don't concern yourself with him. And if he does, and you bury the trey, you're looking at that rarest of offensive conquests: the four-point play.

Post-feed kickout

This shooting drill also applies practically to the basics of the game — whether you're playing against a zone defense or man-to-man. The drill requires three people and one ball.

The shooter, who's the off-guard (in hoops numerology, the 2-man), has the ball on the wing and is guarded by a defender. The post player on offense (5) starts from the baseline, flashes to the middle of the lane, and moves to a position between the high and low posts. The shooter passes him the ball. The defender then *doubles down,* that is, leaves Player 2 to guard Player 5, because Player 5 will draw a double team from the wing.

After the 2-man passes the ball into the post, he should move to the corner. He shouldn't stay in the same spot after he makes that pass, because if he does, D2 (second defender) can easily find him. (The same technique applies for avoiding the boss at holiday parties.) If the defender has to look for him, the chances of the 2-man having an open shot increase. The 5-man can then pass the ball to the corner. The 2-man should shoot quickly, before D2 can reach him.

Benefits: *This drill* involves two offensive players working together, incorporates fly-at-the-shooter techniques, and teaches the shooter to move without the ball.

To make this a defensive drill, order that no shot be taken until the players make five passes (also known as *touches* to coaches). In other words, when the 2-man receives the ball back from the 5-man, he returns it and moves back to another spot along the three-point arc. Do this a few times. Doing so is good practice for guards playing defense, who also have double down responsibilities.

Great Shooters: Players to Emulate

For help in visualizing the proper mechanics of shooting, track down videos or even still photos of the following shooting virtuosos. Notice that although they all have distinctive styles, every one of them launches a shot that has good backspin and "grabs the rim" with his shooting hand during the follow-through.

YouTube is a fabulous tool. Take advantage of it to see some of the names on this list when they were in their prime, long before YouTube was invented.

Steve Kerr (1989–2003, with five teams, most recently San Antonio Spurs): Steve Kerr deserves special mention because of his excellence in three-point shooting at all levels. In 1987–88, Kerr overcame the tragedy of his father's death in Beirut during a terrorist attack to shoot 57.4 percent on three-point attempts at the University of Arizona — the best percentage in the nation and still the fifth-best single season percentage in college history. In his 10-year NBA career, he has shot 46.4 percent on three-point shots, the highest percentage in league history.

Pete Maravich (1970–1980, Atlanta Hawks, New Orleans/Utah Jazz, Boston Celtics): Did he like to shoot? Heck, his nickname was Pistol Pete. Maravich was a showman and a revolutionary as well. Nobody took as many crazy shots as this former Louisiana State star. In many ways, especially to folks in the South, he is to basketball what Elvis is to rock 'n' roll.

Despite playing only three seasons at LSU in the late 1960s, Maravich is still the number-one scorer in college history (3,667 points, 44.2 points per game). That record is even more remarkable when you consider that one of the game's all-time long-range bombers compiled those stats before the advent of the three-point shot.

Reggie Miller (1987–2005, Indiana Pacers): Reggie Miller (see Figure 5-5) made 2,560 three-pointers in his legendary career, a record that stood until Ray Allen of the Boston Celtics broke it in 2011. And Reggie always seemed to make them when it mattered most.

Watch footage of Miller and focus on his follow-through with his hands. No one "touched the rim," meaning that no one extended his shooting wrist, in a more exaggerated style than Miller did. It's what made him great.

Ray Allen (1997-present, Milwaukee Bucks, Seattle SuperSonics, Boston Celtics): Kobe Bryant may have scored more points, but no one in the 21st century has had a prettier jump shot than the Celtics' off-guard.

Stephen Curry (2009-present, Golden State Warriors): Curry, whose father, Dell, was an excellent shooter in the NBA, led the NCAA in scoring as a senior at Davidson College in 2008-09. He is the best pure shooter to enter the NBA since Allen and in his second season led the league in free throw shooting.

Jerry West (1960–1974, Los Angeles Lakers): I may have saved the best for last. A natural athlete who had all the elements of a great shooter, West rarely had his shot blocked because he always released it from the top of his jump. Sounds natural, I know, but too many players shoot as they're still ascending. West, whose form in every facet of the game was so flawless that he literally became the model for the NBA logo (a silhouetted player dribbling), may have possessed the most seamless jumper in hoops history.

"Mr. Clutch" could score from anywhere at any time. In the third game of the 1970 NBA Finals against the Knicks, for example, he hit a last-second shot to tie the game — from 74 feet away. (The Lakers won in overtime but lost the series.)

Figure 5-5:
Reggie
Miller.

Chapter 6

Offense

*T*he objective on offense is simple: Put the ball in the basket. But how do you go about doing so?

Offense is equal parts choreography and improvisation. Coaches can design offensive schemes and have players practice them for hours. But this is not a chess match. Each offensive possession allows for a multitude of options, which is one reason why basketball is always captivating. Being in the correct spot on the floor is only half the battle.

In basketball, as opposed to football, the defense dictates the offense. For example, if the defense plays man-to-man — that is, each defensive player covers one offensive player, following him wherever he goes — the offensive scheme usually follows suit. (Chapter 7 explains the major types of defenses and the differences between them.)

In this chapter, I show you how to put your team in the best position to put the ball in the basket. After that, it's up to you.

Establishing Your Position

Each player on the court has a position, and with the position comes a job description. Don't ever send a player into the game without making her aware of her job description. If you do, you set her up to fail. This section gives a typical résumé for each position. As basketball has evolved, these positions have become less distinct from one another. Forwards handle the ball like guards, and centers shoot with the range of forwards. Dirk Nowitzki of the Dallas Mavericks, for example, is 7' tall but is also his team's best outside shooter. Nowitzki has a center's build and shoots like a guard but is listed as a power forward.

I discuss this blending of roles in this chapter, but there are five distinct positions that you need to learn first.

Point guard (alias "Ball Handler")

Prototypes: Bob Cousy (Boston Celtics), Oscar Robertson (Cincinnati Royals, Milwaukee Bucks), Earvin "Magic" Johnson (LA Lakers), John Stockton (Utah Jazz), Jason Kidd (Dallas Mavericks)

Flavor of the Day: Chris Paul (New Orleans Hornets), Rajon Rondo (Boston Celtics), Steve Nash (Phoenix Suns), Derrick Rose (Chicago Bulls), Sue Bird (Seattle Storm)

Physique/Skills: The point guard is usually the shortest player among the starting five (Chris Paul is 6'0"), but more importantly, he or she should be the team's premier ball handler and have a leader's demeanor.

Tell-All Stat: Assist-to-turnover ratio

Job Description: The quarterback on offense, the point guard's traditional role is to push the ball up court and start the offensive wheels turning, either by dribble penetration into the lane or by passing. Though not primarily a shooter, he can be. The point guard is the coach on the floor; his job is to correct teammates if they forget their responsibilities. He should be the most level-headed player on the court, if not the one who's most respected by his teammates. Unless he takes the ball to the basket himself, he should remain near the top of the key, ready to retreat on defense.

At the NBA level especially, teams must have a great point guard. NBA playoff contests are slower and more half-court oriented than their regular-season precursors, meaning that fewer fast breaks occur. That usually translates to lower-scoring games. Teams need a point guard who is a brilliant creator on the floor because, in tense situations, offensive players have a bad habit of standing around. The point guard must have superior court vision. It is his job to find teammates who are open and to reward them by passing them the ball. A point guard who does not look to pass the ball first quickly becomes very unpopular with his teammates.

The point guard stands tall for several reasons:

- 🗸 **A good point guard can dribble through a full-court press all by himself.** Not only does this demoralize the defense, but it also creates four-on-three or three-on-two situations (which give the offense an advantage) and easy baskets. (Watch Chris Paul of the New Orleans Hornets, for example.)

- 🗸 **The point guard is a double threat because he can pass or shoot.** If he beats his defender one-on-one, he penetrates to score. If another defender tries to help out, one of the point guard's teammates is open for a pass. No one in the NBA has been better at this the past decade than Steve Nash of the Phoenix Suns.

- 🗸 **The point guard runs the fast break off a rebound or steal, or by beating the press.** Fast-break baskets are easy baskets; you want as many of those as possible. Magic Johnson attempted to make every offensive possession a fast break. On turnover violations, for example, Magic scooted to the sideline and tried to hurry the official into handing him the ball. Then he pushed the ball up court while the other team was still hanging its head about the turnover. Magic had what's known as a high basketball IQ; all great point guards do.

Shooting guard (alias "Two-Guard")

Prototypes: Jerry West (LA Lakers), Pete Maravich (Atlanta Hawks, New Orleans Jazz, Boston Celtics) Michael Jordan (Chicago Bulls), Reggie Miller (Indiana Pacers)

Flavor of the Day: Kobe Bryant (Los Angeles Lakers), Dwyane Wade (Miami Heat), Diana Taurasi (Phoenix Mercury)

Physique/Skills: The ideal height in professional ball seems to be anywhere from 6'4" to 6'7" for men, and 5'9" to 6'1" for women, but again, it's more important that this player have a scorer's mentality. The shooting guard must be fearless, have a quick release on the jumper, and be a good three-point shooter.

Tell-All Stat: Points per game

Job Description: The shooting guard, known as the two-guard, is not necessarily a great ball handler. However, he is normally the team's best perimeter shooter. The shooting guard frees himself up for shots by working off screens set by larger teammates. The best two-guards come off screens prepared to react to the defense: shoot, pass, or drive. The two-guard tries to crash the boards while the point guard stays back and defends the fast break. Two guards have been the principal beneficiaries of the three-point line. When a point guard penetrates and draws a double team, he frequently "kicks out" a pass to his open back court mate.

The two-guard is often number one for these reasons:

- ✔ **The three-pointer:** A shooting guard can single-handedly destroy the opponent by scoring three-pointers in the clutch moments of a game.
- ✔ **The Jordan/Kobe Effect:** More people pattern their games after MJ and Kobe than they do after Tim Duncan or Shaq. Simply put, the majority of people fall into the two-guard height range as opposed to the center height range. Most NBA two-guards are 6'4" to 6'7", but in a pickup game between adults, the two-guard is more likely to be between 5'10" and 6'1".

Small forward (alias "Swingman")

Prototypes: Elgin Baylor (LA Lakers), Julius Erving/"Dr. J" (Philadelphia 76ers), Larry Bird (Boston Celtics)

Flavor of the Day: LeBron James (Miami Heat), Kevin Durant (Oklahoma City Thunder), Carmelo Anthony (Denver Nuggets)

Physique/Skills: The decathlete of hoops, the small forward should be 6'4" to 6'10" for men at the NBA level (5'10" to 6'2" for women in the WNBA; it's not so much of a requirement as a general observation). The difference between a small forward and a two-guard is nearly non–existent on some NBA squads. Both positions require a player to be able to shoot well from beyond the arc, for example, and to create off the dribble. Most often the reason that one player is a two-guard and the other a swingman, also known as a "3," depends on who's taller or more physical.

Tell-All Stat: Triple doubles

Job Description: Small forwards must be able to score from both the perimeter and the inside. They're all-purpose players on offense and should be too tall, physical, or tenacious for a defense's two-guard to handle.

Adrian Dantley was the best small forward I ever coached. After playing at Notre Dame, he went on to many years of success in the NBA and is still one of the top 25 scorers in the history of the league. Adrian could score inside and hit the 15-foot jumper. He would have to increase his range today to include the three-point shot, but he was the best I've seen at getting fouled and going to the line, where he was an 81.8-percent free throw shooter.

Power forward (alias "The Enforcer" or "Four-Spot")

Prototype: Bob Pettit (St. Louis Hawks), Elvin Hayes (Washington Bullets), Karl Malone (Utah Jazz), Dennis Rodman (five different teams)

Flavor of the Day: Blake Griffin (Los Angeles Clippers), Kevin Love (Minnesota Timberwolves), DeJuan Blair (San Antonio Spurs), Chris Bosh (Miami Heat)

Physique/Skills: The power forward is a Humvee or 18-wheeler on the court. (Appropriately enough, Karl Malone used to moonlight as the driver of his own big rig.) A player in this position should be anywhere from 6'7" to 6'11" for men or 6'1" to 6'4" for women, with a muscular build or at least a little bulk. The power forward must be a good rebounder and able to handle passes and hit shots near the basket.

Tell-All Stat: Rebounds

Job Description: The power forward, known as the *four-spot,* is a rugged rebounder but athletic enough to move with some degree of quickness around the painted area (the free throw lane) offensively and defensively. He is expected to score when given the opportunity at the baseline, much like a center, but he usually has a range of up to 15 feet, 180 degrees around the basket. The prototype power forward scores from the baseline, scores from in front of the basket, and, most importantly, scores via offensive rebounds.

Twenty years ago, not much difference existed between a power forward and a center. But today, power forwards run the floor well and move farther out from the basket.

Watch Kevin Love of the Minnesota Timberwolves. On November 12, 2010, Love grabbed 31 rebounds in a 112–103 win against the New York Knicks. Love is 6'10" and has a chiseled physique, but his rebounding prowess has more to do with desire than anything else. In the third quarter of that contest, Love, who would lead the league in rebounding during the 2010–11 season with 15.2 per game, told teammate Michael Beasley, "I'm going for 30 tonight." He meant rebounds. As it turned out, Love also scored 31 points. It was the first time in 28 years that an NBA player had scored at least 30 points and grabbed 30 boards in the same game.

Center (alias "The Big Man")

Prototype: Wilt Chamberlain (LA Lakers), Kareem Abdul-Jabbar (LA Lakers), Hakeem Olajuwon (Houston Rockets), Shaquille O'Neal (five different teams)

Flavor of the Day: Dwight Howard (Orlando Magic), Joakim, Noah (Chicago Bulls), Nicky Anosike (Washington Mystics), Andrew Bynum (Los Angeles Lakers), Ruth Riley (San Antonio Silver Stars)

Physique/Skills: Typically the tallest player on the team, the center should be able to post up offensively — that is, receive the ball with his back to the basket and use pivot moves to hit a variety of short jumpers, hook shots, and dunks. Great centers, such as Olajuwon and Howard, are also able to pass from the pivot.

Tell-All Stat: Blocked shots and scoring

Job Description: Consider San Antonio's Tim Duncan, who is listed as a forward but plays like a center. Duncan is the best of all worlds because he's also a point guard in the paint. He can shoot the jumper, face the basket, and (because of the length of his arms) go over the top of his opponents to get offensive rebounds. He can power in for the dunk, make the baseline move for a little jumper, and score from the outside — even three-point range. But most important, in the paint, he knows how to find the open man. Back in college he ranked first in assists for Wake Forest his senior year.

The center may not be as important on offense as he is on defense. This fact may surprise people since Wilt Chamberlain was the most dominant offensive presence in NBA history and Abdul-Jabbar the league's career leader in points.

But these two are the exception. More often than not, centers are on the court to clog the middle, block shots, and grab rebounds. Hall of Fame center Bill Russell, who led the Boston Celtics to 11 NBA championships, is considered the greatest shot-blocker and defensive player in league history.

Because of the three-point line, passing ability is an increasingly important asset for a center. Watch a center receive the ball in the post: If the center has any scoring ability, a defensive guard will *double down* on him (in other words, leave the player he's guarding to double team the center). When this happens, the center must locate the open teammate, usually stationed just beyond the three-point arc, with a soft pass. Passing the ball to a center used to be like throwing it into a black hole. Not anymore.

Playing to Your Strength

As a coach, your first move in setting up an offense is to evaluate the talents of your players. The bottom line is that you need to score. It would be nice if the five players who hustled the most were also your five best shooters, but that's almost never the case. Take what's available — understand the makeup of your team and develop your offense around it.

The best teams have offensive balance: an inside scorer, good perimeter shooting, and a penetrating guard. But the majority of teams are deficient in one of those areas or, at the very least, lack balance. Know your strengths and play to them.

In 2010–11, the San Antonio Spurs had the most balanced offense (and best record) in the NBA because every starter had a different role, and each one understood his role. Tim Duncan was in the pivot. Tony Parker was the slashing point guard. Manu Ginobili and Matt Bonner were the kick-out shooters beyond the arc. And power forward DeJuan Blair scored the "garbage points," putbacks after offensive rebounds. It helped that all were incredibly talented, but the Spurs' balance is what made them so difficult to defend against.

Offensive Plays and Maneuvers

The best-known plays and maneuvers involve just two offensive players. (But don't interpret that to mean that their three teammates simply stand around and do nothing.) A single offensive possession may use one or more of the plays and maneuvers that I discuss in this section.

You may hear coaches or broadcasters talk about "proper spacing." Whether you are playing a half-court game of three-on-three or a league game of five-on-five, offensive players need to be spread out from one another. If you cluster two players together, one defender can effectively guard them both. Make the defense work harder than that. Space yourselves far apart from one another.

The pass

A *pass* involves one player throwing the ball to a teammate, either through the air or by bouncing it off the floor. Simple, yes, but a pass is the first step in playing great offense.

A great one-on-one offensive player may score 40 points every once in a while, but he does so usually to the detriment of his team. Scoring legends such as Pete Maravich and George Gervin played for NBA teams that never advanced to the NBA Finals. The LA Lakers, on the other hand, won five titles in the 1980s largely on the strength of Magic Johnson's ability to find the open teammate. A fine pass that leads to a layup is more demoralizing to a defense than an 18-foot jumper.

What about Michael Jordan, you ask? Jordan was a scorer, yes, but he also knew how to find the open teammate. In a March 1995 game, Jordan — recently returning from baseball's Birmingham Barons — torched the New York Knicks for 55 points. With the game tied in the final seconds, Jordan took the ball to the hoop. As three Knicks converged on him, he dished it to center Bill Wennington for the easy, winning bucket.

No player on earth is fast enough to dribble the ball to a teammate faster than he can pass that ball to his teammate. A pass is the quickest, and thus most effective, way to transfer the ball from one player to another.

The screen

A screen frees up a dribbler or an intended receiver. To set a screen, an offensive player without the ball uses her body as a shield to ward off a defender who tries to follow an offensive player. For a screen to be legal, the screener must remain stationary for at least a full second and must have her arms in toward her torso. Otherwise, the referee charges the screener with an illegal screen foul.

To see an offense that knows the value of screening, watch video of Bob Knight's Indiana Hoosiers. On every half-court possession, IU's offense ran at least two screens. Often, IU set up three screens on one play just to free one shooter. If you can't set a screen, you can't play for the "General." Screens are frustrating for a defense. Offenses that diligently set screens on every half-court play are often able to wear down a defender's will. The great Reggie Miller, who played 17 seasons for the Indiana Pacers, would often run around two or three screens per possession until his teammate was able to find him for an open shot.

The give-and-go

A play that every school yard hoopster knows, the *give-and-go* burns the lazy defender. As shown in Figure 6-1, Player 1 on offense passes to Player 3 and then cuts sharply to the basket. Player 3 returns the ball to Player 1 using a bounce pass (because Player 1 is moving quickly). Player 1 beats the defender because the defender makes the mistake of relaxing after his man passes the ball.

The pass and screen away

Okay, you've passed the ball. Now what do you do? You can stay where you are, but that makes you easy to defend. You can move toward the player you passed to with the idea of setting a pick (explained in the next section). You can try the give-and-go. Or as Figure 6-2 shows, you can try the *pass and screen away* play. To run this play, you (1) move *away* from where you passed the ball (3), toward another teammate (4), and set a pick (or screen). Player 4 then receives a pass from 3.

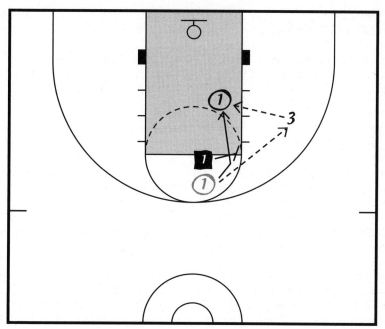

Figure 6-1:
The give-
and-go.

An effective offense always has movement, but the movement must create
space for each player.

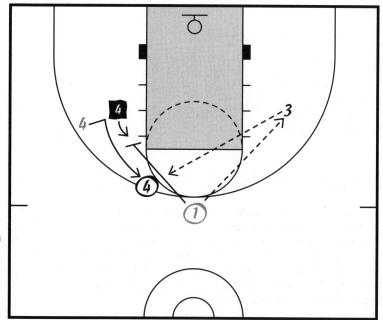

Figure 6-2:
The pass
and screen
away play.

The pick and roll

A *pick* is simply a screen for the player with the ball. The *pick and roll* play is nearly as old as Dr. Naismith's peach baskets (see Chapter 3), but it's still very valuable today. The Utah Jazz, specifically point guard John Stockton and power forward Karl Malone, ran the pick and roll for more than a decade, and no one ever figured out how to stop them.

How effective were Stockton and Malone at the pick and roll? The former is the NBA's all-time assists leader (15,806 . . . no one else is within 4,000 assists of him) and the latter is No. 2 all-time in total points scored (36,928) behind only the legendary Kareem Abdul-Jabbar.

To execute a pick and roll (as shown in Figure 6-3), one offensive player (5) sets a pick for the player with the ball (1), who's almost always dribbling it at the time. When the dribbler comes around his teammate (who is setting the pick), the latter player rolls away from that spot and toward the basket. Why is such a simple play so difficult to defend? Because it creates chaos on defense.

When Malone would set a pick, the defender on Stockton would have to decide if he was going to "fight over" the pick (chase Stockton) or go under. If he went under, Stockton was open for a shot. If Malone's defender jumped out to stop Stockton, Malone would roll toward the hoop, leaving the smaller guard to defend Malone. In this example, you usually see one of three outcomes of the pick and roll:

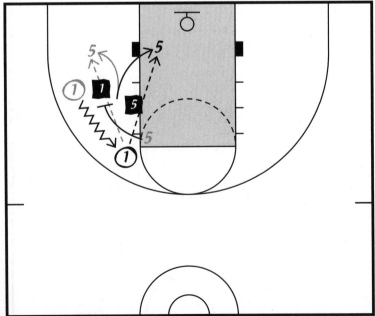

Figure 6-3:
The pick
and roll.

✔ Stockton beats his man off the screen and drives for a layup or short jumper.

✔ Stockton creates a mismatch, whereby he passes to Malone as he rolled toward the hoop.

✔ Both defenders follow Stockton, who again passes to Malone for an easy layup.

There are numerous clips of Stockton and Malone's wizardry on YouTube. Watch them and learn from the greatest pick-and-roll duo in NBA history.

The back door

If you and your teammates are not as quick as the opposing team, you must play smarter than they do. No offensive play is smarter than the *back door* play.

As Figure 6-4 shows, a player on the wing (3) usually receives the pass in the back door play. If the receiver's defender attempts to deny her the pass, the receiver takes a step higher up on the wing as if she's going toward the dribbler. When the defender moves to deny that pass, the receiver reverses direction toward the basket. This is known as a "V-cut," the "V" referring to the pattern you run on the floor: moving in one direction, then sharply changing direction. "V" also stands for victory, which comes easier to those who move smartly without the ball in their hands.

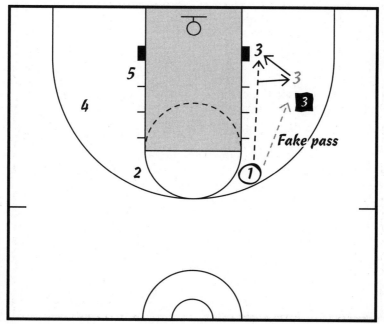

Figure 6-4:
The back door play.

As a defender, you have no excuse for allowing this play. The fundamental concept of man-to-man defense is to keep yourself between your assigned player and the bucket. If the back door play works, the defender took a risk — going for a steal — and the offense duly burned her.

Being Alert (The World Needs Lerts) on Offense

Your alertness can make a huge difference in whether an offensive possession results in a bucket or not. A few things that smart offensive players look for include:

- ✔ Pay attention to off-the-ball defenders who are not watching both the player they are guarding and the ball simultaneously. If he is watching only the ball, his man should cut to get open. If he is only watching his man, you can pass the ball to that man at any time.

- ✔ If you have the ball and are being double-teamed, someone else is open. Pass the ball!

- ✔ If you have to jump to catch a pass, land on both feet at the same time. I'm not telling you this for safety reasons. By landing with both feet on the floor, you may establish either foot as your pivot foot.

Setting the Tempo

Talent precedes tempo. Most up-tempo teams are better offensive teams — and certainly more athletic — than slow-tempo teams. If you sense that your team is in better shape or is more athletically gifted than your opponent, push the pace. (We rarely had such a team at Notre Dame, so I preferred to play more of a half-court game.)

If you get a chance, read Jack McCallum's book ":07 Seconds or Less." It is a chronicle of a season with the 2005–06 Phoenix Suns, who led the NBA in scoring at 108.4 points per game. The title comes from then coach Mike D'Antoni's credo that no offensive possession should last longer than seven seconds before someone was open to attempt a shot.

In 2010, Notre Dame lost its best player and leading scorer, Luke Harangody, to a midseason injury. Coach Mike Brey instituted what became known as his Slow Burn offense. The idea was to milk the clock on each offensive possession, to slow the game down.

It worked as the Irish won six of their final seven games to barely qualify for the NCAA tournament. The following season the Irish visited second-ranked Pittsburgh, which had a 20-game home win streak. Again using the Slow Burn, the Irish won.

"The one thing about being patient and burning it like that is you have to have a group that believes in it," said Brey. "The mental concentration of it is underrated. Fortunately we won last year doing it, so that's a great selling point."

Man-to-Man Offense

As I mention at the beginning of this chapter, teams run a man-to-man offense when the defense is playing them man-to-man. Man-to-man offense involves a lot of cutting and screening, give-and-go's, and pick and rolls. (For more on pick and rolls, see Chapter 7.) Why? Because the offensive players have to work to lose their defenders and get free.

A few offensive guidelines

Not everyone can shoot like Kevin Durant, but that does not mean you cannot be a dangerous offensive player. If you adhere to these rules, you'll be known as a smart player on offense, which is nearly as valuable to your coach.

1. After you pass the ball, move. Either cut toward the basket, or move away from where you passed the ball to set a screen for another teammate.

2. The most dangerous spot on the court is the free throw line. If you can pass the ball to your center or a forward at the free throw line, (also known as the high post in this situation), you have the most options. The post can pivot and because he is in the center of the half court, the defense must respect that he can pass the ball in any direction.

3. It is easier to guard a statue. If you do not have the ball, either set a pick for someone or cut to get free. If you run to a space where a teammate already is, then set a pick. Otherwise, run to a spot where no one is, but a spot from which you are able to attempt a shot.

4. When someone passes the ball to you, do not dribble unless or until you have a plan. You're more dangerous holding the ball because at that point you still have three options: pass, dribble, or shoot. Great offensive players don't need to dribble until they're driving to the basket to score.

5. If you don't have the ball, don't run toward the player who does have the ball. Move to get open, or set a screen for a third teammate so that she can get open.

Patterns and continuity

There are many types of half-court offenses to run against a man-to-man defense. The overriding principle, however, is that each "play" is more like a self-repeating pattern that includes plenty of options. It's almost like a flow chart, or an algorithm. For example, the point guard at the top of the key may either pass the ball to a man on the wing or to the center who flares up to the high post. Depending on who receives the pass, a new set of choices exists.

The difference between basketball and football offense

In football an offensive player will run a specific play in which every player knows exactly where he is supposed to go, whom to block, what pass route to run, and so on. A football play rarely lasts more than eight seconds.

Basketball plays, however, are much different. At certain times, such as when setting up a last-second shot, a basketball play is just like a football play. Most of the time, a half-court offense is more like a choreographed dance that has room for improvisation.

Each player may have an established spot on the court when the play begins, but from there it depends upon who's open, where a pass is thrown, or how the defense breaks down. The best way to learn where you should be or what you should do in a half-court offense is simply to play more basketball. Soon it will become second nature to you.

HALL OF FAME

LSU versus Kentucky, 1994

When you have a potent offense, as former Kentucky coach Rick Pitino knows, you're never out of the game. On February 15, 1994, Pitino's 11th-ranked Wildcats traveled to Baton Rouge to play Louisiana State. These were the weary days of the tough SEC (Southeastern Conference) schedule, late in the regular season, and Kentucky came out onto the court flat.

Already down 48–32 at halftime, the Wildcats surrendered 18 straight points early in the second half to trail 68–37. Only one other team in NCAA history (Duke in 1950, versus Tulane) had recovered from a 31-point deficit to win a game. Pitino called a time-out.

He told his team to show its character. He also told team members to shoot three-pointers and nothing but. Kentucky attempted 23 treys in the second half, making 12 of them. A 24–4 run cut the lead to eight points with more than six minutes left, and the Wildcats eventually won 99–95 to tie Duke for the greatest comeback in NCAA history.

In basketball, offense is more of a philosophy (Princeton, for example, runs a *motion offense* in which all five players move constantly and may handle the ball at any spot on the court). It's less about where you should be as opposed to how you play in relation to your four teammates.

North Carolina's high post-passing game (Four Corners) was one of the most devastating offenses ever created with the intent *not* to score. When run by superb point guard Phil Ford back in the mid-1970s, North Carolina's Four Corners offense, which was nothing more than a form of keep-away, was almost impossible to stop. Or should I say start?

The Tar Heels simply spread the floor, putting one player in each of the four corners of the frontcourt and its fifth, Ford, in the middle. Ford dribbled around the court like a water bug until a second defender left his man to trap Ford. When that happened, Ford passed to the player left open in the corner. The corner player held onto the ball until someone approached him; then he dribbled into the middle, and Ford assumed his corner spot. The idea, however, was to have the ball in Ford's hands as much as possible. UNC was not looking to score, but rather to take time off the clock. If UNC had the lead and the ball with four minutes left, the game was over.

Perhaps the only thing capable of stopping the Four Corners was itself. This offense was so effective that it hastened the advent of the shot clock. Fans became too bored with this offense, and opposing coaches became too frustrated.

Teams run more than one offense in the course of a game. If you happen to have nosebleed seats high up in the stands, use your high vantage point to observe how the offense develops. Watch which players set screens, who moves toward the ball and who moves away, and who runs the baseline. Bring a notepad and pen, and diagram an offensive formation that you see repeatedly.

If you happen to sit at court level, look at the game through the offensive players' eyes. What passing lanes are open? Should a player have cut high up on the wing to receive the ball, or should she have gone through the back door? Should she have shot the ball, dribbled it, or made the pass?

Zone Offense

Zone defenses (defenses where players defend an area instead of a specific player) force an offense to alter its style. Why would opponents play a zone against you?

✔ They don't believe that your perimeter, or outside, shooting is accurate enough to beat the zone. (Shooting over the zone normally forces the zone to come apart because the defense has to come out and get right up on the shooters.)

✔ You have a terrific scorer in the post who cannot be stopped by just one defender. In a zone, your opponent can surround him with three players.

How the zone bothers the offense

A disciplined zone defense virtually negates screens, back doors, and pick-and- roll plays because individual defenders guard areas, not people. Facing a zone defense, the offense must work the ball around (pass it), find openings in the defense, and penetrate to the basket.

How to attack the zone

Zone defense works best when the ball is on the perimeter. If you can get the ball inside to your post player (the center), particularly in the high post, you force the defense to converge on him, which creates new passing lanes and open teammates. It is very important for your post player to understand that he can pivot in any direction and to look for open teammates with a 360-degree view.

Wake Forest's Tim Duncan was a valuable college player for just this reason: A big target inside, he was also a deft passer against a zone.

A zone defense always tries to maintain its arrangement. Quick, crisp passes catch the zone off-guard, and eventually someone overcommits or fails to recover in time. Six quick passes before a shot are not too many — you want to keep the defense moving.

Remember, it's not just about passing the ball. It's about catching the ball and then making the next pass before the defense has time to recover.

A passed basketball moves faster than you do when dribbling it. A passed ball also moves faster than a defender. Passes beat the zone, not dribbles.

Another tactic to try: Start draining three-pointers, or at least outside shots. You force the zone to come out and play you. That, in turn, opens things up inside, not only for post players but also for *dribble-drive penetration* (dribbling to the basket, forcing a second man to guard you, and kicking out to an open teammate).

Playing against a 2–3 zone

The 2–3 zone (explained in Chapter 7) is the most common zone that teams employ. Against a 2–3 zone, most offenses often use a 1–3–1 alignment. As Figure 6-5 shows, the point guard (1) up top may throw to either a wing (2 or 3) or a post player (4). (So in the 1–3–1 alignment, you have the point guard representing "1" and the two wings and one post player representing "3.") If the wing receives the pass, she can either look for the player running the baseline (5, who is the other "1" in the 1–3–1 alignment) or throw the ball to the post (4).

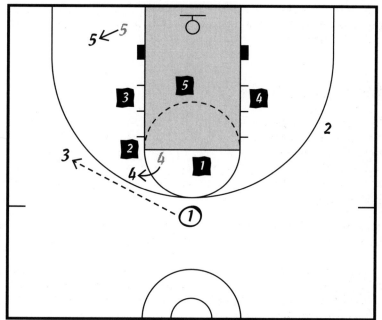

Figure 6-5:
The 1–3–1 set versus a 2–3 zone defense.

On the pass from point guard to wing, the high post player dives to the low post on the side of the ball, and the baseline player takes her place. It's like an X move, low to high and high to low.

If the wing passes back to the point, the point may want to consider penetrating. A talented and lightning-quick point guard forces the zone to collapse or overcommit. That means that someone else is open.

Playing against a 1–3–1 (point) zone

When facing a 1–3–1 zone defense (described in Chapter 7), coaches usually run two guards out on the perimeter and keep three on the baseline (two big players and one shooter). The offense is thus a 2–1–2 set or a 2–3 set. Some teams keep the low post player low. Some teams also run a double low post with two out (two guards out) and have the shooter going from sideline to sideline.

The skip pass is an effective weapon against a zone. A skip pass is one pass that ordinarily would have necessitated two passes. For example, if a player has a ball on the right wing, the safest way to get it to the left wing will take two passes: the first to the point guard at the top of the key, who then relays it to the left wing. A skip pass would have the right wing toss the ball over the zone and directly to the left wing.

It's a risky pass, but if it works, the zone will begin to break down. Once a zone loses its formation discipline, finding an open shot becomes much easier.

Getting the ball inside against a zone

Some teams send a cutter through, but screen off the defender near their big player so that he can loop around to the post and go get the ball. In a 1–3–1 zone (because the zone makes certain slides) or a 1–2–2 zone, the middle is open. When you get a skip pass and the zone slides, the center sees the gap in the post, goes to that gap, and looks for the ball.

Take a look at what happens after the skip pass. The ball leaves the fingertips of the passer and goes to the opposite wing. The center follows the pass. Before the receiver catches the ball, the center is already at the opposite wing. Essentially, the center follows the pass, reads the passer, knows that the ball is going opposite, looks for a gap in the zone, and gets to the spot. As a result, the pass is almost a touch pass.

The receiver throws the ball into the post. The post player must work to get open. Sometimes he must step out of the lane to get the ball high, and at other times, he must step out low to get the ball low. He can't lock himself in; otherwise, defending him is too easy.

Centers must move and work to get open, but the perimeter passers must be patient and read and wait. One of the weaknesses of the zone offense, no matter whether it's against a 2–3 or a point zone defense, is that the wing players don't look into the baseline or to the foul line area before they reverse the ball. Remember, any post feed bothers a zone. A post feed is the toughest thing for a zone to defend; someone will be open, either on the baseline opposite or the wing opposite, and the post can even toss the ball back to the point.

Fast Break Offense

To *fast break* means simply to push the ball up court before the defense has a chance to set up. The key to running an effective fast break is to get the ball to the middle of the floor (that is, away from the sidelines). The defense then must play one of three options: a pass to the left, a pass to the right, or the player with the ball keeping it.

The player with the ball must decide what to do by the time she reaches the foul line: pass it, continue driving, or stop and shoot. Don't force a shot on a fast break if it's not there. Good teams transfer right into their set offense.

When Sonny Allen was coaching at Old Dominion, he numbered certain spots on the floor and assigned individual players to run to each spot — such as a corner or wing — on the fast break. Even after allowing a score, Sonny had his players do this. This drill gave new meaning to the phrase, "See Spot run."

Why the fast break works

The offense usually outnumbers the defense, whether it's three on two, three on one, or two on one. The job of the ball handler on the fast break, especially in the latter two scenarios, is to force the defender to commit and then to hit the open teammate.

The three-man weave drill

This drill involves no dribbling. Three players, spaced about 15 feet apart, start out on the baseline. The player in the middle passes to a wing and then runs toward that player and *behind* him. The player who caught the pass throws it across to the third player, running toward and behind him as well. And so on. Do this until the player who catches the ball is just above the far foul line, and then treat the situation like a fast break: The receiver passes to one of his two teammates on the wing (a bounce pass, I say) or keeps it and shoots or drives.

The benefit of this drill is that players learn to pass on the run and understand the concept of filling the lanes on the fast break.

Paul Westhead and Loyola Marymount's offense

When Paul Westhead was coaching at Loyola Marymount (LMU), he imposed a rule on his players: When playing offense, move the ball past half court in three seconds and shoot it within seven.

Preseason camp at LMU resembled Marine boot camp, as Westhead threw all sorts of conditioning drills at his players to mold them into top shape for the running (and gunning) they'd be doing. One drill involved players running with small parachutes on their backs to maximize wind resistance, a tactic that many other college and pro teams have since adopted.

From the opening tip-off, LMU did nothing but fast breaks and three-pointers. Westhead recruited players who could run and shoot the outside jumper. In 1989–1990, his third year at the Los Angeles school, he had his athletes in place. Against Louisiana State that season, LMU won 148–141. (Westhead's sprinters gave up a load of points as well.) That game was temporarily stopped when the play-by-play typewriter broke, apparently from exhaustion.

The LMU team averaged 122.4 points per game that season. A glance at the record books reveals LMU's impact on the game during Westhead's grand experiment. While he was coach there (1987 to 1991), Loyola notched five of the ten highest-scoring games in NCAA history. Each of its four seasons are included among the top ten highest-scoring seasons in NCAA history as well.

The three-on-two, two-on-one drill

Position two defenders at the far end of the court — one at the foul line and one in the lane. Then start your three offensive players up court, either in a three-man weave or passing back and forth to simulate a fast break. When they approach the far end, you have a three-on-two situation. The offense must take the ball to the basket immediately.

When the defense retrieves the ball, either on a rebound or after a made basket, the two defenders run a fast break against the former offensive player who was closest to the offense's basket when the offense lost possession of the ball. The two other players remain on defense when the ball returns to that end of the court.

Press Offense

The press offense is less concerned with scoring than with simply getting the ball past mid court before committing a ten-second violation. (In the NBA, teams have only eight seconds to advance the ball past mid court.) This offense is used when the defense employs a full-court press, which usually involves double-teaming the player with the ball, the objective being to force the offense into a turnover in its own back court.

When taking the ball out of bounds in your back court against a full-court press, what do you need to know?

✔ If you in-bound the ball after a made basket (either a field goal or a free throw), you can run the length of the baseline. You cannot do so after a violation, however, or after a ball has been knocked out of bounds. In those situations, you must have a pivot foot just as if you were on the court and had already given up your dribble.

✔ Envision this scenario. You in-bound the ball after your opponent makes a basket and run the baseline. Your pass is deflected out of bounds. Your team retains possession, and again you in-bound from the baseline. Are you still allowed to run along the baseline? Answer: No.

✔ The backboard is a blocker. Be aware of the backboard, especially if you attempt to in-bound a pass to beyond half court. If you stand directly under the backboard, your pass may hit it.

✔ The corner is a deadly place. If you receive the inbound pass, stay away from the corner. The defense can easily trap you with two players. If you are attempting to get open to receive an inbounds pass, avoid running to the corner.

✔ Set a screen for a teammate and then cut to open space.

✔ Don't wait for the pass to come to you. Be aggressive.

✔ After you have the ball and start to dribble, do not pick up the dribble (in other words, don't stop dribbling and hold the ball) until you know to whom you're going to pass the ball. If you dribble toward a trap, pull yourself back and *arc your dribble* — attempt to go around the trap. Or back up and look for an open teammate. Passing or dribbling backward in the back court is not a sin. Sometimes you have to take a step back to move ahead (see also *Philosophy For Dummies*).

✔ Too often, an offense becomes so obsessed with beating a full-court press that it stops working after the ball passes the mid court line. If you beat the press and have a man advantage on the defense (that is, you beat them down the court and have more players there than the defense does), the situation is no different than a fast break. Unless your coach has ordered you not to shoot, take the ball to the hoop.

Breaking Half-Court Traps

Defenses run half-court traps for different reasons. They may be trailing late in the game and trying to force a turnover. Or they may simply be trying to give their own lethargic offense a shot in the arm. In a Lakers-Rockets game a few years ago, for example, Del Harris, then the Los Angeles coach, ordered a half-court trap in the second quarter. Harris hoped that if he could awaken his team defensively, that liveliness would spread to the other end of the floor. His ploy worked.

To beat the half-court trap, an offense must spread out, almost as if playing the four corners. Some other tips include:

- ✔ **Ball fake prior to passing.** The defense is playing so over-aggressively that they usually fall for the ball fake.

- ✔ **Bounce pass when the defender has his arms outstretched high.** A bounce pass is much harder to intercept and much easier to make.

- ✔ **Don't pick up your dribble.** You have less freedom to move against a half-court trap because you can no longer venture into the back court. The defense has to guard only half as much space.

- ✔ **Always have someone flashing to the foul line.** In a half court, the foul line is the epicenter. If you position one player in each of the four corners and the fifth as a rover, the free throw line is an open area. It offers the best combination for a short pass — if the player with the ball is trapped in a corner — with adequate spacing. The rover should move to the area vacated by the player who flashes to the foul line.

Chapter 7

Defense

Good defensive players are good defensive players because they want to be. Playing defense is hard — I'm not going to kid you — and rarely is it glamorous. How often do you see ESPN's SportsCenter devote even one of its nightly Top 10 Plays to a forward denying his man a pass on the wing? Or to a center fronting her opponent in the low post? It just does not happen.

Nevertheless, defense is literally half the game. It is every bit as instrumental in winning — perhaps more so — as offense. The objective of basketball, remember, is not just to score but to outscore your opponent. The less your opponent scores, the less you need to. Two reasons why defense may be *more* important than offense are

▸ **Great defense begets instant offense.** Defensive plays, such as steals and blocked shots, often lead to easy fast-break baskets — for your team, that is.

▸ **Defense relies on attitude, not aptitude.** In some games, your jump shot just isn't going to drop — even Kobe Bryant has the occasional 7-of-24 shooting night. Good defense, however, is as reliable as the tides, because its foundation is effort. You can count on this facet of your game every time you suit up.

So how do you play defense? An old coach once said, "You play defense with three things — your head, your heart, and your feet." That's funny, considering how often coaches tell their players to keep their hands up on defense, but it's true. You play with your head because a good defender outsmarts his man. You play with your heart because a good defender outhustles his man. And you play with your feet because, as this chapter explains, defense is mostly about establishing position. You establish position with your feet, not your hands.

Playing with Your Head

To play defense with your head, you must know your opponent. Offensive players are creatures of habit. For example, a player may always dribble to his right or favor the jump shot from the free throw line. Like bad poker players, these opponents can be "read." Be aware of your opponent's tendencies, and you'll play better defense.

But remember that defense is also a *team* concept. Because of screens and *double teams* (where two defenders guard one player), you'll *guard* (defend against; not to be confused with the position of guard) various players on the court. Good defenders know the strengths and weaknesses of at least a few players on the opposing team.

A smart defender's checklist includes

- ✔ **Quickness:** Is your man quicker than you are? If so, give him enough room in front of you to take a full step — you want to be able to retreat quickly and reestablish your defensive position.

- ✔ **Range:** Is your man a better-than-average shooter? Just as important, *from how far away* is he a good shooter? When a marksman gets within his range, you must play him close.

- ✔ **Weaknesses:** Most offensive players — including you, when you're on the other end of the floor — have flaws in their game. Maybe the player you're guarding doesn't like to dribble to his left. If that's the case, move over to his right side, forcing him to go left. Or if he has little confidence in his 15-footer, dare him to beat you with it. Good defensive players always capitalize on their opponents' weaknesses.

Playing with Your Heart

In a 1996 article that appeared in *Sports Illustrated Presents,* All-Star guard Latrell Sprewell, then with the Golden State Warriors, blamed his poor defensive season of 1994–95 on indifference. Sprewell, who had established a reputation as a tenacious defender as a rookie, admitted that the Warriors' trade of his best buddy, Chris Webber, affected his play. "I admit that my heart wasn't into it that season," said Sprewell, "and that's what defense mainly is — heart and dedication."

When I watch Duke games from the ESPN Studios in Bristol, Connecticut, I notice that coach Mike Krzyzewski has his players perform a gesture that, though symbolic, acts as a reminder to play tough defense. When the Blue Devils need to make a big defensive stop, here is what they do as they retreat past mid court to play defense: Each player crouches and slaps both hands against the hardwood. Bending that low requires extra effort, which may be Coach K's point: Defense requires extra effort.

Playing with Your Feet

The most important aspect of defense is making sure that your feet do the work to keep your body in balance. If you play too far up on the balls of your feet, you lean forward. That's bad. If you play on your heels, you lean backward. That's bad, too.

Balance, therefore, is the key.

The *defensive stance,* as it's known in hoops, is the fundamental position for a defender to assume. Your feet are shoulder width apart. Your knees are bent, but your back is not; you move on the balls of your feet. Your arms are low — not hanging at your sides, but slightly outstretched — with your elbows bent and your palms upward, almost as if you're ready to catch a baby.

In-the-paint drill

Place three players in defensive stances in the free throw lane: one at the baseline, another in the middle of the key, and a third just below the free throw line. All of them face you, the coach, standing at the top of the key with the ball. Why three players? Competition. If you have just one player, he won't try to beat anyone.

Blow the whistle and point the ball in one direction. All three players shuffle-step (slide their feet swiftly sideways, never crossing their feet) across the lane until they reach its boundary; then they shuffle-step to the other side of the lane and return. Run them back and forth for 15 to 30 seconds and then blow the whistle and have three more players step in. Speed is the objective.

Never cross your feet on defense. N-e-v-e-r. If the dribbler sees you do that, he's going to switch direction and blow right by you. When shuffling your feet, kick your front, or stride, leg out to the side. Make this your big stride, pushing off your back leg. Then kick your trail leg over to meet your stride leg. By "meet," I don't mean that the two feet need to touch. The faster you need to move, the bigger kick you need your stride leg to make and the closer your trail leg must come to it on the follow-through.

On-the-diagonal drill

The defender lines up at the right corner, facing mid court. He shuffle-steps toward the right end of the free throw line, his left leg in front. At that point, he turns his hips and heads to the opposite corner of the lane, facing the baseline on a diagonal. Upon reaching that point, he swings his hips again so that his right leg is now the lead leg of the shuffle-step. The player shuffle-steps to where the sideline meets the free throw line extended. The goal here is not speed but rather form.

The width of your stance is the most important aspect in determining balance. As the shooting principle explains in Chapter 5, if you put both feet together and someone pushes your chest, you'll fall over. The same principle applies to defense. Spreading your feet the width of your shoulders gives you better balance.

Man-to-Man Defense

Of the two types of team defense, man-to-man is the defense that purists respect — the all-natural-ingredients, no-preservatives defense. It is *Defense Unplugged,* if you will — the way the game is meant to be played. You defend one person, as does each of your teammates. Theoretically, if every player wins his individual battle, the defense prevents the opposing team from scoring a basket.

You must remember two simple rules at all times when playing man-to-man:

- **If your man has the ball:** Stay between your man and the basket at all times. If your man has the ball, his objective is to penetrate closer to the basket for an easier shot. Your objective is to prevent that.

- **If your man does not have the ball:** Stay between your man and the ball at all times. Without the ball, he cannot score. Maintain that state of affairs by denying him the ball.

Simple, eh?

The three stages of an offensive player's possession

As a defender in a man-to-man defense, you must keep in mind the three stages of any offensive player's possession of the ball: the pre-dribble stage, the dribble stage, and the post-dribble stage. Adjust your defensive technique accordingly.

Pre-dribble stage

When a player has just caught the ball, she is the most dangerous because she has the most options: She can pass, dribble, or shoot. Do the following as you guard a player who has just caught the ball but has not yet begun to dribble:

- ✔ **Assume your defensive stance** (unless you're defending a player in the post, which I discuss later in this chapter). You must stay low. The lower your center of gravity, the easier it is for you to move in quick, short bursts as well as change direction. Defense more often entails moving laterally than sprinting forward.

- ✔ **Keep your eyes on her midsection.** You gain nothing as a defender by looking into your opponent's eyes, at any of her limbs, or at the basketball itself. The offensive player uses her head, her limbs and feet, and the ball to *fake you out* — that is, to fool you into committing one way so that she can go the other. However, an offensive player's belly button is like her shadow: She can never shake it. The belly button cannot fake you out, so keep your eyes on it.

- ✔ **Know your opponent.** If she's quicker than you — this is no time for pride — back off a step so that she can't dribble past you. Then again, if she's a deadly outside shot, you have to guard her more closely. If she is both quicker than you *and* a great shooter . . . well, that's why some players are called unstoppable.

In college ball (but not in the NBA), the player with the ball has five seconds to make, in the official's judgment, a positive move on offense. She can't just stand still holding the ball for six seconds. Remember that as you defend her. If she's pushing the five-second mark, look for her to start dribbling or pass the ball.

Dribble stage

After receiving the ball, the player you're guarding may decide to dribble in an attempt to drive toward the basket. He can still pass or shoot off the dribble, but unless he is still dribbling in front of you, he is not the triple threat that he was before putting the ball on the floor. Play him closer.

Most players, even at the high school and college level, prefer to dribble with the same hand, and thus are more dangerous heading in that direction. For example, a lefty will prefer to dribble to his left. So, go ahead and overplay that side when guarding the dribble. Force a lefty to dribble toward his right.

The sideline or baseline is your best friend as a defender. Always try to force the dribbler toward the sideline if he's up top — or the baseline if he's dribbling from the wing or corner. If the dribbler beats you to the middle, he can pass in either direction. If he beats you along the sideline, you can at least dictate where the pass must go.

Post-dribble stage

After the player picks up his dribble, he can only pass or shoot. At this point, he may move only his pivot foot, which he sets by moving his opposite foot. Play as close to him as possible without fouling him.

If your man attempts a shot, remember the principle of verticality. You may legally jump straight up with your arms straight over your head when contesting an opponent's shot.

The principle of verticality is especially important for the defender to keep in mind when guarding the post player (see the section "Playing post defense" later in this chapter). Not only can you alter the shot's trajectory, but if the referee notices that you're leaping straight up with your arms straight up, he's far less likely to whistle you for a foul.

Having said that, I should warn you that most referees know this rule but do not respect it. If you jump straight up in the air, and the offensive player initiates contact, the zebras are likely to whistle you for a foul . . . even though you are allowed to jump straight upward.

The first day of practice

If you want to make your point as a coach about the importance of defense, begin every practice with man-to-man defense drills. Don't give defense the perfunctory attention that you might to, say, mailing out thank-you letters. Emphasize defense and insist that players do every drill correctly.

Zigzag dribble drill

This should be your principal man-to-man drill — it drives home the fundamentals of good footwork. Run it at three speeds: walking, at half speed, and then at full speed.

Players pair off, with one player getting the ball. The player with the ball dribbles from baseline to baseline in a zigzag motion, reversing the dribble every few steps. (Make sure that he zigs before zagging; don't ever zag first. I'm kidding.)

The defender's job is to assume a defensive stance, using the *shuffle-step* to head off the dribbler's intended direction and force him the other way. When the offensive player dribbles to the right, the defender "drops" his left foot backward and shuffles to the left. When the dribbler changes direction and moves to the left, the defender drops his right foot and shuffles right. (See Figure 7-1.) The defender does not try to steal the ball, and the dribbler does not try to blow past the defender. When the pair reach the far baseline, they switch roles and return.

After a walk-through of the zigzag, players should go at half speed. The defender's job is still to keep his man in front of him (between himself and the basket) and to force a change in direction by shuffling his feet. Finally, the players run the drill at full speed. If the dribbler beats the defender — as often happens — the defender must turn and pursue the dribbler.

Figure 7-1:
The zigzag dribble drill.

Few, if any, players can out-shuffle-step a player who's dribbling the ball at full speed. So if the dribbler beats the defender, the defender abandons his shuffle, turning and sprinting to cut him off — known as the *turn* and *go*. A defender sprinting all-out should be faster than a player dribbling. The defender's intent is to pick a spot up court to which he can beat the dribbler, sort of like heading him off at the pass. If he can do that, he can resume his defensive stance or shuffle.

Do not let the dribbler beat you to the middle; force him to the sideline instead. When you "force sideline," you give yourself defensive help because the sideline acts as a wall — the dribbler can't go beyond it. If you're going to overplay the dribbler in one direction, overplay to the middle.

Defense is TEAM defense

To play great team defense, each defender must know where the ball is at all times. Covering your man in a man-to-man defense is not enough. If you focus on your man alone, you'll soon be the victim of a screen (explained in Chapter 6). If you know where the ball is, on the other hand, you can surmise your man's next move. Will he cut toward the basket? Is he going to set a pick for a teammate? Anticipating his next move is half the battle.

The triangle principle of man-to-man defense

The triangle principle, shown in Figure 7-2, is simple: Imagine yourself as one point of a triangle, the other two points being the person you're guarding and the ball. Now use your peripheral vision to see both the man and the ball.

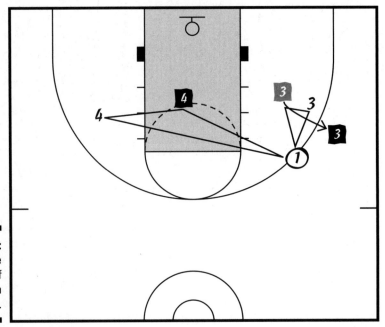

Figure 7-2:
Triangle
principle of
man-to-man
defense.

When you're guarding the player with the ball, you stay between that player and the basket. Your job is to prevent the offensive player from penetrating to the basket. When you're guarding a player without the ball, on the other hand, you're playing both the ball and the person you're assigned to defend. Sound, solid defense gets back to peripheral vision: watching your man closely in a position from which you can also see the ball out of the corner of your eye.

Playing guard in a man-to-man defense

Key Stat: Steals

A guard who's defending the player *with* the ball should stay in a low defensive stance. Why? Your man is more of a threat to drive to the basket than the players being guarded by a forward or center. And, as discussed earlier, the lower your center of gravity, the quicker you will be. Also, a guard's man probably has the ball farther away from the basket than a center's man or forward's man would.

The defending guard has three big responsibilities:

- ✔ Don't let your man beat you on the dribble.
- ✔ Don't give up an uncontested three-pointer.
- ✔ Force the man away from the middle to one side of the floor.

A guard defending a guard *without* the ball (known as the *off guard*) has two ways to play the situation:

- ✔ **Deny the passing lane:** The off guard often guards the opposition's best outside shooter, so he may choose a *closed* stance on defense. His lead foot is in the passing lane (the path via which the ball would travel to get to his man), and he may guard him closely and overplay the pass, knowing that his teammates will help him if his man goes back door, or cuts behind him to the hoop. (See Figure 7-3.)

- ✔ **Play help defense:** Here the guard uses an *open* stance, meaning that he is in position to react to the ball just as much as to react to his man. His foot is not in the passing lane. (See Figure 7-4.) You use this method if you don't consider your man to be a major outside scoring threat. You want to be in position to help a teammate if necessary.

Figure 7-3:
Denying
the passing
lane.

A

B

C

Figure 7-4: The weakside guard: helping to the ball on penetration (left), and recovering to the player who receives the ball (right).

Guards don't receive enough credit for being great defenders because the statistics that fans associate with defense, rebounds and blocked shots, are not guard-related Only one true guard, Gary Payton of the Seattle SuperSonics (a franchise that no longer even exists), has been named the NBA's Defensive Player of the Year since 1988–89. Payton's nickname was "The Glove" because of how well he covered opponents.

Having said that, Michael Jordan was an outstanding one-on-one defender, as is Kobe Bryant. Chris Paul is often thought of as a terrific scorer and assists man, but the New Orleans Hornet point guard has led the NBA in steals in four of his six seasons.

Rotation defense

Rotation defense is one of the best innovations of the past decade. In any discussion about why scoring is down, someone usually mentions improved defense — and rotation is at the forefront of this revolution. The idea behind rotation defense is to leave your man to help the defender who got beat, with the understanding that one of your teammates will pick up the player you were guarding. The rule of rotation is to leave your man (when necessary) and find a player who's more likely to receive the next pass.

The Detroit Pistons teams of the late 1980s, which won two NBA titles under the guidance of Chuck Daly, were the first practitioners of this rotation defense, and they elevated it to an art. Blessed with athletic and eager defenders — such as Isiah Thomas, Joe Dumars, and Dennis Rodman — Detroit always seemed to have six men playing defense. Watch an NBA or college game today, and you'll see that every team plays this sophisticated defense.

Rotation defense is easier to understand if you see it happening. Take a look at Figure 7-5, where you have two guards (1 and 2) and two forwards (3 and

4). If the strongside guard (1) passes to the strongside forward (3), the weakside guard (D2) slides down to take the weakside forward (4), and the weakside forward (D4) goes over to help on 3. For the guard on top playing 1 (D1), the first thing is to take away the passing lane with a closed stance.

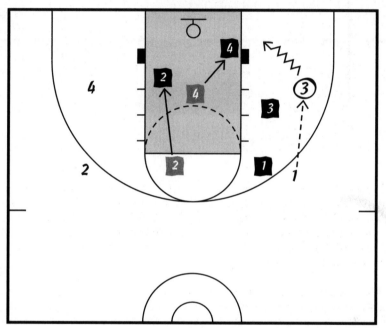

Figure 7-5:
Rotation
defense.

This is a difficult rotation for the D2 guard because she ends up defending a taller forward. After the ball leaves the fingertips of the passer, the D2 guard must react defensively, although she's not guarding the ball. After the ball goes from guard to forward, the defender has to anticipate, cheating a little toward the baseline. She can do so because the ball is now two passes away from her player.

Shutout defense

When the ball handler picks up his dribble, both guards instantly switch to *shutout defense* mode, which means that they both face-guard the ball handler, denying him the pass or even much of a view of the court. In college ball, if the player who picks up his dribble does not pass the ball within five seconds, a turnover results. Sometimes a defender will yell "dead" to alert his teammates of the situation.

Playing forward in a man-to-man defense

Key Stat: Rebounds

The responsibilities of a forward in a man-to-man "D" are fairly straightforward (see Figure 7-6):

- ✔ **Defend the pass to the post player:** If the man you are guarding posts up, you either attempt to deny the entry pass to him or you force him to receive the ball farther from the basket than he would like to receive it.

- ✔ **Defend the high and low cuts:** As a power forward, you must anticipate where your opponent is trying to go to receive a pass. Try to thwart his advance, be it when he cuts up high or down low. But beware of him using a fake-step and then cutting in the other direction.

Figure 7-6:
If the guard picks up the dribble, all defenders play shutout defense, denying all passing lanes.

Don't make the mistake of giving the forward you're guarding an option to go high or low after faking the opposite way. (You'd better not give him low, because he may dunk on you!) Be in a balanced defensive position when guarding a forward with the ball. (See Figure 7-7.)

Ben Wallace

In more than 11 NBA seasons Ben Wallace, a 6'9" NBA power forward whose arms are the size of tree trunks, has proven that he cannot shoot. Wallace makes only 41.5 percent of his free throws and just 47 percent of his field goals, an abnormally low number, which is why he rarely shoots anything other than dunks or put-backs.

So why is he a four-time NBA All-Star? Because nobody plays better defense in the paint. Wallace is a four-time NBA Defensive Player of the Year who has twice led the league in rebounds and once in blocked shots. That's how he has survived so long among the greatest basketball players in the world.

When playing a forward one-on-one, apply the same principles as when playing guard on defense. Know the strengths and weaknesses of the shooter. If the forward is a good shooter, keep a hand up in his face; if he's not a threat to score, play tough defense but be more careful about committing a foul and sending him to the free throw line. Remember, especially when defending a forward, to turn and box out (see Chapter 8) after he shoots — he's in a position to rebound.

When defending a player on the weak side of the court (opposite the side of the ball), a forward must be ready to slide over and help the other forward or center. Sometimes the other forward's man beats him. On the other hand, the center may need help on a double team (where two defenders guard a player) because the two defenders physically overmatch him.

Watch when teams attempt to defend muscle-bound Dwight Howard of the Orlando Magic — who can overpower anyone not allergic to Kryptonite. (Howard once wore a Superman jersey and cape during the NBA dunk contest.) The weakside forward usually slides over to "seal off" Howard — at least the forward honestly tries.

When the forward slides over, he leaves his man and yells, "Rotate!" Normally, the off guard slides over to take the forward's man because the forward on offense is now a more viable scoring threat than a guard who's positioned up top.

Figure 7-7:
The strong-side forward (3) must help to the ball but also be ready to deny the flash pivot.

Playing center in a man-to-man defense

Key Stat: Blocked shots

Centers need help — more than most of us, actually. The center is normally a team's tallest player. Inherently, fewer centers populate basketball teams than forwards or guards, which means that a greater disparity in talent exists at the center position.

Some centers have an offensive arsenal – think of Pau Gasol of the Los Angeles Lakers – while others are thought of as simply having six fouls to give. On most teams at any level the least skilled player is the center (actually, the back-up center), but even a Hall of Famer such as John Stockton, who was barely 6'1", could never guard a back-up seven-footer.

Hence, coaches sometimes keep the tallest kid who tries out, simply because they need someone to defend the other team's tallest kid. At worst, he can foul the other player and compel him to earn his points from the free-throw line. Here's a defensive cheat sheet for centers:

- Do *not* react to the ball fake. That is, do not leave your feet.
- Do not lean on the opposing center; instead, keep a hand or forearm on his back.
- Once your opponent commits to a move, beat him to the spot to which you anticipate he wants to go.
- Keep your arms straight up (not at 45 degrees) when contesting a shot.
- After a player releases a shot, box out.

Boxing out

Simply put, *boxing out* is how you keep the player whom you are guarding from getting the rebound. When the ball is shot, whether your man or someone else shot it, you do the same thing. First, turn and face the basket, and put your backside into that player. Keep your body low and wide and stick your butt as far out as you can, maintaining contact with him. Why? This way you know where he is without having to look at him. You can have your eyes trained on the basket to look for the ball.

Establishing position by boxing out will get you more rebounds than being taller or jumping higher.

If the center attempts to play in front of a physically dominant or taller center, the offense will often attempt a lob pass over the center's head. A forward needs to slide over from the weak side, or a guard needs to slide down from the elbow, to intercept the lob. This defensive play often works because a good lob pass requires ultimate precision.

Double-team the center

Most pivot players are not very good passers. When double-teamed, they often panic and have trouble finding the open teammate. The center on defense usually double-teams with a forward and the other three defenders play against that center's four offensive outlets.

Double down off the passer

Another way to neutralize the post player is to *double down* (a guard leaves his man on the perimeter to double-team a forward or center on the blocks). You see this all the time in the NBA. The player defending the entry passer follows the pass and collapses on the center, who finds himself with a big body on his back and a pesky guard or forward in front, swiping at the ball. (See Figure 7-8.) The offensive center's best bet is to return the pass to the player who fed him the ball.

Note: Doubling down can lead to a bonanza of three-pointers for the wing player left unattended. You have to factor how dangerous a shooter that wing player is when considering the double-down or rotation out of the double.

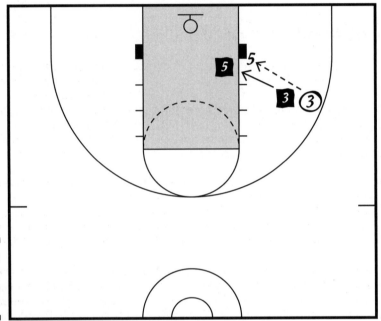

Figure 7-8:
Doubling
down on the
post player.

As the player doubling down, don't lose sight of the offensive player who made the entry pass. Smart players slide to another spot when you leave them to double down. When you go to help, keep yourself in a triangle between your man and the ball. If your man cuts to the basket or to the weak side of the court, either follow him or yell, "Rotate!" so that your teammates help you out.

The shot block: The center's last-resort weapon

When all else fails for the center — when he has allowed his man to get the ball on the low post and a shot is imminent — he has one last line of defense: the blocked shot. Sure, guards and forwards can block shots, too, but almost without exception, a team's shot-block leader is its center.

Some shot blockers are smart and others less so. The smart shot blocker merely deflects the ball, allowing himself or a teammate to gain possession of the ball. No one did this better than Bill Russell of the Boston Celtics. "Russ" would catch an opponent's shot in midair and toss it to a teammate to initiate a fast break. The unwise shot blocker tries to swipe the ball into the third row of the stands (while simultaneously bellowing some tough-guy line like "Not in my house!"). The crowd gets fired up, the defender bumps a teammate, and . . . the opponent retains possession of the ball.

Even if you are not a natural-born shot blocker, it's still important to contest a shot. Leap high and get a hand in the air to distract the shooter. If you have no chance of blocking a shot, the next best thing you can do is to box out the shooter after he releases the ball.

Playing post defense

Offensive players *post up* a defender (face away from the basket and then turn and shoot) if they think they can outmuscle or shoot over him. Some post players just prefer playing with their backs to the basket. Most post players are centers, but guards or small forwards occasionally play the post if they feel that doing so is to their advantage. Charles Barkley, whose vast derriere gave him a huge advantage over any player his height (6'5"), loved to post up on offense.

Post defense is different from perimeter defense because the player you're guarding has his back to you. Keep a loose hand or forearm on her back but don't apply pressure or you may be whistled for a foul. Don't place your body against his, though. Why not? Because then he knows exactly how you're leaning — vital information for helping her spin around you to the basket.

When a player gets the ball in the post, his first option is to shoot. When he attempts the shot, don't leave your feet. Post players often fake a shot to get the defender airborne so that he can either dribble around her defender or draw contact — and a foul. The best advice is to wait until the offensive player leaves his feet before you leave yours. It's not even a bad idea to keep your feet planted and raise your arms straight up. Then, box out.

Defending the entry pass

The entry pass is *one pass away* — it's the pass that the ball handler intends to make to the player you're guarding. The following applies primarily to anyone defending a player on the perimeter.

As the defender, you attempt to deny the passing lane (the lane through which the ball handler can pass the ball to the player you're guarding), but you must be aware that, if you overplay the passing lane, your man may slip by you in the other direction.

When defending one pass away, place your lead foot (the one closer to your man) forward and extend your corresponding arm, with your elbow bent.

You want your hand — but not your foot — in the passing lane to deflect the bounce pass or chest pass.

Why put your hand and not your foot in the passing lane? Two reasons:

- ✔ The offensive player will aim the pass toward the player's chest, not the lower half of his body.
- ✔ By keeping your foot back, you minimize the chance of your opponent cutting behind you and receiving a back door pass.

An entry pass from, say, above the top of the key to the wing encompasses many of the defensive elements I've described. The defender guarding the dribbler is between the dribbler and the bucket. The defender who is one pass away is between his man and the ball.

Another element to consider: Has the ball handler dribbled yet, or has he already picked up his dribble? If the answer is the latter, the one-pass-away defender can play his own man more tightly, knowing that the ball handler is eager to pass the ball.

Defenders often err by putting both their hand and their foot in the passing lane. A smart wing player will coax you into leaning forward and then back-cut to the hoop (that is, escape through the dreaded back door) for a pass that leads to an easy lay-up.

Defending screens: To switch or not to switch?

Switching on defense means exchanging defensive assignments with a teammate during a play. That is, you guard his man and he guards yours.

Switching is an option when one offensive player sets a screen for his teammate, which causes his defender to become separated from him. The two defenders may switch; that is, pick up each other's man, so that neither offensive player is left open.

The result, however, is often a mismatch in favor of the offense. Say your favorite team is playing the New Orleans Hornets. Watch as 6'10" Emeka Okafor sets a pick for 6'0" Chris Paul. The defender who had Okafor is probably too slow to guard Paul, whereas the one who had Paul is probably too small to guard Okafor.

The benefit of switching is that defenders don't get lost trying to find their men after a pick. The disadvantage is that, as illustrated above, it can create mismatches.

How do you defend a screen? First, anticipate the screen before it occurs. Anticipating a screen is like watching traffic ahead of you on the freeway and sensing when a car will change lanes.

Coaches train their defenders to call out — different coaches use different terms — to alert the teammate being screened. Then the two defenders involved have two options: The defender being screened may yell "Switch!" and exchange men (see Figure 7-9), or the defender being screened can try to fight through the screen and stay with his man.

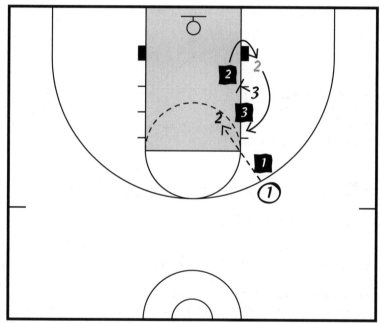

Figure 7-9:
The defenders may switch when one becomes the victim of a screen.

Screens work because they create a moment of indecision for the defense. No single formula exists for defending them. Defenders must learn to work together well and have a sense of what each one likes to do. The most important element of successfully defending screens: communication between the two defenders. The defense must talk.

Defending the pick and roll

A *pick* and *roll* is simply a screen that's set for the player with the ball, as Figure 7-10 shows. The screener rolls off the screen, to the hoop, and catches a pass from the player with the ball. How do you defend it?

Say the offensive center drifts up from the post to screen for the guard who has the ball. The defensive center must help by stepping out, or *hedging,* on the dribbler — doing so slows down the dribbler and gives the dribbler's defender extra time to fight over the screen and stay with the dribbler. The defensive center, having halted the guard momentarily, recovers and slides down to defend the screener, who is rolling to the hoop. If the defensive center gets beaten on the roll, the weak side forward must be prepared to slide over to help.

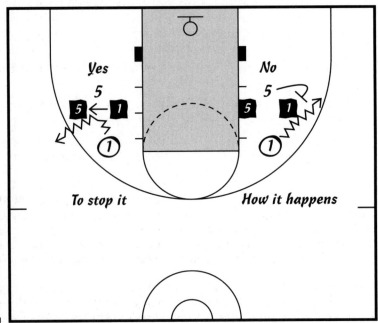

Figure 7-10:
A pick and roll is a screen set for the player with the ball (1).

Never go behind (around) a screen to find your man. Anytime you do so, whether or not your man has the ball, he'll have room and time enough to bury you with an open jumper. Always go above the screen, between the offensive players. In basketball parlance, the term is "fighting over the screen." That's a good term because it is a struggle to do so, but it is also better defense.

Fighting over a screen is a terrific metaphor for defense in general. Great defense requires extra effort and tenacity.

Digger's switching rule

If you switch and find yourself in a physical mismatch ("Mr. Boykins [who is 5'6"], meet Mr. Garnett [who is 6'11"]"), *front* the player you're guarding (that is, get between him and the ball, still facing the ball). Play in front of him, and expect the cavalry (your teammates) to provide weak side help against the lob pass over your head. If you play behind him, you make it easier for the entry pass to arrive, and he can score easily over the top of you.

Here are some basic principles of switching on man-to-man defense:

- ✔ **Don't switch if you can effectively slide through the screen, using your teammate to help you recover.** The defender who is free from the screen gives his teammate room to slide through the screen closer to the ball.

- ✔ **If a switch occurs, the screener is often the player left open.** Jump in front of him as soon as possible.

- ✔ **The defender of the screener should look to step in front of the player coming off the screen and draw a charging foul.**

- ✔ **Communicate.** You must talk to each other to let each other know whether to switch and where the screen is coming from.

Switch on a pick and roll? Never. The post defender must step out and go over the top, or trap the ball handler. The reason that Amar'e Stoudemire and Steve Nash, the most lethal pick-and-roll tandem of this millennium, were so effective is that Nash was impossible to trap even with two defenders. Chances are, though, that the player you'll be defending is not Steve Nash. The trap is a good, proactive defensive counter to the pick and roll.

Always switch when a screen is set at the three-point line. Size is not the big factor out there; the shot is. Guards usually attempt threes, so if a forward is setting the pick, switching is to the defense's advantage: The shooting guard now faces a taller defender. If you are the guard who's switched to defending the forward, don't worry. A pick and roll from 23 feet away is harmless.

The Last Word on Man-to-Man

Eventually, despite all your defensive tenacity (or even elevenacity . . . one degree beyond tenacity!), the offense will get off a shot. *Box out!* Grab the rebound. Two seconds of laziness can spoil 24 or 35 seconds of solid defense. The reward for well-played defense is offense, not more defense. (See Chapter 8 for more information about rebounding.)

And another thing — you can always foul. In theory, a player should never intentionally foul an opponent, but it happens all the time. You foul a player intentionally (making it look unintentional) under two circumstances:

✔ The player has an otherwise uncontested basket, and you'd rather see him earn his two points on the free throw line.

✔ The player being fouled is a notoriously poor free throw shooter. If you ever have Shaquille O'Neal in your rec league some day, remember this.

Some of the best defenders in NBA history almost never fouled out. Center Moses Malone, for example, played 20 seasons and fouled out only five times. Wilt Chamberlain *never* fouled out in the 1,205 games he played over 14 seasons. That statistic is as amazing as any of the other eye-popping numbers attributed to "Wilt the Stilt."

Zone Defense

The word *zone* is synonymous with *area.* In a *zone defense,* each defender covers an *area* as opposed to a player. When an offensive player moves from one area to another, the defensive player in the first area does not follow; instead, she remains in her zone (area).

How do you know when a team is playing a zone? Watch an offensive player move around the court. If one defensive player does not shadow her, the defense is playing a zone.

Why play zone?

✔ The opponent is a poor outside shooting team. You can pack a zone defense into the lane, making passing the ball inside difficult for your opponents, which forces your opponents to take outside shots.

✔ Your team is slow afoot and the other team will beat you on defense by cuts and screens (explained in Chapter 6).

✔ One of your players is in foul trouble. The zone protects her from having to defend a player one-on-one and lessens her chances of fouling out.

✔ Your zone takes your opponents out of their man-to-man offense.

For example, during a 1984 Notre Dame game against the University of Washington, we used a zone press (a full-court zone defense) to combat UW's Detlef Schrempf (who went on to a fruitful 16-season NBA career). Detlef liked to take the ball in the backcourt and go one-on-one against his man, and he became frustrated when he couldn't do that versus our press.

Today, the illegal defense has been scrapped in favor of the "Defensive Three Seconds" rule. That rule stipulates that a defender may not remain in the free throw lane for more than three seconds unless he is within arm's reach of an offensive player and in a guarding position. Zone defenses usually take their names from their configurations, beginning with the defender positioned closest to mid court/farthest from the basket. Thus a 2–3 zone, the most common form of zone defense, features two players up (near the foul line) and three below (closer to the basket). Other zones you see include the 1–3–1 and the 1–2–2. If the numbers add up to a number other than five, you've got a problem.

2–3 zone

Most teams play a 2–3 zone (shown in Figure 7-11) as a means to defend against a potent offensive post player. The 2–3 zone allows more than one defender to surround that player at all times. What you cede to the offense by playing a 2–3 zone is perimeter shooting. (See Chapter 5 for details on this type of shooting.)

Illegal defense

For the longest time, playing a zone defense in the NBA was illegal. The conventional wisdom was that a zone would inhibit offenses, and fans don't buy tickets to watch defense.

In 2001 the NBA made the illegal defense . . . wait for it . . . illegal. That is, the league allowed teams to play a zone. Because of the popularity of the three-point shot, and the increasing acumen that players have with the shot, the zone is largely antiquated anyway.

Guard responsibilities in a 2–3 zone

The two guards in a 2–3 zone are responsible for covering the three perimeter players. "Wait a second," you may be saying, "I thought you said that defenders guard an *area* in a zone, not *people!*" That's correct. The two guards are responsible for the *area* that those three players inhabit — that is, the perimeter. If two of those three players converge in the lane, they are no longer the guards' responsibility (because they moved out of the perimeter).

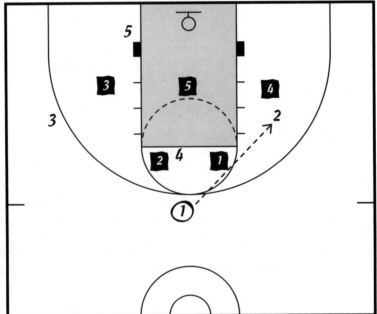

Figure 7-11:
The 2–3
zone.

Guards work hard in a zone, and guarding three perimeter players requires a lot of legwork. The guards must chase the ball within the perimeter, not giving up an uncontested three-pointer.

Here are some hints for guards playing a 2–3 zone:

- **Drift to the center.** When the ball is on the opposite wing, you should drift into the middle of the free throw lane, but never cross that imaginary line that cuts the half court in two.

- **Prevent dribble penetration.** The cardinal sin for guards playing a zone is to allow the ball handler to dribble between them, called *splitting the zone.* Allowing the split forces other defenders to converge on the ball handler, leaving one (or more) opponents open for an easy shot.

Forward responsibilities in a 2–3 zone

The forward must do the following in a 2–3 zone:

- ✔ **Defend the wing.** If the ball is passed to the wing, the defender must guard the man with the ball until the guard on his side has shifted over to help. Normally, the ball comes to the wing from the top of the circle, meaning the defensive guard on that side needs time to slide over after the pass to provide help.

- ✔ **Defend the baseline.** Nobody with the ball should get around the forward on the baseline. The idea is to force the action back to the middle, where a teammate can help.

- ✔ **Guard the post player if he steps to the baseline.** If the center receives a pass on the baseline and has no shot, he looks for the high post player, who cuts to the hoop. The defensive center's job is to seal off that route.

Center responsibilities in a 2–3 zone

Centers have the following responsibilities in a 2–3 zone:

- ✔ **Defend the paint.** The center, in the middle of the back line of three defenders, is responsible for the post area.

- ✔ **Seal off drives.** If a guard splits the zone or a wing eludes the forward and *drives the baseline* (dribbles at full speed along the baseline to the basket), the center must step in to halt the penetration.

- ✔ **Rebound.** The center rarely has to worry about solo coverage in a zone. Even when defending the post, he has a teammate to help. Thus he needs to shoulder more of the rebounding burden.

1–3–1 zone

The 1–3–1 defense, shown in Figure 7-12, forces the offense to one side of the court. It also attempts to force shots from the baseline. For this defense to be effective, you must be wary of the skip pass. The weak side wing defender as well as the low "1" defender must also anticipate skip passes.

If the opposing point guard is not much of a scoring or penetration threat, the 1–3–1 is also effective. If the point guard is able to dribble past the "1" defender up top, drawing one of the three men in the second line of defense to stop him, the zone will fail.

Figure 7-12:
The 1–3–1
zone.

Matchup zone

Bill Green, the longtime successful coach at Marion High School in Marion, Indiana, was a master teacher of the matchup zone. Before the 1976–77 season, I invited him to South Bend to teach the matchup zone to my players. That season, we jumped out to a 7–0 record and beat top-ten teams Indiana, Maryland, and UCLA with the matchup zone. We finished at 22–7 before losing in the Sweet 16 in the NCAA tournament.

The matchup zone is a combination of the zone and man-to-man defense. It may be better suited to *Basketball For Smarties*, but if you hear an announcer use the term, just know that the center guards a man and that the other four defenders work in unison to guard different areas.

Gadget defenses

Gadget defenses are not long-term solutions, but they may be effective in specific situations or against a team that relies on one player to do most of its scoring. A gadget defense is rarely used throughout an entire game.

Stopping Stephen Curry

On November 25, 2008, Davidson met Loyola. Davidson guard Stephen Curry, a 6'3" guard with outstanding shooting range, finished leading the nation in scoring that season. On this particular night he was held scoreless.

Whenever Davidson had the ball, Loyola's coach Jimmy Patsos decided to put two defenders on Curry no matter where he went. After a few possessions, Curry figured out the tactic, so he stood in the corner — with two defenders flanking him — and allowed his teammates to exploit the four-on-three advantage.

Davidson won by 30 points. Curry was held scoreless for the only time in his career, though; as we noted, he still would lead the nation in scoring that season. Afterward, Patsos defended his dubious strategy by saying, "I'm a history major. They're going to remember that we held him scoreless or that we lost by 30?"

Box and one

Play a box and one when the opposition has one monstrous scorer on whom they rely almost exclusively. In a box and one, you set up four defenders in a box around the three-second lane (a 2–2 zone, in effect). You deploy your fifth player to cover — and by "cover," I mean that he should be able to tell you how many fillings that player has in his teeth — the opposition's go-to guy. (See Figure 7-13.) In other words, four people play zone, and the fifth chases the big scorer all over the court man-to-man.

Install your best defender in the "one" position in the box and one. If the opposing player is a dangerous enough scorer, you may want to start a non-starter if she's your best defensive stopper.

Keep in mind that the "one" is likely to get (a) in foul trouble and (b) very tired. Is he a valuable scorer for your team? If so, measure how important it is to sacrifice his offensive output — which suffers due to (a) and (b) above — to have him defend the opponent's dead-eye shooter.

Triangle and two

In a triangle and two, three defenders (3, 4, and 5) play a zone in the paint — a guard up top, two big players down low — in the shape of a triangle, as Figure 7-14 shows. The two other defenders (1 and 2) have man-to-man assignments. The guard in the triangle plays just above the free throw line, and the two others position themselves along the blocks on the back line.

This defense is for a *short* period. Play it on a key possession to throw off the offense; the offense will not be prepared for it. Stay with this defense only until the offense figures out a way to beat it.

Figure 7-13:
The box
and one
defense.

Beating the triangle and two

Yes, you're in the defense chapter, but this is the only place where I discuss the triangle and two, so I may as well tell you how to beat it. Follow these steps:

1. Isolate the two guarded players man-to-man on the same side of the court. One of them should be handling the ball.

2. Have a third player set a weakside screen against the guard on the triangle. The player on the weakside wing should have an open jumper. As is the case with all zones, the best way to break a triangle and two is to bury your outside jump shots.

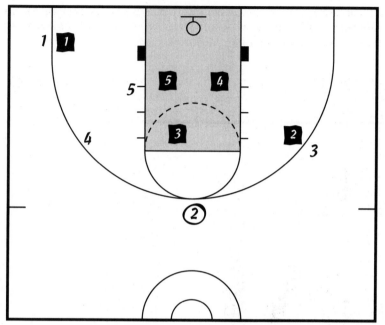

Figure 7-14:
The triangle
and two
defense.

And that concludes our geometry lesson. Don't worry; no rhombus and one or pentagon zone exists — at least not yet.

Meet the Press

Press is short for *pressure,* which is what a press defense is designed to inflict. A press (often called a *full-court press*) is an attacking defense employed in the backcourt, where the objective is not so much to defend against a bucket as it is to force a turnover. A press is only called after a made basket or after a dead ball situation (such as when the offense must inbound the ball). The pressing defense swarms all over the opponents in the backcourt.

In men's college basketball, the offense must advance the ball beyond mid court within ten seconds. In the NBA, the offense has 8 seconds. In women's basketball, no such rule exists (but there was a proposal to change this in 2011).

If the offense advances the ball past mid court (called *breaking the press*) without turning it over or committing a 10-second (or 8-second) violation, also known as a backcourt violation, the pressing team usually falls back into their normal defense. The strategy of the press is to force the ball handler to make a decision before he wants to do so.

Why press? The short answer is, "To create turnovers." But there's a little more to it than that.

- ✔ **Because the opposition are not good ball handlers.** A poor ball handler is anyone who commits turnovers. It has less to do with dribbling ability than it does decision-making prowess.

- ✔ **Because you hope to disrupt the opponent's offensive rhythm.** Some teams prefer to play a deliberate, half-court offense (the "Slow Burn" offense of Notre Dame, for example, to which we alluded in Chapter 6). Opposing teams may press them to hasten the tempo, but the Irish usually slow down as soon as they get the ball past mid court.

- ✔ **Because you want to increase the tempo of the game.** When playing against a slow, methodical team, your offense may need a jump-start. By changing the game pace with a press, your offense is more likely to get steals and easy baskets, which helps their confidence.

- ✔ **Because your players believe in it.** Former Arkansas coach Nolan Richardson used to use the term "40 minutes of hell" to describe playing his team. His players bought into the concept of pressing from start to finish — of turning the game into a war of attrition. If your players love to press and you have the bench depth to do it, pressing is a great way to play. Full-court pressure results in lots of turnovers and, hence, easy baskets. But pressing is also physically demanding and can tire players quickly.

- ✔ **Because it's something different.** Few hoops teams have the athletic ability and bench depth to press all game; hence most teams devote little practice time to breaking the press.

Figures 7-15 and 7-16 show two common press formations: the 2–2–1 full-court press and the 1–3–1 half-court press.

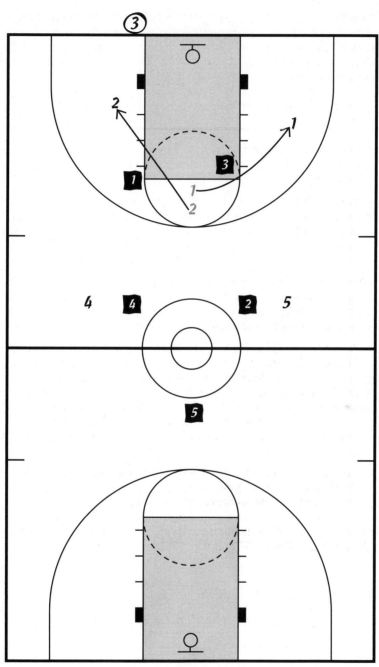

Figure 7-15:
The 2–2–1
press: a
common
full-court
press.

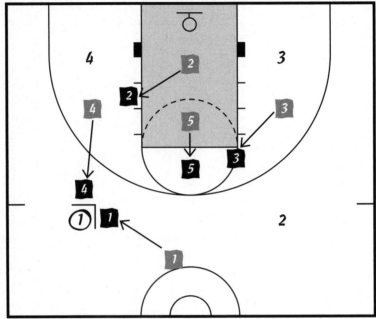

Figure 7-16:
The 1–3–1
half-court
press.

The trap press

The purpose of a press is to double team, or *trap,* a player, using the sideline as a third defender. The trap areas (shown in Figure 7-17) follow:

- The primary trap area is the spot where a player receives the inbounds pass.
- The secondary trap area is between the foul lines and half court on both sides of the mid-court line.
- The third trap area is deep in either corner in the front court.

The trap press involves three steps:

1. **Trap the ball.**

   After your opponent in-bounds the ball, trap the player who receives the pass. Two players attack him (not literally), forcing him toward the sideline. Don't give the player with the ball an opportunity to look for an open teammate; attack the ball immediately.

   What about the defender guarding the inbounds pass? He should not leave his man to help trap until the player who received the pass begins to dribble. If the defender leaves his man, the player with the ball can simply toss it back to the player who in-bounded it.

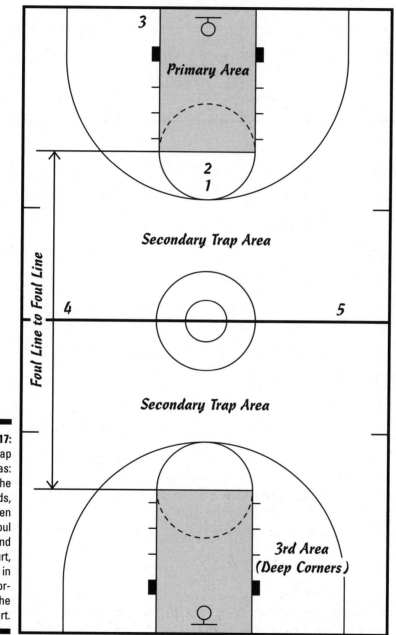

Figure 7-17: The trap areas: on the inbounds, between the foul lines and mid court, and deep in either corner in the front court.

Digger and presses

I first learned about presses in 1965–66 when I was coaching at St. Gabriel's High School. In the summer of 1965, I was working Bill Foster's basketball camp in the Poconos. John Wooden visited the camp that summer. His Bruins had won the NCAA title that year with a small, pressing team. The Wizard of Westwood enlightened us on the entire system.

When I first arrived at St. Gabriel's, the local folks told me that teams only pressed when they were behind in the fourth quarter. So I decided to do something different. We pressed for 32 minutes (the entire game) at St. Gabriel's and won a state championship.

When I arrived at Fordham, I too had a small team; not one of my players stood over 6'5". So my players pressed the entire game — 40 minutes of hell. That year, my only season at the Bronx school, Fordham's record was 26–3. Why did the press work so well that year? Yes, I had quick players. But those players believed in the press and the coach who was teaching it to them. That's half the battle.

2. **Keep the player surrounded in the trap.**

   After the player with the ball puts the ball on the floor and begins her dribble, the defender in front of her must force her to the sideline. The inbounds pass defender approaches from behind to effect the trap. If she picks up her dribble, converge on her and hound her.

DIGGER SAYS

   When she picks up her dribble, she should reach in for the ball with two hands. The player with the ball is holding it on the sides to make a pass. If you reach in, reach with one hand on top and the other on the bottom of the ball; don't try to slap the ball out, or the ref may whistle you for a foul. If the opportunity to put two hands on the ball — to either steal it or get a held-ball call — is not there, don't risk it. Better to try to force a five-second violation.

3. **Anticipate the desperation pass.**

   But do *not* foul the trapped player.

COACH TIP

Teach all your defensive players every spot on the floor in the trap defense. When they're familiar with every spot, they get a feel for where everyone is supposed to be in this defensive alignment, and they know when to make the interception. The players have more confidence in what their teammates are doing, and you can sub each player in for anyone during a game.

Defending the break

Every team would love to have tall, athletically gifted players, but in reality, most teams have to play at least one center in the press who's not as quick. If you're the deep man on defense — or one of the two — you're usually positioned at the foul line in the frontcourt. If no offensive player happens to be behind you, gamble. Move up to the top of the circle. Unless the offense tests you, tighten the press by moving up as far as its deepest player. But be careful: A desperate player trapped in the backcourt will throw the home-run ball (long pass) to a streaking teammate. Don't get beat deep.

If you're the center facing a 2-on-1 fast break, point out to your teammate who's recovering on defense where she should go. That way, you neutralize the 2-on-1 into an evenly balanced 2-on-2 situation.

Defensive superlatives

Fewest points allowed in an NBA game: 49. The Miami Heat beat the Chicago Bulls 82–49 on April 10, 1999. This was during the strike-shortened NBA season and also, as every Bulls fan knows, the year after Michael Jordan left.

Fewest points allowed in a quarter of an NBA game: 2. Twice. In the more recent of the two, the Toronto Raptors held the Golden State Warriors to just 1–13 shooting in the fourth quarter. The Raptors overcame a 16-point deficit at the start of the period, forced overtime, and then won.

Fewest points allowed in a Division I NCAA men's game, pre-shot clock era: 6. Tennessee beat Temple, 11–6, on December 15, 1973.

Fewest points allowed in a Division I NCAA men's game since 1986 (shot-clock era): 20. George Washington University beat St. Louis, 49–20, on January 20, 2008.

Fewest points allowed in a Division I NCAA women's game: 11. Georgia Tech beat Mercer 82–11 on December 30, 2010.

Chapter 8

Rebounding

- -

In This Chapter

▶ Examining offensive and defensive rebounding strategies

▶ Practicing with rebounding drills

▶ Emulating the great rebounders in basketball history

- -

*H*ow valuable is rebounding? In 1956 Red Auerbach, the coach of the Boston Celtics, took aside his rookie center, Bill Russell, and gave him the following instructions: "Your game is to get me the ball. You get the ball and throw it up there for the shooters."

Then Auerbach, who understood that he was asking Russell to sacrifice individual stardom for the benefit of the team, dangled this carrot in front of his gifted player. Auerbach said, "We'll count rebounds as baskets for you."

Had the NBA bean counters conspired with Auerbach's scheme, Russell, on the strength of rebounds alone, would be the NBA's all-time career scoring leader with 43,240 points. Instead, the 6'11" center had to satisfy himself with leading the Celtics to 11 NBA championships (including eight in a row at one point), winning the league's Most Valuable Player award five times, and retiring with 21,620 rebounds — second only to Wilt Chamberlain on the career list.

Even more than 35 years since both Hall of Famers retired, Chamberlain and Russell remain one-two on that list.

How valuable is rebounding? Consider that, with the exception of Michael Jordan, only three players in NBA history have won the league's MVP award four or more times. They are Chamberlain (four times), Russell (five times), and Kareem Abdul-Jabbar (six times). Is it just a coincidence that Chamberlain, Russell, and Abdul-Jabbar rank one, two, and three, respectively, on the NBA's Most Rebounds, Career list? Or that the teams on which they played won 17 NBA titles? I don't think so.

Rebounding is hard work. Because many a rebound ricochets off the backboard (referred to both as the *board* and the *glass*), the phrases *clearing the boards* and *wiping the glass* have become slang for grabbing a rebound. Both terms imply blue-collar duties; the latter implies that a good rebounder, like good domestic help, does do windows.

Board-dom: A Glossary

Before I talk about rebounding techniques, I need to define a few terms:

- **Boxing out:** Establishing a position between your opponent and the basket while a shot is in the air.
- **Offensive rebound:** Gaining possession of an errant shot that either you or one of your teammates attempted.
- **Defensive rebound:** Gaining possession of an opponent's missed shot.

Rebounding: The Key to Victory

Kareem Abdul-Jabbar once said that if his team outrebounded its opponent, his team would win. It really is that simple. Just as in baseball, where the team with fewer errors usually wins, winning teams in basketball outrebound their foes. Consider this: You have four ways to regain possession of the ball when playing defense:

- Your team rebounds a missed shot.
- Your team steals the ball.
- The offense turns the ball over via a violation. (See Chapter 3 for information about offensive violations.)
- The offense scores.

Clearly, your job as a defender is to prevent your opponent from scoring. Steals happen, as do offensive violations such as traveling, but steals are less common than missed shots. The more defensive rebounds you grab, the fewer shots your opponent attempts. That translates to fewer opportunities for scoring. You're right, Kareem; winning a game *is* that simple.

Rebounding involves all five players on the floor. Every player is a potential rebounder on each missed shot. Thus, to out-rebound the other team, each player must neutralize the player he's guarding. Even if you do not grab the rebound, you are doing your job if the man you are guarding does not collect it, either.

The Team Concept of Rebounding

As a player, you need to work individually, but rebounding is a team effort. Here's how the teamwork plays out on each end of the floor:

✔ **On defense:** All three front-line players (that is, the two forwards and the center) must put a body on the player they are guarding. Use your derriere to feel where that player is and make a wide base to keep him from getting around you.

The guards must prevent the perimeter offensive players from swooping in, grabbing an offensive rebound, and making an easy bucket.

✔ **On offense:** If all five players crash the boards and no one remains at the top of the key, the defense will make you pay if they get the rebound. A defender, upon grabbing the rebound, will throw a quick pass (known as an *outlet pass*) to a teammate. That's how fast breaks, which lead to easy transition buckets, are born.

How do you prevent a breakaway? If you're out on top of the key when your team takes a shot, your first obligation is to retreat on defense. Only go for the rebound if the ball caroms out toward you and you have an excellent chance to be the first one to retrieve it.

If you're down low near the bucket, think of that missed shot off as belonging to you and nobody else. If you're outrebounded, don't allow the rebounder to throw the outlet pass immediately. Get in his face with your arms extended skyward.

Rebounding Physics

Good rebounders understand shots and anticipate the outcome. For example, the longer the shot, the farther the miss bounces. That's simple physics. A longer shot has more velocity *and* a higher arc than a shot taken near the basket, so players most likely will have to rebound the ball farther from the hoop.

Rims can be *hard* or *soft*. I'm not talking about the iron of the rim itself; by hard or soft, I'm referring to how tightly the rim is affixed to the backboard. A rim that is tightly affixed has no give and is considered *hard*. A loosely affixed rim has plenty of give and is known to hoopsters as being *soft* (or generous). This varies from facility to facility. Tightly affixed rims not only result in errant shots that bounce farther away from the rim, but they also result in more missed shots.

Oddly enough, you will become a much better shooter if you are able to practice on a hard, or "unforgiving," rim. It compels you to put more of an arc on your shots.

Dayton place

The University of Dayton had the hardest rims I ever encountered as a coach. On a court like that, it doesn't matter where the shot is taken; the ball comes off the rim long. My strategy was to have our front-line players box out a foot or two outside their normal perimeter when on defense. Rather than being 6 feet from the basket when boxing out, we'd go back to 7 or 8 feet, because the ball came out that long.

Missed three-point shots used to bounce all the way back to the three-point line.

In 1973–74, Notre Dame arrived in Dayton as one of the top rebounding teams in the nation with a 24–1 record. Although we had played there a year earlier, I forgot to remind my players about the gym's hard rims. Dayton outrebounded us, and we lost 97–82.

Be sure to scout the rims of the facility in which you're going to play. You can do some rim scouting during pregame warm-ups. Watch the opposition shoot with two objectives in mind:

✔ To discover how hard the rims are.

✔ To observe which players, especially which guards, take low-arc shots, which bounce off the rim farther and faster.

Defensive Rebounding

On defense, the perfect rebound hits the floor. *Uh oh, Digger's losing it.* No, really — think about it. As a defensive player, your job is to prevent the offensive player you're guarding from grabbing the rebound. That part of your job actually takes priority over grabbing the rebound yourself. Why? Imagine that the ball bounces off the rim and you're unable to grab it. As long as the player you're guarding fails to grab it as well, you've done your job.

If all five defenders are unable to grab the rebound, and each defender keeps the offensive player she's guarding from getting the ball, then the ball hits the floor. Theoretically, the ball rolls out of bounds, and the defense gets the ball. Perfect.

Don't misunderstand me: Players should go after the rebound. My point is that, defensively, your *top* priority is to keep your opponent from getting the rebound. If all five players do that, the ball hits the floor. In real life, that almost never happens, but then again, physics professors like to discuss frictionless surfaces. Humor me.

The key to defensive rebounding starts in pregame shooting practice. A great defensive rebounder watches how the other team shoots. Some shooters are *soft shooters* (they shoot with a high arc); others shoot *on the line* (with a low arc). Your job is to know the shooter, especially the player you're guarding. Here's what you can look for from either type of shooter:

- ✔ **High arc:** A missed shot may not bounce off the rim as far, but it may bounce off higher. The ball has a tendency to take a second bounce off the rim or backboard.

- ✔ **Low arc:** Fooore! This shot usually comes off as more of a line drive and is less likely to take a second bounce off the rim. More important than the distance the ball travels is its speed. Your reflexes must be faster for this shot than for a high-arc shot.

Listen to Kevin Love, the NBA's next great rebounder, discuss his craft. In a 2010 article in *Sports Illustrated*, the Minnesota Timberwolves' 6'10" forward told writer Lee Jenkins, "A different sense knocks into me when the ball is in the air. I know where it will hit and where it will land. I'm playing percentages, but it's not a guessing game. Most of the time I'm right."

Using your time wisely

Most shots taken from the perimeter travel in the air for *two seconds* from the moment the shooter releases the ball until it bounces off the rim or the backboard (or goes in). Two ticks: one-thousand-one, one-thousand-two. What should you be doing during these two seconds? Read on.

Find someone

Say your team is playing man-to-man defense. After the shot leaves the shooter's fingertips, your job is simple: Find the player you're guarding — hopefully he's nearby, or else you have other problems. If your team is in a *zone defense* — where each player guards an area instead of an opponent — locate the player near you who is moving toward the basket.

Everyone on defense should fight for a rebound with equal intensity. "Designated rebounders" do not exist on defense; rebounding is everyone's job.

Make contact

Rebounding is the most physical aspect of basketball. If you're squeamish about a little bumping and bruising, you won't become a good rebounder. But if you prioritize getting the ball above personal safety, you may become a great rebounder.

Two methods of making contact exist: the *reverse method* and *the step-in-the-path method.*

The reverse method: By *reverse,* I mean that when you play defense, you always face the player you're guarding. However, after the ball is shot, the ball takes priority over your opponent: You must know where the ball is, but you don't want to lose your opponent, either — so, you reverse yourself. Turn your body so that you're facing the hoop. Now your eyes can follow the path of the shot. (See Figure 8-1.)

Use your backside — and by backside, I mean your rear end — to stay with your opponent. Put your body on him and use your butt for two purposes:

- ✔ To block out your opponent.
- ✔ To be aware of your opponent's movements.

Figure 8-1:
The reverse method.

The step-in-the-path method: You may find yourself away from the player you're guarding at the moment the shooter releases his shot. (Perhaps you were helping out on a double team or were simply out of position.) Hence, when the shot is attempted, you may not be able to use the reverse method. Instead, you must anticipate your opponent's path to the basket to keep him from getting the rebound. Find the spot where you'll be able to intercept that player as he heads toward the basket, and race to that spot.

Think of the player you're guarding as a missile en route to a target and pretend that you've been sent as an anti-attack missile. Your trajectory is not toward the target; rather, your aim is to intercept the missile *on its way* to the target.

Maintain contact

After you successfully box out an offensive player, maintain contact until you locate the ball, and then go get it. The offensive player is attempting to elude you because you have the more advantageous position. When you lose contact, the offensive player's task becomes that much simpler.

Kevin Love's middle name is Wesley. Love, the NBA's first dominant rebounder since Dennis Rodman, was given that name in honor of Wesley "Wes" Unseld, a former teammate of his dad, Stan Love, when both played for the Washington Bullets. Wes Unseld is currently 11th all-time in career rebounds in the NBA. He also threw the best outlet passes anyone had ever seen . . . until Kevin Love arrived.

Gaining leverage

You often hear coaches urging their players to "Box out!" — a phrase that condenses the three rules above (that is, find someone, make contact, and maintain contact). As with so many basketball skills, you must use the proper form for boxing out. Maintaining proper form is a matter of *leverage*.

Charles Barkley was one of the best rebounders in the NBA for more than a decade, despite the fact that he was only listed as 6'6" (he was actually a hair shorter than 6'5", which is curious because Sir Charles was bald for most of his career). Barkley's lower back problems hindered his jumping prowess, but he still managed to collect 33 rebounds in a single game in 1996. (Ten rebounds per game will rank you among the Top 6 rebounders in the NBA these days.) Why? Because nobody — not even Archimedes — understood leverage better than the bulky Barkley, whose other nickname, a most apt one, was "The Round Mound of Rebound".

Try this experiment: Stand as erect as possible and have someone push you from behind. See how you move. Now bend your knees and stick out your derriere to establish a wider base. Keep your torso erect, but lean slightly forward. Have someone push you again. Notice that your wider base gives you more stability, that you are not as easy to budge.

You want to crouch down and make yourself more horizontal when boxing out. Making yourself shorter to grab a rebound may seem paradoxical, but it isn't. Barkley had an airbag for a butt, and he used his gluteus maximus to maximum advantage. In essence, his backside was telling opposing players to "butt out."

Keep your knees bent, butt out, and arms out and bent upward at the elbows at a 90-degree angle. Your palms should face the rim. Ideally, your butt is sitting on the offensive player's knees.

Think of it this way: You grab a rebound with your hands. Thus your hands should be as far *in front* of the player you're boxing out as possible. If he tries to jump over your back to grab the rebound, he'll be whistled for a foul. He may be taller than you and able to jump higher than you, but he can't jump over you.

If there is one unpardonable sin of defensive rebounding, it is allowing the shooter to rebound his own shot. If you're guarding the shooter and attempt to block the shot, that's great. But don't lose control of your body. Use the reverse method described above to box out the shooter, who must occupy himself with his follow-through before he can concentrate on rebounding.

Rebounding in a zone defense

When playing a zone defense, you guard an area rather than a player. You can't really box out an area. Therefore, in a zone, the emphasis is on *forming a three-defender triangle* around the basket, no matter what type of zone you're playing. The triangle protects the middle of the three-second lane and the two block areas from offensive interlopers. (See Figure 8-2.)

Even in a zone, however, you must find somebody to box out. You have an area to protect in that triangle, and someone will try to infiltrate. When that offensive player comes at you, box him out.

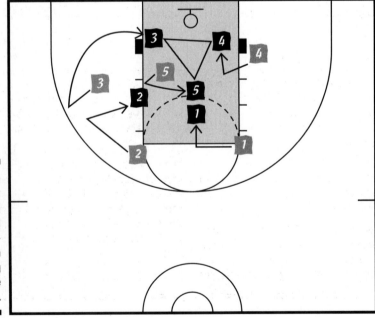

Figure 8-2:
Forming a triangle around the basket when rebounding in a zone defense.

Offensive Rebounding

In the 1995 NCAA Championship Game, UCLA beat a favored Arkansas squad, the defending national champs, 89–78. Despite having a team composed of smaller players, the Bruins won the game because their players outrebounded the Razorbacks 50–31. UCLA hit the offensive boards especially hard, collecting 21 offensive rebounds that resulted in 27 points. If you're the coach of the losing team, those types of numbers can lead to ulcers.

A good offensive rebounder does four things:

- ✔ Anticipates where a miss will land
- ✔ Looks for the quickest route to the ball
- ✔ Avoids contact with the defender via quickness
- ✔ Knows that he has two seconds to retrieve the ball after the shooter releases it

The keys to defensive rebounding are positioning and leverage; the key to offensive rebounding is quickness.

Dennis Rodman: Chairman of the Boards

Dennis Rodman, a key player on five NBA championship teams (twice with the Detroit Pistons, three times with the Chicago Bulls) was inducted into the Basketball Hall of Fame in Springfield, Massachusetts, in September 2011. Rodman's shooting and dribbling skills were, at best, on par with those of a middling college player (and that is being generous).

On the other hand, "the Worm," as he was known, led the NBA in rebounding for seven consecutive years (ending 1997–1998), and no one else can say that.

What exactly made the 6'8" Rodman, who played 14 seasons, the Chairman of the Boards for half his career? First, he was a fabulous physical specimen, a stunning combination of quickness and strength, not to mention that he was blessed with disproportionately long arms. Rodman was also a pogo-stick jumper — he was able to leap two or three times in the span it took most of his peers to leap once. That skill often allowed him to tap the ball to a place where he was able to get to it first.

Most rebounders try to go get the ball with two hands, which is a sound principle. But if you can only get close enough to tip the ball into a vacant area, and if you're quicker than your defender, go ahead and do it. When Rodman tipped the ball into the corner, he was going to get it, because the Worm was quicker than his foes.

Always follow your shot. The moment a shot leaves your hands, you should prepare to rebound it. I'm not trying to instill pessimism here, but you don't do your team much good just standing and admiring the ball in flight. As a shooter, you're often close to the rebound, and because you're the one who shot the ball, you should realize before anyone else whether the shot will be long, short, off to the side, or — hopefully — good.

Offensive rebounding is a mindset: When that ball is in the air, it's a free ball. If you're on offense, assume that every shot is a missed shot. Go get that rebound!

Rebounding Drills

Rebounding does not avail itself to drills as well as other hoops skills, such as shooting or dribbling. First, you need someone to shoot the ball — *and* to miss it. Then you never know where the ball will go. The best rebounding drills are actually live scrimmages.

As a coach, never be afraid to trade ideas. Remember drills — especially those you witness at clinics. Write them down and include them in your repertoire. They'll be useful for years to come. And when another coach asks about one of your drills, be willing to share.

During practice, keep rebounding simple. Emphasize that your players need to do two seconds of work to get a rebound. I used to tell my players, "Your parents work a 40-hour week. I'm asking you to work for two seconds." If you work hard on defense for 25 seconds and force the offense into taking a poor shot, two seconds of lax play can cause the previous 25 seconds to go for naught: The offense gets the rebound and converts the miss into a bucket. If that happens, I don't want to hear any excuses; you're on the bench.

Circle the wagons drill

Circle the wagons is a four-on-four drill. The four offensive players stand stationary outside the three-point arc, while the coach holds the ball. The four defensive players rotate in a square around the free throw lane (see Figure 8-3). As the defensive players move around the square, the coach shoots the ball. The defensive players must match up to an offensive player and box out. The offensive players can do whatever they want — push, grab, anything — to get the ball. The idea is to teach defensive rebounding. Have the defense get three straight rebounds. If the defense misses a rebound before reaching the third, they must start over from zero (or run sprints).

Then switch the offensive and defensive players.

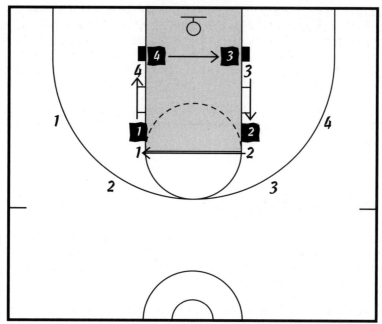

One-on-one rebounding drill

The shooter takes a perimeter jumpshot over a defender in a one-on-one situation. You may have the shooter begin from either wing or the top of the key, and allow him no more than two dribbles in either direction. He cannot attempt to drive past the defender. The defender should have his hands up as the shooter takes the jumper. After the ball leaves the shooter's fingertips, the defender boxes out the shooter by making and maintaining contact. The rebounder must use all the principles in this drill: go right or left, step in the path, and reverse into the opponent. He should make contact, hold position, and look for the ball.

This is a fantastic drill for both offensive and defensive rebounding. The defender must hone his reverse method boxing out skills. Because this is a one-on-one situation, the shooter uses his speed to pursue the loose ball.

Forward Bob Pettit grabbed 12,948 rebounds in 11 NBA seasons with the Milwaukee and later St. Louis Hawks (1954–65).That total does not put him anywhere near the top ten all-time, but in terms of rebounds per game (16.22), the thin 6'9" forward ranks third behind only Chamberlain (22.89) and Russell (22.45). Those who saw Pettit play say it was because he was willing to work harder than anyone else.

Dan Mara drill

Dan Mara, a very successful former coach on the women's junior college level (see Chapter 13 for more on junior college basketball), developed this drill. Split the squad into three teams, each with an equal number of players. Each team lines up outside the three-point circle and sends one representative into the free throw, or "three-second," lane. The coach takes a shot. Whoever grabs the rebound returns it to the coach. That player goes to the end of his team's line, and the next player from that line enters the fray. The other two players remain in the paint until they get a rebound. The first team to have all of its players get a rebound wins; the other two teams get to run laps.

Manhattan drill

I learned this drill from Jack Powers, the former coach at Manhattan College, when I attended one of his clinics in the 1960s. This survival-of-the-fittest drill is useful in finding out which players are true scrappers.

This drill may not be suitable for young kids.

Take three players and put them in the paint. The coach has the ball on the foul line and shoots. The three players vie for the rebound; whoever recovers it attempts to score. Allow the other two players to foul the rebounder, though not flagrantly — they should be physical. When a player makes a shot, the ball becomes live again as soon as it goes through the net. The first player to score three times gets to go out, and a new player joins the other two, who start again from zero.

This drill is great for teaching the conventional three-point play: The shooter is fouled, so she gets two points for the basket plus one free throw. You want players to become accustomed to being fouled and scoring on the same play. You want them to go up strong and expect contact.

As you may have recognized, this is a bear of a drill as far as testing players' stamina. Nobody can relax after a shot, even if it's good. I've seen players who were stuck in that drill for ten minutes look as if they'd just completed a triathlon. With any luck, that fatigue motivates them to be a tad feistier the next time through.

Just how dominant were Chamberlain and Russell as rebounders? Only 28 times in NBA history has a player grabbed 40 rebounds in a single game. In 26 of those instances, that player was Wilt or Bill (Chamberlain holds the single-game record with 55, oddly enough against Russell's Celtics, on November 24, 1960).

The bubble

In the 1970s, Notre Dame led the nation in rebounding three times and was ranked in the top ten nationally for three other seasons. One reason we were so successful was the bubble.

During practice, especially in preseason, we used a rebounding drill in which we put a plastic bubble over the basket. The bubble prevented shots from going into the basket, so every shot required a rebound. Shot after shot had to be rebounded, which led to some fierce rebounding action.

If you choose to use the bubble with your team, never keep it on the hoop for a long period. Doing so depresses your players, who constantly take shots that have no prayer of going through the hoop. To solve this problem, have a coach or manager put up shots.

The only other two players to grab at least 40 boards in one night were Nate Thurmond of the San Francisco Warriors (42, in 1965, versus the Detroit Pistons) and Jerry Lucas of the Cincinnati Royals (40, in 1964, versus the Philadelphia 76ers).

Four-player full-court rebounding drill

Here's a drill guaranteed to get the heart pumping. Play four-on-four and run live (that is, pretend that you're in a real game) as if it's a fast break. A coach shoots the ball, and play continues until the defense gets the rebound. Then the defense becomes the offense and runs the fast break. Play continues until the team playing defense gets the rebound or until the fast-break unit scores.

Why four-on-four instead of five-on-five? The reduced number leaves more space on the floor.

Out-rebounding a Taller Player

You may do a great job of positioning, blocking out, and maintaining contact, but the other player still gets the rebound. Why? That person reaches over you and plucks the ball out of the sky before you can reach it. What can you do to prevent that? Go out to meet him with your backside; don't wait for him to come to you. (You neutralize the extra inches on a taller player by initiating contact farther away from the basket.) Use your butt. After you position yourself against him (using the reverse method), stick out your butt to keep him as far away from the basket as you are able.

If you were using your hands to hinder your opponent's movement, the referee would whistle a foul against you. But no referee will ever call a foul against your butt. Consider it your arsenal against a taller player.

Your butt is the most important part of your anatomy in terms of out-rebounding a taller player.

Great Rebounders to Emulate

Rebounding determines so much about the end result of a game. Rebounding is the meat of this book to me and the aspect of the game I believe in the most. In my 19 seasons at Notre Dame we led the nation in rebounding margin — that is, the difference between the number of rebounds we grabbed versus our opponents — four times. No other school led the nation more than three different years. I'm proud of that.

You don't have to be 7 feet tall (and I doubt that you are) to be a great rebounder. Just look at Table 8-1, which lists the all-time leading rebounders in NBA history. Only three of the top ten players are 7 feet or taller; four are 6'9" or shorter. At George Washington University in 1997, for example, a guard named Shontay Rogers stood 5'4" and still grabbed 11 boards in one game.

Table 8-1	All-Time NBA Rebounding Leaders			
Name	**Height**	**Rebounds**	**Years**	**Average**
Wilt Chamberlain	7'1"	23,924	14	21.9
Bill Russell	6'9"	21,620	13	22.5
Kareem Abdul-Jabbar	7'2"	17,440	20	11.2
Elvin Hayes	6'9"	16,279	16	12.5
Moses Malone	6'10"	16,166	20	12.3
Karl Malone	6'9"	14,968	19	9.8
Nate Thurmond	6'1"	14,464	14	15.0
Robert Parish	7'0"	14,715	20	9.1
Walt Bellamy	6'10"	14,241	14	13.7
Wes Unseld	6''7"	13,769	13	14.0

On the rebound

Valentine's Day has been the single best day for both men and women on the rebound. On Valentine's Day, 1953, Bill Chambers of William & Mary set the single-game collegiate rebounding record, grabbing 51 in a win over Virginia.

Thirty years later, on February 14, Deborah Temple of Delta State pulled down 40 boards in a win against the University of Alabama-Birmingham. Both records still stand.

Chapter 9

Moves, Plays, and Strategies

Shaquille O'Neal and Ray Allen were keys to the success of the Boston Celtics in 2010–11. They are both in the top 25 in the history of the NBA in scoring, but both score their points in different ways.

Shaq finished his career after the 2010–11 season with 28,596 points, seventh in NBA history. He had over 11,300 field goals, but only one was a three-point goal (he attempted 22 and the only one he made came in his third season in 1995–96).

Allen is 29th in NBA history in scoring with over 22,200 points. He has over 7,800 career field goals, but he has over 2,600 career three-point goals, more than any other player in NBA history.

Shaq's best spot on the floor to score has been near the basket. Allen's most effective spot has been 23 feet away from the hoop. But they are both very effective in their own ways.

The tale of Shaq and Allen is the NBA version of a lyric from the musical *Showboat*: "Fish gotta swim / birds gotta fly." You position your players on offense at the spots where they are most likely to score. This positioning is usually determined by the player's position (center, forward, or guard), which is almost always determined by height. I said *almost* always. Los Angeles Lakers player Kobe Bryant is a 6'6" guard who can score from the outside, but much of his success comes on shots from underneath the hoop where he can post up against a smaller player. Channing Frye of the Phoenix Suns is a 6'11" center who ranked in the top 10 in the NBA in three-point goals in 2009–10 (see sidebar).

Twin Towers

The game at all levels has evolved with the implementation of the three-point shot. It has become more and more of a perimeter game as players become bigger and faster, making the court effectively more constricted on the inside, forcing players to the perimeter to get open shots.

But there have been some lineups over the years, even recently, where using two centers, or "Twin Towers" have been effective. In 1984, the Houston Rockets reached the NBA championship round behind 7'4" center Ralph Sampson and 7'1" Hakeem Olajuwon. Both were young players who had been top selections in recent drafts.

The Twin Towers combination of 7'1" David Robinson and 6'11" Tim Duncan took it the extra step in 1999 and 2003, winning the NBA title both years. Robinson had been a star for San Antonio between 1991 and 1998, leading the team to the playoffs nearly every year. But, there was something missing.

The final piece of the puzzle was Duncan, who like Robinson, was the first pick in the draft (1998) and won NBA Rookie of the Year honors. In Duncan's second year, in a strike shortened season, San Antonio won the title. They did it again four years later and both were named co-recipients of *Sports Illustrated's* Sportsman of the Year Award.

Both players had a lot in common off the court as well. Both were not stars coming out of high school, as Robinson had a late growth spurt growing from 6'7" to 7'0" over his career at the Naval Academy. Duncan grew up in the Virgin Islands where his goal was to play on the 1992 United States Olympic Team . . . in swimming, not basketball. That changed when a hurricane destroyed the local pool and he didn't want to practice in the ocean because of his fear of sharks.

Duncan and the Spurs won two world championships since Robinson retired in 2003. Duncan is still going strong, leading the Spurs to two more NBA titles through the 2011 season.

As a coach, you must know where your players like to be, keeping in mind that you must space the players well. You need shooters out on the perimeter and at least one player inside who can play with his back to the basket. The most productive offenses have an array of weapons in their arsenals.

Playing Center

Whether your center is a 7-foot pro, a 5-foot sixth grader, or, most likely, somewhere in between, he must discover three concepts in order to excel in the role of playing with his back to the basket. This section outlines these concepts.

Working to get open inside

A center on offense sets up along the free throw (or three-second) lane with her back to the basket. She does not set up inside the lane itself, because remaining in there for three or more seconds is a violation causing the offense to lose the ball. The area where the center sets up is called the post. If she sets up near the basket, normally within 10 feet, she's in the *low post*. If she positions herself farther up the lane, even on the elbow or free throw line, she's in the *high post*. (Refer to Chapter 3 for an illustration of these areas.)

The low post is a tight space. "Getting open" doesn't translate to losing your defender so much as it does to knowing which side of the center the defender is favoring. Rarely does a defender play directly behind the center. Instead, the defender overcompensates to one side in hopes of batting away an *entry pass* — that is, a pass thrown to the center from the perimeter area. Dwight Howard of the Orlando Magic is especially proficient at stealing the entry pass. If you are the center, use your body to know where the defender is. That way, when a pass is thrown to you, you can use your back, butt, and arm to keep the defender from deflecting the pass.

Breaking contact with the defender

Assume that the ball is on the wing and that you, the center, are looking for the entry pass. You must break contact with the defender to get open. You break contact with your defender as the ball leaves the fingertips of the passer. Use your elbows or butt to create space between you and your defender. With your body, create a wide base by spreading your legs and bending your knees. Because the entry pass is often a bounce pass, prepare to catch the ball as low as possible.

Moving without the ball

Perhaps the defender has chosen to front you — that is, to position himself between you and the ball rather than you and the basket — or, for some other reason, the player with the ball can't get it to you. *Do not become a statue.* When folks referred to Hakeem Olajuwon and Ralph Sampson as the Twin Towers, they never meant it literally. A post player should never remain in the same spot for more than three seconds. Move within the paint (the free throw lane). Chris Bosh of the Miami Heat is very good when it comes to moving without the ball.

Think of the free throw lane as a rectangle — after all, it is (unless you're playing outside the United States). You are positioned at one of the four corners. When something doesn't work, move to one of the other three corners. You can

✔ Slide to the other low post

✔ Cross over to the opposite high post

✔ Slide up to the high post (or down to the low post) on the same side

Move, plant, wait a few seconds, and then move again. If you can, set a pick for a teammate when you move to a new spot — or if she can set one for you, even better. But stay in and around the paint. That's your turf as a center.

For years, "big men" were never taught how to move without the ball. Too often, coaches just stationed a tall player in the low post and hoped that he'd win a wrestling contest with his defender. This has changed in recent years as big men have become more proficient at shooting from the outside, and offenses have become more perimeter oriented.

John Wooden's eight things you can do on offense when you don't have the ball

John Wooden is the standard by which all college coaches are measured. Within a 12-year span (1964–75), his UCLA Bruins won ten NCAA championships. Here are eight tips from "The Wizard of Westwood" for what to do on offense when the ball is not in your hands:

1. Be ready to screen at the proper time if the play or the situation calls for it.

2. Set up your man to run him into a screen if the play or the situation calls for it.

3. Keep your defender so busy that he will not be in position to help out a teammate defensively.

4. Make your defensive man turn his eyes away from the ball at the proper time.

5. Constantly work to get open to provide an outlet pass for the player with the ball.

6. Constantly work to get open to receive a pass where you will be a triple threat player with the ball. In other words, try to get the ball in position where you are a threat as a shooter, as a driver, or as a passer.

7. Be ready and in position to cover the proper territory as a rebounder or as a protector in case someone takes a shot.

8. Be thinking constantly, because your moves will probably be predicated on the moves of the player who has the ball or the player who just passed the ball.

Source: Jerry Krause, ed., *Coaching Basketball* (National Association of Basketball Coaches).

Moves for a Center

You've worked hard to have the ball passed to you; now what? Fortunately, for centers, the first option is to shoot the ball. Hey, you're close to the bucket, so why not? The more shots you make, the more often your team-mates will *feed* you (pass you the ball) in the future. This section outlines a few moves to help set you up to take shots.

A cardinal rule for big men with the ball: Do *not* dribble unless you absolutely, positively must. Your height is a disadvantage when you dribble. When you put the ball on the floor, you give smaller defenders an opportunity to steal it. You put the ball on the floor only to keep your balance or to keep from traveling.

The drop step

When you receive the ball in the post, be sure to have both feet planted; jump-stop when you catch the ball. This way, you can use either foot as your pivot foot. (***Note:*** If you're an NBA All-Star center, don't worry about this; the refs will never call traveling on you.) Remember, your back is to the basket.

Say that you're situated on the right side of the lane on the low block, and your left foot is near the baseline. With two hands, show the ball away and high from your shoulder, with your back to the basket and the defender. As you show the ball, drop step your left foot to hook your defender so that she can't get in defensive position to stop you. "Wait," you say. "If my foot is already planted, how can I drop it any farther?" Good question.

When I say "drop step," I mean move your left foot closer to the baseline and inward. Your right foot is your pivot foot; it stays planted. Your left foot can move. You're taking the step to your side and back, but because your back is already to the hoop, it's actually a step *to* the hoop. (See Figure 9-1.)

After you drop step, notice that you have effectively hooked the defender and are using your backside as a shield as you move toward the basket. Now swing your right foot around outside to the left and face the basket, hopefully close enough to execute a lay-up or dunk.

Establish position on the *low block* (the tiny square along the three-second lane close to the baseline, used for positioning rebounders on free throws) close enough to the basket so that you can shoot a lay-up after taking the drop step without having to dribble.

Figure 9-1:
Executing
the drop
step: at left,
hooking the
defender,
and at right,
taking a
step to the
hoop.

Power move through the hoop

Sometimes you lose the battle of position and receive the entry pass farther from the hoop than you'd like. You can still drop step, but follow it with one power dribble. As you drop step, pull the ball with you — two hands on it — and then dribble. Use your inside shoulder to shield the ball from the defender.

Now you're closer to the basket. Actually, many post players like to put the ball on the floor to establish a rhythm as they go to the hole. The danger is that you leave yourself open to pesky guards swiping at the ball from the outside.

Finish up strong. You worked like a lion to get this shot so close to the hoop; don't become a lamb now. If you're able to dunk the ball, do so with two hands. If you can't, jump as high as possible — explode to the basket — and lay the ball off the glass at the top of your leap. No one takes it to the hole with more *oomph* than Shaquille O'Neal did in his 18 years in the NBA. Emulate him.

The pull-up jumper

Suppose that the defender anticipates the drop step and is playing a step off you. In other words, he is not placing his body against yours but instead is playing a step closer to the basket than he normally would so that you cannot drive past him as easily. To keep the defender honest, burn him by squaring up right where you receive the pass and burying a quick jumper from 10 feet.

You catch the pass with your back to the basket, but I don't advise shooting it that way. You must turn and square the front of your torso to the hoop. But in which direction? If you make sure that your feet are planted when you catch the ball, you can use either foot as your pivot foot. Practice so that you're equally deft at pivoting off your left and right foot. If you are, the defender can't anticipate your move. Also practice faking the pivot one way and then going the other: Use your head to fake in one direction, and then go the opposite direction.

If you're a large player, I must warn you against too many fakes. Referees will be quick to whistle you for traveling, especially at levels below professional, and often they'll be right.

Most shooting fouls are called in the lane. As a post player, look to draw contact when you shoot. Don't be shy. If your defender makes sufficient contact, the referees will almost never call the foul on you. Be prepared to be fouled when you shoot the ball — and if you hear the whistle, *always* follow through on your shot. You may make the shot and earn a free throw for a three-point play.

No one is better at this than Dwight Howard of Orlando Magic (see Figure 9-2). He uses his strength to force up a shot when the whistle blows. If he makes 1 shot out of 20, that's one more than if he didn't heave up that prayer.

Figure 9-2:
Dwight
Howard.

Hook shot

This was the best move by the all-time leading scorer in the history of the NBA, Kareem Abdul Jabbar. Why more centers don't use it is a mystery to me. When you execute it correctly, especially with either hand, it is unstoppable. One player who does use it today is Pau Gasol, who ironically plays for the Los Angeles Lakers, the same franchise Jabbar played on during most of his NBA career.

The up-and-under move

For the up-and-under move, you *pump-fake* a shot — that is, you move your arms as if you're taking a shot but do not actually release the ball. This action brings the defender up into the air. You then drive around her — which is very embarrassing for the defender. Follow these steps:

1. **Catch the ball.**

2. **Pivot 180 degrees to face the defender.**

3. **Fake the ball upward with both hands.** The quicker the fake, the more likely that she'll buy it. Remember to lift both arms above your head in order to really "sell" the fake.

4. **The second the defender leaves her feet, drive past her.**

Hakeem Olajuwon's not-yet-patented-but-oughta-be "Dream Shake" move was the best up-and-under maneuver in the business when he starred for the Houston Rockets in the 1990s.

Pass to the open player

If you catch the ball in the low post and find yourself double teamed, do the math: One of your teammates is open. Pass the ball to that teammate. It's a great way to garner an assist — and make friends.

Note: Tim Duncan is the best passing big man in the NBA and has had that title for many years. If you want to see the way to beat a double team and find the open shooter, watch any San Antonio Spurs game.

The atypical center

There are exceptions to every rule in life and that applies to basketball. Channing Frye of the Phoenix Suns is not your typical center. The 6'11", 245-pounder from the nearby University of Arizona campus camps out much of the game at the three-point line, not on the baseline.

During the 2009–10 season, he became the first center in 13 years to be invited to the NBA Three-Point Shooting competition during All-Star Weekend. For that season, he made 172 of 392 three-point shots, 82 more made three-point goals than any other NBA center, and .his 44 percent three-point shooting percentage was sixth best in the NBA among all statistical qualifiers.

Frye's three-point shooting prowess is a function of the Phoenix Suns unique offense that encourages all five players to shoot from just about anywhere on the court, making it the top scoring offense in the league in 2010. Frye led the Phoenix team in three-point goals in 2009–10, 48 more than all-star point guard Steve Nash.

Frye did not come into the NBA with the reputation of a great shooter. He made just six three-pointers in his career at the University of Arizona and made just 20 three-point shots in his first four years in the NBA combined. But he benefited from the open court style of first year coach Alvin Gentry in 2009–10 when the Suns reached the NBA Western Conference finals.

Moves for a Guard

Unlike a center, a guard usually already has the ball as the offense proceeds up court. Her forte is *beating her defender off the dribble* — that is, dribbling past her to drive to the basket for either a score or an assist.

Tips for going one-on-one with a defender:

- **Take the optimum spot: the top of the key.** From there, you can go either left or right. Great guards (and they are rare) are just as strong dribbling and shooting the lay-up with either hand. If you can go only to your right, starting from the top of the key loses its efficacy. The defender will cheat to that side.

- **Read the defender's hands.** If the defender's hands are low, pull up and shoot the jumper. Good guards practice the quick pull-up jump shot from just inside the top of the key. The difference between a good shooting guard and a poor one: A good shooter jump-stops (both feet planted), gets her feet underneath her torso, and jumps straight upward, not forward. A poor shooting guard stops without curbing her momentum, forcing her to jump forward as opposed to straight upward. It's very difficult to have the proper balance to take a good shot this way. Ben Hansbrough, who led Notre Dame as a senior guard in 2011, was especially proficient at this at the college level.

✔ **Read the defender's quickness.** If you can drive by the defender, by all means do so. You can still pull up anytime and take the jumper, but if you can go all the way to the basket, you have an easier shot.

Defenses do not surrender lay-ups to guards gladly. Expect some company — that is, a second defender — if you beat your man off the dribble. When this happens, be ready to dish a pass to your center underneath, who is now open when her defender comes over to stop you. Watch Rajan Rondo of the Boston Celtics; he's a genius at the last-second dish.

The crossover move

You just received a pass on the wing and face the defender. If his hands are low, shoot the jumper immediately. If not, you can fake one direction and then go the other. As you do this, you cross over the ball quickly in front of your defender, going from the right to the left. It is a *crossover* because you start your pivot foot in one direction, but, once you make your move, it heads in the other.

For example, say you're on the right block and just turned to square up to (face) the defender. You decide to fake right and then go left (toward the center of the lane). To do so, step with your right foot to your right; the defender will react. As he does, take the next step with your *right* foot across the front of your body — dribble with your left hand to use your body as a shield against the defender — as you drive toward the middle of the lane. Allen Iverson made the crossover famous at the guard position. But be careful — don't get called for palming.

The pick and roll

As a guard handling the ball through a pick and roll (see Chapter 6), you have three options:

✔ **Pull up behind the pick, and shoot the jumper.**

✔ **Stutter your dribble.** To stutter your dribble, wait until the ball reaches its apex in the air off the dribble, and instead of bouncing it again, cradle it in your hand for the briefest of moments. Then drive past the pick either for a lay-up or to dish off when defensive help arrives.

✔ **Pass to the screener.** If the defender guarding the player who is screening for you leaves his man to cover you, pass the ball to your screener.

Stockton to Malone

No two players are more synonymous with a basketball play than John Stockton and Karl Malone. As teammates for 18 years with the Utah Jazz, they perfected the pick and roll play, leading the Jazz to the playoffs all 18 years, including two trips to the finals where they had to face the Michael Jordan Bulls.

The Stockton to Malone call by Hall of Fame Jazz announcer Hot Rod Hundley in legendary staccato calls brought the legend to light in the 1980s. Hundley was a good friend and broadcast Notre Dame's win over UCLA in 1974 that broke the 88-game streak. He started a 35-year career with the Jazz the next season.

Malone finished his career as the number-two leading scorer in the history of the NBA with 36,928 points. Only Kareem Abdul Jabbar had more than this behemoth power forward, Stockton established the NBA career record for assists with 15,806 — 4,000 more than any other player — and in steals with 3,265 — 700 more than Michael Jordan. Both were first ballot Naismith Hall of Fame selections, Stockton in 2009 and Malone in 2010, and they were both on the 1992 United States Dream Team.

The legend has continued for years. Stockton to Malone Honda is a top-selling car dealership in Draper, Utah. You can also become a member of the Stockton to Malone Facebook page.

They will forever be a part of the Utah Jazz history. They have side-by-side statues erected outside the Energy Solutions Arena, the home of the Jazz. The statues stand at the intersection of Stockton and Malone Streets.

Setting screens for the shooting guard

A common way to set up a good shooting guard for an open shot is by sending him through a series of screens, first by a center and then by another guard.

A move for a forward

For this move, called a *screen for the screener,* the power forward positions himself at the foul line. The center is on the low right block, facing the basket, and the shooting guard stands on the opposite low block (in this case, the left block).

The point guard takes the dribble entry to the left wing. The power forward moves down the right side of the lane to set a *down screen* (where a player moves toward the basket to set a screen) for his center to come up. You may think that the center is going to shoot the jumper at the foul line, but instead, the shooting guard moves across the lane, from the left low block to the right, and screens for the power forward at the baseline. The screen set by the off guard is called a *screen for the screener* because the power forward sets the first screen. Now you can pass the ball to the power forward.

Step back, step in

The step back, step in is the signature move of Boston Celtics eight-time All-Star Paul Pierce. The former Kansas All-American is the master of stopping on a dime, ball faking with a bit of a backwards lean to draw the defender closer to him, then jumping forward into the defender to draw the foul. Because the defender jumps at Pierce at an angle, Pierce always gets the call when he jumps forward.

Pierce has used this move to become the number-three scorer in the history of the Boston Celtics (only Larry Bird and John Havlicek have more). He has averaged 22.2 points a game over 13 years, and many have come from the foul line where he is an 80.5 percent shooter.

But this is not Pierce's only move; he is an outstanding three-point shooter and won the Three-Point Shootout at the 2010 All-Star game.

The point forward

The point forward is a unique player who shares the attributes of a point guard and a forward. He is someone with good ball handling skills and court vision, who can bring the ball up, and initiate the offense.

Why would a coach use a point forward? Teams that have outstanding wing shooting guards can set up at different areas of the court and spread out the opposing team's offense.

The consummate point forward in today's NBA game would be LeBron James of the Miami Heat. He averaged seven assists per game in 2011 and had the ability to create openings for teammate Dwayne Wade on the perimeter and for Chris Bosh on the inside.

The first point forward was John Johnson, who played with the Seattle Supersonics in the 1970s. Other modern point forwards are Lamar Odom of the Los Angeles Lakers and Grant Hill of the Phoenix Suns.

Last-Second Plays

You're sitting at home on the couch, feet up, potato chip bag within arm's reach. Ten seconds remain, and your favorite team has the ball and is down by a point. Okay, maybe your feet aren't up. Maybe you're leaning forward and gnawing your fingernails down to nubs.

At this moment, you probably don't envy your team's coach. You aren't bellyaching, "How can they pay a college coach that much money when a prof makes one-tenth of that?" If anything, you're glad that you don't have to think of what play to call. They couldn't pay you enough to take on that kind of pressure. You just hope that the coach can figure out a great play during the time-out.

Fact is, he drew up the play a long time ago. Coaches include last-second plays in their game plans for these very moments. This section describes some of my favorites.

Length-of-the-court game-winning play

You have to be prepared for last-second plays, and preparation starts in preseason practice. At Notre Dame, we practiced our last-second play once a week, and we reviewed it at shoot-arounds just to refresh the players' minds. I doubt that any of the players really believed that we'd ever need this "emergency chute."

In 1989–90, I coached Notre Dame against Syracuse. In the final seconds of the game, Syracuse scored to take the lead. We called time-out. The last-second play we used was a play that we'd practiced during the fall. Our center, Keith Robinson, in-bounded the ball from the endline and threw it to half-court to LaPhonso Ellis, who had cut up from the foul line. Ellis threw the ball to Elmer Bennett at the top of the key, who hit the three-pointer that won the game. The key to the play's execution was having Keith and LaPhonso work on that inbounds pass in the preseason.

Digger's tips on last-second plays

In any season, at least a few games are going to be won or lost in the last ten seconds of the contest. (This time period is usually referred to as the "last second.") In these tense moments, a team needs all the poise and maturity it can muster. One way to avoid epic — or so they will seem at the time — blunders is to be prepared. Remember these points:

✔ **Go to the basket.** It blows me away when a team, trailing by only one point, chooses to shoot an outside jumpshot in the final seconds. *Why?!?* The defensive team, leading by a point, has a tremendous fear of fouling. So take the ball inside. You get a closer shot, you have a chance of being fouled, and your chances of tipping in a missed shot are greater. If you take a jumper from the outside, on the other hand, the defense has an easier time boxing out your players and rebounding a missed shot.

✔ **Don't wait too long to shoot.** The score is tied, and you have the ball for the last shot. Most coaches advocate taking the shot with so little time remaining that, if the defense rebounds the ball, the defense won't have a chance to call time-out and take a shot.

But I disagree. Teams wait too long to start a possible game-winning play. Why wait until only seven seconds remain to begin your move to the basket? You should start with at least 12 ticks showing on the clock. Give yourself time for an offensive rebound or two. More important, give yourself enough time to take a good shot if the first option fails, which it often does in these situations. Too many teams force shots because the clock is running down.

Note: Know your officials. Some officials swallow their whistles on last second plays. They have the theory, "Let the players decide the game." If your lead official has this reputation, take it into account with your last second strategy.

Last-second defense

There are books and entire clinics devoted to last-second shots by teams on offense. But, sometimes the game deciding strategy can come from the defensive end of the court.

That was the case when I attended the Louisville at Notre Dame game in South Bend on February 9, 2011. Louisville had the ball with 25 seconds left and the score tied at 74, Rick Pitino called a time-out to set up a last second shot to win the game.

The Cardinals inbounded the ball to top guard Kyle Kuric, who had already scored 28 points in the game, and was guarded by Notre Dame star guard Ben Hansbrough, who had four fouls. With that four-foul mind-set it was going to be difficult for Hansbrough to have a defensive approach because he knew one more foul and he was done.

Figuring Pitino was going to set for one shot late in the clock, Notre Dame Coach Mike Brey had

his team line up in a man-for-man defense. With just 10 seconds left, his team switched to a zone defense. Hansbrough dropped back to the top of the key and was at the top of the zone with fellow guard, Eric Atkins.

Now, when Kyric started his drive to the basket, he faced a zone that double teamed him at the top of the key. He gave up the ball to Preston Knowles, who was not prepared mentally or physically, to take the game winner. His three-point shot missed and the game went to overtime. Notre Dame scored the first 14 points in overtime and won the game, 89–79.

Coaches Notes: This is not an easy switch defensively and you need to have a veteran team to pull it off. Brey had the luxury of having five players in at least their fourth year of college on the floor at the time.

To call time-out or not to call time-out: That is the question

Here's the scenario: You're down one with ten seconds left in the game, and your team just grabbed a defensive rebound. Do you take a time-out, or do you just let the players run the fast break and ad lib? If you call time-out, you can set up a play. But does the time-out help the defense more?

My gut reaction as a coach: Go to the hole. The offense knows where it's going, and the defense has to react. Basketball is a game of matchups, and a time-out before a last possession is to the defense's advantage. Plus, a coach can have her team play a matchup zone or some defense you haven't seen before, and your offense won't have an opportunity to react to it. With no time-out, the scene is too chaotic for your opponent to set up anything more than its most basic defense. You also run the risk of not getting the ball in-bounds or committing a turnover.

In your last time-out in a close game, plan ahead. If you call time-out with 30 seconds or less remaining, set up what you will do on offense and defense if you need to pull out a last-second play.

Preparing for the Big Game

All conscientious coaches prepare to the best of their ability for each game. But every schedule includes games that loom just a little bit bigger than the rest. Whether it be your big rival, the number-one team in your conference or league, or the number-one team in the nation, these games require special preparation.

My Notre Dame players always knew which games were the big ones. As a coach, you don't want your players to look past lesser teams, but you do want them to be ready for the big games. At the college level, these contests determine your seed in the NCAA tournament, not to mention the morale of your squad.

Scout the opposition — and yourself

I usually watched three videotapes of the upcoming opponent and then met with my assistants to develop a game plan. Today coaches have video available for all games, but they still just try to view the five most recent games when they get into the middle of the season.

Sure, you need to know your enemy. But you also need to take an honest look at your own team. Doing that is just as important, if not more so, as preparing to face a particular opponent.

Before a big game during a Notre Dame season, we would pay an outside service to scout our team and identify the areas in which we needed work. On my own, I liked to review our last two or three losses (which hopefully required more long-term than short-term memory skills) and see what needed fixing. If we weren't getting the ball into the post, for example, I tried to figure out why.

Challenge the opposing team's star

A big game means a tough opponent, who probably has at least one outstanding player. That's why the team is a good team. In many ways, that's how they got to be a good team.

Look at the mindset of the opposing team, opposing coach, and opposing star; then decide whether you can challenge that star player. Doing so has its benefits: First, it tells your players that you have confidence that they can stop the star. Second, it often forces your opponent to find alternative options on offense, which can spell trouble at any level of play.

For example, in 1978, my Notre Dame squad beat #1 ranked Marquette because we placed our 6'7" forward, Bill Hanzlik, against Butch Lee, Marquette's All-American guard. Hanzlik was not naturally suited to defending a point guard, but he was the best defender we had. Plus, with his long arms and rangy style, he gave Lee fits. Hanzlik shut down Lee (who went 3–15 in field goal shooting), and Lee's Marquette teammates were unable to pick up the slack.

Play up a sense of rivalry

Talking about revenge seems to be taboo in athletics today — at least publicly. Inside a locker room, however. . . . Well, let's just say coaches are a little less politically correct. Revenge is a great motivator.

Sometimes, the best thing a coach can say to players is nothing. In the 1987 game against North Carolina in South Bend, for example, I knew that junior David Rivers was ready. Two years earlier, as a frosh playing in his first NCAA tournament contest, Rivers had been stripped of the ball by North Carolina's Kenny Smith, who drove in for the winning bucket. Final score: 60–58.

I knew that I would not need to motivate Rivers for this game. Instead, I let his teammates feed off their leader's energy. Rivers indeed got his payback, and we even won by the same 60–58 score.

Of course, the thing about revenge is that after you exact it, you become a target once again. Six weeks later, Carolina beat us in the NCAA tournament to end our season.

Prepare your team mentally

There are many stories about the intangible aspects of mental preparation. One of the best psychological ploys that I used at Notre Dame took place in 1974 when we practiced cutting down the nets the day *before* the UCLA game.

After a big win, such as a tournament championship, it's customary to cut down the nets: Players take two snips and keep a strand for themselves. I wanted our guys to look as if they knew what they were doing when the moment came the following day. Because I was less afraid of them being cocky than of them being timid, I felt that I had to do something to let them know that their coach truly believed that they could snap college basketball's longest winning streak ever. They may have believed that I was nuts, too, but I didn't care.

Years later, Gary Brokaw, who scored a game-high 25 points in the win, told me that cutting down the nets made the difference in our mental preparation for that game.

Note: If you're a high school or junior high coach, make sure that your school has another set of nets before attempting this ploy!

Lean on your support groups

Students are the base of any college or high school support group, and I never forgot that. When we beat San Francisco in 1977, for example, the Notre Dame students were the key. The Dons entered the contest 29–0 and ranked number one in the nation. On the eve of the game, we staged a pep rally (I love pep rallies), and I told the students to arrive half an hour before the game and start chanting "29 and 1." We told them that San Francisco was going to leave Notre Dame with a mark in the loss column.

This strategy seems brash now, but it created an atmosphere. The place was packed half an hour before warm-ups, and I have to think that the USF players were somewhat intimidated.

Notre Dame won that game 93–82. For the first and still only time in history, NBC named our student body the Player of the Game — that's how enthusiastic the students were that day.

Part III
The Game

In this part . . .

There are so many ways that you can be a fan. This part delves into the world of organized basketball, from pickup games in your driveway to exploring basketball around the world. Whether you're a high school, college, or pro-ball enthusiast, these chapters tell you everything you need to know to enjoy the game year 'round.

Chapter 10

Pickup Basketball

"*M*ake it, take it." "Winners." "Win by two?" "Wanna run?"

Pickup basketball has its own lexicon, one that crosses state lines and time zones. Soda may be "pop" in some parts of the country, and Europeans may drive on the opposite side of the road than we Americans do, but the language and etiquette of pickup basketball is universal.

Pickup basketball — games that seem to spontaneously arise anywhere a basketball hoop exists — may be the best example of the game's robust health. Unorganized and unscheduled, pickup games not only pop up everywhere, but their partisans adhere to a uniform code of rules, lingo, and even fashion (adroitly captured in the 1992 film *White Men Can't Jump*).

No national governing body of pickup basketball exists, thank goodness. But you can visit any playground, gym, or driveway in the United States and say, "We got next!" or call "Winners!" (meaning the team that wins retains possession of the ball) and be understood. That's the beauty of pickup basketball: A society of hoops exists through the sheer passion that folks possess for the game.

The Traits of Pickup Basketball

Considering how loosely defined the society of pickup hoopsters is, the rules and characteristics of pickup games are surprisingly uniform. The following sections describe what you see and hear in a typical pickup game.

Gimme the ball

No player ever remembers how many assists or rebounds she had after a pickup game; everyone wants to score. On the playground, the highest tribute for a player is to be told that she "has game" — meaning she has the ability to play well and score.

As David Letterman might say at the end of a top ten list of Things You Won't Hear After a Pickup Basketball Game, "And the number-one phrase you won't hear after a pickup basketball game: 'Wow, your defense was just outstanding today.'"

Pass — or shoot — the rock!

You won't find a shot clock in pickup hoops, but that doesn't mean that the game moves slowly. Holding on to the ball too long is a cardinal sin; players want to play. Any team that makes more than five passes on one possession will find itself jeered at best and possibly even pummeled by the guys on the sideline who have next.

Trash talk

The very title of Ronnie Shelton's film *White Men Can't Jump* is trash talk — an indelible part of pickup hoops. Your manhood (or womanhood) is on the line when you step onto the court. Talking trash is one way to gain an advantage.

Trash talk is not politically correct, but it does not need to be profane. The best trash talk is brash, puts down the opponent or exalts the speaker, and — most important — is funny.

For example, in *White Men Can't Jump,* Billy Hoyle (Woody Harrelson) uses a double putdown after watching an opponent miss a string of shots: "Why don't we take all these bricks (missed shots) and build a shelter for the homeless, so maybe your mother will have a place to stay?" That's a brilliant putdown, because it mocks the opponent's hoops skills and his mother (though not too harshly) all in one sentence.

The lane — No place for the faint of heart

So you think that the NBA is rough! If you try to dribble down into the three-second lane for a layup (or "take your game down the lane"), expect to be *hammered* (or fouled). In pickup hoops, nobody fouls out or shoots free throws. If someone fouls you, you just take the ball out again. Don't expect the guys playing defense to surrender an easy shot without *hacking* (that is, fouling) you.

HALL OF FAME

Kevin and Kobe

Even though NBA players compete for much more than respect, they still talk trash. To me, that shows that, despite their wealth, they play because they love the game. Larry Bird and Michael Jordan, arguably the best players of the 1980s and '90s, respectively, were also two of the most notorious trash talkers in hoops lore.

These days, Kobe Bryant of the Lakers and Kevin Garnett of the Boston Celtics are the game's two best trash talkers. Of course, because each of them has led their respective franchises to an NBA championship in just the past three seasons (Kobe has led the Lakers to a pair), they have earned the right to chirp.

"Trash talking is fine," Bryant said before the Lakers visited the Celtics in February of 2011. "I love to talk. Paul (Pierce, of the Celtics) likes to talk. KG likes to talk. I'm probably the only one on my team that likes to talk so I'll probably be jawing with all of them. It's fun."

Bird. Jordan. Kobe. KG. Can you find four more competitive NBA players in the past 30 years? That may be the key to both their greatness and their affinity for trash talking.

Arguments

You won't find any refs in pickup basketball, either. Every matter, from who touched the ball last to what is the accurate score, is contested. ("We were up by two *before* that basket!") The lesson here: Pickup basketball does not so much *build* character as it *reveals* it.

Don't expect to run Coach K's offense

Most of the time you don't even know who your teammates are until minutes before the game begins. There will be no set plays. However, the more pickup basketball you play, the better you will learn fundamental tenets such as good spacing, back-door cuts, or setting screens.

Midnight basketball

In Chicago, Gil Walker of the Chicago Housing Authority has used basketball to help reduce crime. Walker founded the Midnight Basketball program, wherein gyms open late on weekend nights so kids can play hoops instead of hanging out on the streets. Walker's idea was that hoops is a religion, and it can instill some of the same benefits, such as creating friendships and building community.

It's too much to hope for that all of your teammates will be a cohesive unit on offense. On the other hand, no one likes to play with a ball hog, either. Don't be that guy.

Other pickup basketball customs and terms

And one: A player calls this when he is fouled and makes the basket. Although he won't actually shoot a free throw (the "and one" to which he refers), it's a way of letting the defense know that they cannot stop him even by fouling him.

'baller: This is another name for a serious player.

Black hole: Derogative term ascribed to someone who never passes the ball once he or she receives it ("The ball disappeared into a black hole").

Bucket: A basket.

Cherry picking: In a full-court game, this refers to the practice of not returning to the defensive end of the court or simply heading toward the offensive end of the court the moment your opponent takes a shot. In theory, your team will get the rebound and feed you, the cherry picker, for an easy layup.

Courtesy: Whether you are warming up before a game or simply shooting around with others, the shooter keeps shooting until he misses. This is known as courtesy. Layups do not count, however.

D-up: This is an exhortation to your teammates to find an opposing player to guard. You "D-up" before the opening possession, usually based on comparative size and/or skill level.

Firsts: Without a referee, players must have a way to determine a jump ball situation. Unless someone brings an arrow to the court, players determine who gets the ball after a tie-up by yelling "Firsts." Whoever has the presence of mind to say "firsts" first gets possession.

Free-ins: On courts with little out-of-bounds room, some people play games using the *free-ins* rule. According to this rule, defenders may neither intercept the inbounds pass nor harass the inbounder. In a half-court game, the inbounds pass must be above the foul line. Otherwise, teams would have a lob pass for a free layup.

Game: When the winning shot goes in the hoop, the winning team says, "Game," as in "We just scored the game-winning point."

Hack: This is another term for a foul.

Hacker: A hacker is a player who indiscriminately fouls. No one likes to be guarded by a hacker.

Hold court: *Hold court* refers to a team remaining in successive pickup games by virtue of consecutive victories.

Make it, take it: In a half-court game, which normally involves three or fewer players per team, you retain possession after making a shot. That's what this term refers to.

My bad: This is what a player says after he commits a turnover or makes a mistake.

Out front: *Out front* (or *up top*) is the area, usually beyond the foul line or the three-point line (if one exists), where players *check* the ball (when a defender handles the ball) before being in-bounded in half-court play.

Rock: This a term for the ball, as in "shoot the rock."

Skunk: *Skunk* is a term for a game that ends in a shutout — 11–0, 15–0, 21–0, or whatever the point total goal was when the game started. A skunk game can also be called before a team reaches the final score. For example, a skunk game to 15 can be called at 7–0. There is no set rule on which a team calls skunk; often the trailing team is grateful for the reprieve.

Half court or full court?

Two factors determine whether you'll be playing a half-court pickup game or having a full-court run: Not enough players, and too many players.

"We got next!"

During the NBA playoffs in 1997, the WNBA, which was preparing to launch its fledgling league, shrewdly used a pickup basketball term as their slogan: "We got next!" In the culture of pickup hoops, players say "We got next!" to let everyone know that their team has dibs on the following game.

Because the term is familiar to pickup hoopsters nationwide, the WNBA got across its point that, as soon as the NBA completed its season, the women would be taking the court. It was a savvy wink to a skeptical male audience that these women, by knowing that term, were genuine 'ballers — almost as if the WNBA was letting the boys know that this league was no charlatan. To borrow another pickup hoops phrase, the women were saying, "We got game."

You need at least eight — usually ten — players for a full-court game to be worth it. However, if you do have ten players but there happen to be two dozen more waiting to play, the court is usually split into two half-court games of three-on-three or four-on-four. This way, more players are able to participate simultaneously.

Both types of games have plenty to offer for the hoops-obsessed. The half-court game rewards good fundamentals, particularly a game of three-on-three. Players learn to set picks, using both ball screens and picks involving the two players who do not have the ball, in order to get open. Also, you learn to use the backdoor cut and the simple pleasures of passing and cutting. On defense, you learn to switch, fight through screens, and communicate.

The full-court game is less about fundamentals and more about sucking wind. Full-court games are a lot of fun if everyone is in decent shape. If not, however, the game quickly devolves as the bigger-bellied 'ballers stop running up and down the court on every possession. You can't get away with that in the NBA or college . . . or even high school. But in a pickup game, well, who's going to bench them?

Gentleman's Rules of Pickup Basketball

As I alluded to earlier in the chapter, no evidence exists of a Continental Congress of pickup basketball having ever convened. No latter-day Thomas Jefferson framed a Bill of Rights for the playground game. The customs and rules that have taken hold are the product of millions upon millions of pickup games having occurred; players gradually conform to the ideas that make the most sense. The following rules of pickup basketball are the ones most universally accepted.

To 11, 15, or 21 by ones

The first team to score 11, 15, or 21 baskets wins. Each basket is worth one point in pickup games. If you have a lot of time, 21 is a satisfying run. If other players are waiting to play or if time is short, 15 or 11 is better. Sometimes games only go to 7. I don't know why these numbers are universally recognized or why they're all odd numbers, but that's the way it is.

With the advent of the three-point shot, scoring has changed, however. Some people prefer to let a three-pointer count as two points. Others prefer to use the same point system as a regulation game, so that a bucket is worth either two or, if from beyond the arc, three points.

Winners

Also referred to as *possession, winners* applies only to a half-court pickup game. The team that scores retains possession of the basketball. I'm not sure how this rule started, but it forces a team to play defense. If you don't play defense in a game of possession, you never see the ball on offense.

This rule keeps the game entertaining. Say you're playing to 15 and are down 14–9. If you get the ball, you can *make a run* (score a few baskets in a row) without ever having to surrender the ball to your opponent.

Gotta win by two

There is no timekeeper in pickup hoops. The game ends when one team reaches an agreed-upon point total.

Also, the winning team must win by a margin of two baskets. If you're playing to 21 and the score is tied 20–20, for example, you must score two straight to win. (If you trail 20–19, you need to score three in a row.) This rule is fun because it allows for the possibility of a game that lasts into infinity — although, last time I checked, no such game was taking place.

Call your own fouls

By *call your own fouls,* I don't mean to call a foul that you committed. Sometimes a player does that, but the gesture is so noble that it causes other players to wonder about that player's sanity. Call your own fouls means that you, and only you, call the foul when one is committed against you.

If you're fouled in the act of shooting, make sure to call "Foul" *immediately.* (Sometimes you hear players say, "I got it," which is fine.) Don't wait to see whether the ball goes in and then call the foul if it misses. You don't deserve the call if you do that.

Take it back

Take it back is an expression used in half-court pickup games. This rule states that when a change of possession occurs via a rebound or turnover, the team that gains possession must take the ball back beyond the three-point arc. The player with the ball must have both feet behind the arc before his team can begin its offensive possession.

The rule acts as an orderly way for teams to switch from offense to defense in a half-court setting. With quick changes of possession, you need to have a rule that allows teams to identify themselves as offensive or defensive entities on a possession. Taking it back allows players to catch their breath, too. But in many a pickup game, you don't have to take the ball back on a turnover; you can take it straight to the hoop. This is the defense's reward for forcing the turnover.

We got next

Say that ten players are playing five-on-five, and you and a buddy arrive. "We got next!" you call. What happens then, assuming that no one else shows up, is that the team who wins remains on the court. Three players from the losing team join you and your buddy to challenge the winners. How do you figure which three? Normally, a free throw contest determines that: The first three players to hit a free throw get to play.

A court in New York City's Upper West Side burgeons with players when the weather turns warm. Watching players keep track of who's got next on this court is like watching the stock exchange at the opening bell. That's why you have to call "next" loudly, and you can't be shy when your turn to play comes.

Check

Check simulates what occurs in an official game. When a referee handles the ball before giving it to a team to in-bound and start play, he is *checking the play* — that is, allowing the defense a reasonable amount of time to prepare itself. As I mentioned earlier, though, refs don't work pickup games. Who needs the grief?

So how do you check the ball? The defender guarding the player in-bounding the ball after a made basket calls "check." (The in-bound takes place above the top of the key.) The player with the ball tosses it to the defender, who must make sure that his teammates are ready. When he is satisfied that they are, he returns the ball to the offensive player and play begins.

No free throws

You won't find any free throws in pickup basketball games. Players call their own fouls, but shooting free throws is out of the question. The team whose player has been fouled in-bounds the ball from the top of the key. (Remember to check the ball first.)

Looking for Good Pickup Facilities

Goldilocks would fit the character profile of a pickup hoops player by sheer finicky nature alone. Pickup players search and search for the perfect game (meaning the site, not the contest itself). Having found it, they're loath to venture anywhere else. Try suggesting an alternative and pickup players may enumerate any number of reasons why it's no good: "Cement's too slippery," "Rims are too soft," "No water fountain," "Too many old men."

A good rule, if you find yourself visiting or relocating somewhere, is to troll the local college or high schools. They almost always have outdoor courts. Sometimes, the gym is also open and available to outsiders looking for a game. These are the best sites for pickup hoops junkies to network among their kind.

As you search for your own Pickup Nirvana, read this section for a few things to keep on your checklist.

A good number of courts

You want a facility with a lot of courts so that you have a better chance of playing. If 20 players are waiting to play on one court, you may be waiting an hour between games if you lose.

Be aware that, while regulation courts in gyms are 94 feet long, most outdoor courts are shorter by at least 10 feet.

A good variety of courts and games

The ideal facility has some half-court games plus a full-court game or two. It also has a side court or two where you can shoot baskets to warm up or cool down.

Many players waiting their turn to play in a full-court game shoot at one basket when the action is on the opposite end of the court. Do so at your own peril. Nothing annoys a player more than when somebody who's not even playing interrupts his fast-break dunk.

When a pickup basketball facility has a lot of courts, you can usually find people playing at different levels of competition. Some facilities have A-game courts and B-game courts, or a college-level court and a high school-level court. This is another reason why facilities with a higher number of courts are usually better pickup spots.

When you arrive at a new facility, just hang out and observe the levels of competition to determine where you belong.

Even baskets with nylon nets and rectangular backboards

Many outdoor courts fall victim to bent rims. Everyone loves to dunk — or at least try to — and over the years, missed dunks equal bent rims. The ideal pickup court (and I don't think it's a lot to ask!) has straight rims that are 10 feet above the ground.

The perfect facility also has nylon nets. Playing without a net throws the full-court game off because a pure swish keeps on going and rolls far off the court, and you have to chase it as though it were an air ball. You can't appreciate the net's purpose until you play a game without one. Nets also help the shooter's eye by giving depth perception.

How about backboards? Most pickup baskets have fan-shaped backboards, which are less expensive. But as a result, bankshots suffer — smaller backboards give you less room to work with.

Some outdoor courts have the preferable rectangular backboards, but they're made of screen material. This type of backboard doesn't give your shot a true bounce. The rims attached to screen backboards also tend to be loose. Such a rim is more forgiving; more bad shots fall in because they don't ricochet far. You get a false sense of confidence in your shot playing with a loose rim. Better not to play on these rims and become a better shooter.

Lights

The perfect outdoor pickup facility has lights. A lighted outside facility means hoops for an additional three hours in the summertime, or even all night.

Because of the summer heat, night basketball produces some of the very best pickup hoops you can find. I can personally attest that along the New Jersey shore, hoopsters are like mosquitoes: dormant all day long and then suddenly appearing in droves after the sun goes down. Of all the things teenagers could be doing while out at night in the summertime, I'd opt for them to be playing hoops.

Cameron hoops

Some of the best summer pickup games in the Carolinas are played in Cameron Indoor Stadium. Most of the summer, the players for Duke, North Carolina, and North Carolina State (three schools just 25 miles apart) play pickup games in this legendary arena. Players from the past often come by and challenge the younger stars of each school. And on some weekends, the players from Wake Forest (just 40 miles away) drive over.

A water fountain

How far to the fountain? Is the water cold? Does it have barely any pressure, or does it shoot 5 feet in the air? Devoted pickup players know exactly where the water fountain is at their favorite spot and can discuss the virtues or drawbacks of the fountains at three courts in the area.

Courtside concerns

Can you leave your watch, radio, or car keys lying near the court without fear of them being taken or smashed? Is there a pond or a busy road adjacent to the court — both of which present danger to a ball that flies out of bounds? Is there a parking lot close to the court? Is there a nice place for you to sit back and watch a game going on in front of you? These are dire quality-of-life issues in the world of pickup hoops.

A chain-link fence surrounding the court area is another good thing to look for. Fences have two distinct advantages:

- ✔ **You survive after running into a chain-link fence.** If you're chasing a loose ball out of bounds and ram into a chain-link fence, at least you live to tell about it. Not so with a concrete wall.

- ✔ **Errant passes go only so far.** Nothing kills a game's momentum like a bad pass that flies off the court and into oblivion. Remember, pickup games don't have ball boys.

Padding on the basket support

You should take into account two aspects of the basket support:

- ✔ **The pole should be padded.** Fast breaks in pickup games often send players careening into the pole as if they'd been tossed from a car wreck. You don't want the poles (or the players) *looking* as if they'd been tossed from a car wreck, too. Padding the support solves that problem.

  During the 1977 Bookstore Basketball Tournament at Notre Dame, Jeff Carpenter, one of Notre Dame's point guards, separated his shoulder when he crashed into a pole. This happened in April, so he was not in danger of missing any time with the varsity, but his injury underlined the fact that the poles needed padding — not just for varsity players, but for everybody on campus. The next year, Jeff's team won the Bookstore Tournament, defeating a team in the semifinals that featured football great Joe Montana.

- ✔ **The basketball support should be recessed from the endline of the court.** On a lot of courts, the basket supports are on the endline. The farther the support can be recessed, the better. When the pole is on the endline, you just don't have much room to maneuver around the baseline.

A level court

You don't need to call a surveyor, but the court should be level enough so that your shot is consistent from all areas. Although each pickup court has its own character that gives players home-court advantages that Boston Garden never afforded the Celtics — such as overhanging tree branches — having a court with a level surface is best.

Non-planar courts also breed puddles after rainstorms. Watching kids who love the game so much that they'll play even when a giant puddle is on the court is always amusing. The puddle acts as a no-man's land during the game. It's the closest basketball ever comes to miniature golf.

Of course, having a court with something like a sloping right side can work to your advantage when an out-of-towner comes to play. Chances are the new guy needs some time to get used to that shot. But by and large, a non-level court is not good for your all-around game.

North-south orientation (if outdoors)

The perfect court runs north and south. If you play on a court that runs east and west, you'll have trouble seeing the rim on your jump shots during early morning or late-in-the-day games when you shoot at the goal that faces the sun. If the court runs north and south, you don't face this problem late in the day, except on wing-to-wing passes.

Bathroom facilities

Most outdoor facilities don't have an outhouse or a substitute. That's where an adjoining indoor gym comes in handy. Although you are probably going to become dehydrated and won't have many occasions to use the facility, it still serves as a place to change clothes after games.

Proper ventilation in the gym

Air-conditioning is not absolutely necessary in a gym, but the gym should at least have enough windows and doors to keep the place relatively habitable. Hey, people sweat in gyms. And they should. But you shouldn't have to play hoops in a sauna, either.

Pickup Shooting Games

You can play the shooting game competitions in this section instead of playing an actual game of basketball. You can play shooting games to kill time while you're waiting for one more player to arrive, if someone in your group doesn't have the stamina for a real game, or just for fun.

H-O-R-S-E

Ideal number of players: 3 to 5

H-O-R-S-E is a simple and popular game. Establish a shooting order; then start the game. When a player hits a shot, every succeeding player must match that shot (in style and court location) until someone misses. As the caller of the shot, you can dictate whether the shot must be a bankshot or whether it should swish through the net. Just make sure that you make the shot as you call it. (If you call "swish" and the shot goes in but fails to swish, you don't get credit for making the shot.) The player who misses is labeled with an H for the first miss, and the next player then introduces a new shot. If all the players make the shot, the player who began the round introduces a new shot.

On your second miss, you receive an O, and so on until you spell out H-O-R-S-E. The last player remaining after everyone else spells out the word wins. Remember, you receive a letter only after missing a shot following a made shot. If you're the first player shooting after a missed shot (or after everyone has made the shot that you introduced), you are not penalized.

If one of the players in the game can dunk and another can't, you can establish a "No Dunk" rule.

Here are some tips that just may help you beat that longtime foe:

✔ When you're not following a made shot, take your favorite shots. As long as you control the shot, someone will eventually slip.

✔ On your own time, develop a gimmick shot or two.

✔ Develop your off hand. In other words, if you're normally right-handed, get comfortable with a left-handed shot and use it. Call "opposite hand" — that way, if a guy is a lefty, he has to shoot with his right.

✔ Know your opponents. What shot do they have trouble making when you play pickup basketball with them? If they can't shoot from the corner, for example, exploit that weakness.

✔ Shoot a shot from the baseline behind the hoop — in other words, a shot that requires an attempt over the top of the backboard. This shot is easier than you think, as long as you give it a really high arc.

✔ Add a special twist to a basic shot. For example, a 5-foot jumpshot is more challenging if you shoot it with your eyes closed.

✔ Call "bank" and then hit a bankshot from the wing.

✔ Call "swish" or "nothing but net" from wherever you feel most confident.

✔ Shoot a behind-the-head shot. Set up in the lane with your back to the basket. Lean back and shoot the ball over your head to the basket.

✔ Shoot a hook shot. Not many people practice the hook — and shooting it when you have H-O-R-S is a tough time to start.

21

Ideal number of players: 3

In 21, your free throw shooting, aggressiveness, and individual offensive talents are put to the test. Although the game is suited for three players, you can play with as few as two or as many as you like. Free throws are worth one point, and shots made during live action are worth two.

Play begins with a player shooting a free throw. The other players may stand wherever they please in preparation to rebound. If the free throw shooter makes the shot, he shoots again. If he misses, the ball is live and the player who gets the rebound attempts to score a basket. All the regular rules of the game apply, except that when the ball goes out of bounds, it goes to the player closest to the ball, even if he was the last one to touch it. And no fouls exist.

After a player scores during live play (two points), he goes to the free throw line and shoots up to three free throws in a row, until he misses. (Each free throw is worth one point, except the free throw that begins the game, which is worth two.) If he makes three in a row (three points), he takes the ball out from the top of the key, and play is live again.

The winner is the first player who scores exactly 21 points. If you are at 20 and miss your free throw, your score is dumped back to 11 points, and you must start from there. You can find true free throw pressure in 21.

Around the World

Ideal number of players: 2 to 5

Players shoot from different designated spots in a semicircle around the basket. If you make a shot, you move to the next spot. If you miss, you choose to either *chance it* — that is, to take a second shot from the same spot — or to stay put until your turn comes up again. If you chance it and make the shot, you advance to the next spot and shoot again. If you miss, you must start from the very beginning.

The game is called Around the World because you circle the basket by moving from spot to spot. Here's the order of the designated spots. (See Chapter 3 for an illustration of these spots.)

> ✔ Layup from the right side (shot with right hand)
>
> ✔ Right corner
>
> ✔ Right wing
>
> ✔ Top of the key
>
> ✔ Foul line
>
> ✔ Left wing
>
> ✔ Left corner
>
> ✔ Layup from the left side (shot with left hand)

But that's not all. The players then must return in the opposite direction — that is, another left layup, then left corner, left wing, and so on. The last shot, the game winner, is a layup from the right side.

Depending on your age and/or skill level, move the orbit shots, such as those from the corners, wings, and top of the key, closer to the basket.

5-3-1

Ideal number of players: 2 to 4

This game is fun for kids under ten years old — and it teaches them addition as well. Five, three, and one are the point values of the three different shots that are taken in each turn. You begin your turn with a foul shot (worth five points). You take your second shot from wherever you grab the rebound of the free throw (three points). You take your final shot from wherever you wish (one point). The first player to reach a certain number — say, 50 — wins.

Two extra rules: If you make all three shots in one turn, you go again. If you miss all three shots in one turn, your score returns to zero.

From Driveways to Tournaments

High school is the last time most of us ever suit up and play for a competitive team. Pickup basketball satisfies the basketball junkie's urge to play, but it's still fun when there is something more at stake if you win than just holding the court for the next game.

What if you could create an annual tournament that allowed pickup 'ballers to play while also generating the excitement you feel at being part of something greater than just the game itself? In the Midwest two such tournaments have evolved in the past few decades.

Bookstore Basketball

Bookstore Basketball is a campus-wide, five-on-five, single-elimination tournament that captivates the Notre Dame community each spring. Upwards of 700 teams compete in this full-court outdoor endeavor that has become as integral to campus life as football Saturdays are. The tourney's name was derived from the original site, a pair of adjacent courts behind the campus bookstore. This tournament is unique because the field is open to anyone currently involved in the Notre Dame community in any manner.

Bookstore Basketball is full-court basketball with no subs during a game. Games are played to 21 baskets. Unlike most pickup games, team fouls are kept by an official scorer, and after the pool is whittled down to 64 teams, free throw shots are allowed after a team has ten fouls.

Because of the overwhelming number of games that must be played in a limited number of days, contests are played regardless of northern Indiana's mercurial weather conditions, and I do mean regardless. The 1975 championship game was played amid tornado warnings. And one year, one of the early rounds was contested in a snowstorm. So much snow was on the court that players couldn't dribble; they had to pass the ball up the court.

Gus Macker

In 1974 Scott McNeal staged a three-on-three tournament with 17 of his friends on his parents' driveway in Lowell, Michigan. The original "prize" was $18.

Over the years McNeal (alias "Gus Macker") continued to hold the tournament. First it outgrew his parents' driveway. Then it outgrew the town of Lowell. Eventually, it outgrew Michigan.

Today the Gus Macker three-on-three tournaments are held in numerous cities each spring and summer. Teams that register are guaranteed at least three games in this double-elimination tournament, and divisions start at the age of eight and up. No dunking allowed.

Chapter 11

High School Basketball

*1*n 2009–10, according to the National Federation of State High School Associations (NFHS), more schools offered basketball than any other sport for both boys and girls. The survey stated that 17,969 schools offered boys basketball and 17,711 schools offered girls basketball. Although outdoor track and field each had more boys and girls participating than basketball, and whereas football still has the most participants of any male sport, basketball remains the most popular sport in grades 9 through 12 in terms of the number of teams fielded.

In case you were wondering, Texas — with 1,478 and 1,425 schools, respectively — is the leader among the 50 states in both boys and girls high school participation. More than 145,000 Texas high school students played high school basketball in 2009–10. Funny, because Texas is widely renowned as being mad for football at the prep level, as the TV late, great television show *Friday Night Lights* illustrated so well.

If you think about it in terms of skill sports, basketball is the most popular in terms of individual participants as well. Track and Field and football, whereas both demanding, are a pair of sports that need a great amount of bodies in order to fill out a team. Rarely is someone cut from a football team, and even less often in track.

In basketball, however, especially with better basketball programs, as few as one in four students who try out may make the team. High school hoops is flourishing all across the country.

And that's just the beginning. Since we last revised this book, AAU (Amateur Athletic Union) basketball has taken off. If you are a junior high or high school basketball player with aspirations of playing college basketball, you are more than likely also playing for an AAU team. We discuss this in greater length later, but AAU teams are not affiliated with any school, and almost anyone with the desire and a few talented teenagers can start an AAU program.

One School, Three Teams

Depending on the size and resources of a high school, each gender can have anywhere from one to four teams. The most common teams at any one high school are freshman, junior varsity, and varsity.

Freshman

For high schools that run from grades 9 through 12, the freshman team is exclusively for ninth graders. It is the only one of the three teams where the players are specified by their academic year. In some public school systems junior high runs from grades 7 through 9, so the freshman team is at the junior high school. To keep it simple, remember that freshman basketball equals ninth grade.

Also, at some schools with a greater number of students or where basketball is highly popular, there will be a freshman A and a freshman B team. The better players participate on the A team. Why have two teams? Because at that age — roughly 13 to 15 years old — an adolescent's body, interests, and maturity level develop at wildly uneven rates. A 5'7" ninth-grade boy may develop into a 6'3" junior in just two years. However, if that ninth grader is cut from the freshman team he may be too discouraged to try basketball ever again, and that would be a shame.

Junior varsity

The "jayvee" team is composed primarily of sophomores and juniors (grades 10 and 11), although often a precocious freshman or two will be on the roster. Seniors are almost never on junior varsity because the primary function of the junior varsity squad is to prepare players for varsity. At most high school programs that have developed a formula for success, the junior varsity head coach is also an assistant coach for the varsity squad and runs the same type of offensive and defensive sets.

MJ on Jayvee

It's a well-known tale in basketball that Michael Jordan, arguably the greatest all-around basketball player ever, was cut from his high school team in Wilmington, North Carolina. Jordan delights in telling the tale himself. However, most fans only know half the story. Yes, MJ was cut from the squad as a sophomore at Laney High School, but he was cut from the varsity squad. Sophomores almost never make varsity.

Still, it is funny that one of Jordan's classmates, a boy named Harvest Leroy Smith, did make the Laney varsity squad that season.

Jordan was only 5'11" as a high school sophomore; he would eventually grow to a height of 6'6". But as a 5'11" sophomore on the Laney jayvee squad, he had several 40-point games.

Varsity

These are usually the big men on campus, and they are always the tall men on campus. The varsity is the school's premier team and is usually composed of seniors, juniors, and a gifted sophomore or two. If a freshman makes varsity, that means either that the school is under stocked in terms of talent or that the freshman is someone who will be earning a college scholarship in four years.

High School Basketball Is All Over the Map

Where in the United States is the high school game the biggest? The answer depends on how you look at basketball:

- **It's a rural game.** In Ohio Valley states such as Indiana, Kentucky, and Ohio, basketball is a religion, and high school hoops is considered the first stage of enlightenment. Here and in agricultural states devoid of NBA teams, towns often equate their identities with their high school hoops programs. Drive along a country road in Indiana: Any town whose team has won the state title advertises it on the sign welcoming motorists.

- **It's a city game.** At big city high school gyms the crowds may not equal those that parade — literally, in half-mile-long processions of cars — to games in Indiana on Friday nights, but the quality of play in cities is outstanding. City kids are raised in asphalt jungles where baseball backstops and football goalposts are rare, but where basketball courts — too many of them whose rims have no nets — are readily available. Plus, inherently the city produces more talent than in the country because the pool of players is larger.

✔ **It's a suburban game.** The 'burbs are home to private schools, which, unlike public schools, are allowed to court students — and in many cases, offer them scholarships — while providing an above-par secondary school education. Take a gander at the perennial nationally ranked high school programs, such as Oak Union Academy (Virginia), Mater Dei (California), Findlay Prep (Las Vegas), and St. Anthony's (New Jersey), and you realize that private schools have nationally respected programs.

No matter whether the high school is in a big city or a small town, basketball remains one of the most popular school sports in the country. Table 11-1 shows the popularity of the game among boys' high school sports; Table 11-2 shows the same for the girls.

Table 11-1	Boys' High School Sports in the United States, 2009–2010		
Ranking	**Sport**	**Teams**	**Participants**
1.	Basketball	17,969	540,207*
2.	Track and field	16,011	572,123
3.	Baseball	15,786	472,644
4.	Football	14,226	1,109,278
5.	Cross country	13,942	239,608**

Basketball is No. 3 in terms of the number of individuals participating, behind football and track and field.

**Cross country is No. 7 in terms of individual participants behind both soccer and wrestling.*

Source: NHSF, 2010

Table 11-2	Girls' High School Sports in the United States, 2009–2010		
Ranking	**Sport**	**Teams**	**Participants**
1.	Basketball	17,711	439,550,
2.	Track and field	15,923	469,177*
3.	Volleyball	15,382	403,985
4.	Softball	15,298	378,211
5.	Cross country	13,809	201.968**

More girls participate in track and field than basketball.

**Soccer is No. 6 in terms of teams, but No. 5 (356,116) in terms of the number of participants.*

Source: NHSF, 2010

Morgan Wootten

The second most successful college coach in men's history is named Wooden. The most successful high school coach in basketball history is named Wootten. For 46 years, from 1956 until 2002, Morgan Wootten was the coach at DeMatha High School in Hyattsville, Maryland. Wootten's teams won 1,274 games, an all-time high school record.

Wootten coached his DeMatha squads to five mythical national championships and 31 conference championships while recording 42 consecutive 20-win seasons. Twelve former players, including Adrian Dantley, the most talented player I ever coached at Notre Dame, ascended to careers in the NBA. Wootten's most memorable on-court achievement occurred in 1965, when DeMatha played Power

Memorial of New York City. Power Memorial, led by gifted (and very, very tall) center Lew Alcindor (now Kareem Abdul-Jabbar), entered the game with a 71-game win streak. DeMatha halted the storied streak.

But it may be the indefatigable Wootten's off-court achievements — he underwent a liver transplant in July 1996 and was back on the bench for the first game of the season — that his players most revere him for. Between 1961 and 1990, for three full decades, every single graduating senior who played for Wootten was offered a college athletic scholarship.

Wootten retired in 2002 with a 1,274–192 record, giving him an incredible .869 win percentage.

High School Is the New College

In 2010–11, the varsity basketball team at Mater Dei, a Catholic high school in Orange County, California, played games in Phoenix, Arizona, Washington, D.C., and Springfield, Massachusetts (home of the Basketball Hall of Fame). This was Mater Dei's *girls* varsity team. The boys team traveled only to Florida.

Every year, the top strata of high school basketball enters frontiers that would have seemed unimaginable less than two decades ago. The elite high school programs travel outside their state for games and tournaments, have sneaker endorsement deals, and even appear on television occasionally.

The greatest aspect of evolution is in the talent. The McDonald's All-American game, an annual contest staged each spring that features some of the nation's best high school players, resembles an NCAA tournament game in terms of the talent on the court. The McDonald's game, by the way, is nationally televised in prime time on ESPN. The contest often takes place in an NBA arena. Soon high school basketball games will be televised nationally on a weekly or even semi-weekly basis. Just wait and see.

Duncanville's big win

On December 28, 1998, the girls' basketball team at ChristWay Academy in Duncanville, Texas, lost 103–0. "I called a couple of time-outs," recalled ChristWay coach Jennifer Marks, then 23, recalling her Little Bighorn, "but there wasn't much I could do."

It was the worst shutout in high school basketball since Logan beat Sugar Grove Berne-Union in Ohio with a score of 106–0 in 1972.

After the 103–0 debacle and losses in the next two games by scores of 86–7 and 76–15, a funny thing happened to the ChristWay girls: Nobody quit. Nobody whined. Nobody, including Marks, blamed anyone else. "Seven of my nine players never played basketball before this season," the coach says. "Sure, they'd like to win a game. But most of them are just learning how to play."

On January 22, ChristWay played Gospel Lighthouse of Dallas, a team with a record of 1–19. Marks' Lady Chaparrals actually had an advantage: Gospel suited up only five players. At halftime, however, Gospel led 21–13.

Early in the third quarter of a physical game, Gospel's Bethany Wall drew a technical foul for tossing aside ChristWay's 4'10", 80-pound Anna Saucedo as if she were a rag doll. Then Gospel players started fouling out, and their lead began to slip. The first player fouled out early in the quarter, with Gospel ahead 31–17. Later a second fouled out. With less than a minute to go, Wall kicked a ChristWay player in frustration, drew her second technical, and was ejected. With 17 seconds left, Gospel led 43–40 but had only two players on the court.

Then one of the two remaining Gospel players committed her fifth and disqualifying foul. Silence filled the gym. "Game over!" shouted the referee, waving his hands. Gospel was left with only one player and was thus unable to pass the ball inbounds. Officially the Lady Chaparrals had a 2–0 win — their first and, as it would turn out, only, victory of the season. "It wasn't pretty," says Marks, "but who deserved a win more?"

Most of high school basketball is still parochial. Today, however, there exists a national elite class of programs, schools whose schedules and talent level are more akin to college than high school. Why? Because it is easier to be a precociously talented athlete in basketball than it is, for example, in baseball or football. Also, a basketball team has fewer members on its roster, so traveling out of state for games is less cost-prohibitive.

Finally, because there is a market for it. A television market. In an age when the best high school players are only a year away from playing in the NBA (currently they must play one year of college ball or sit out a year after high school), there will be plenty of hoops fanatics who want to see them now.

From the Prom to the Pros

Nothing illustrates how swiftly high school basketball has evolved in the past decade than the NBA draft. Between the NBA's inaugural season of 1946–47 and 1994 just three players were drafted directly from high school into the NBA — Reggie Harding, a 7'0" center, by the Detroit Pistons in 1962; Darryl Dawkins, a 6'11" power forward, by the Philadelphia 76ers in 1975; and Bill Willoughby, a 6'8" forward, by the Atlanta Hawks in 1977.

Then along came Kevin Garnett and Kobe Bryant, and those two changed everything. In 1995 Garnett, a 7'0" center, was selected in the first round (number 5 overall) by the Minnesota Timberwolves. The following year Bryant, a 6'6" guard, was selected in the first round as the 13th pick by the Charlotte Hornets and promptly traded to the Los Angeles Lakers.

It sounds silly now, but at the time highly respected hoops minds wondered if any high school student could jump directly to the NBA. Harding, Dawkins, and Willoughby had all cost themselves back-end years of their NBA careers by entering the league before they were ready from a maturity standpoint.

Kevin and Kobe changed all of that. Both are destined to enter the Hall of Fame and as this book goes to publication, both are still NBA All-Stars some 16 and 15 years into their careers, respectively. Garnett has one NBA championship ring; Bryant has five.

Beginning with Kevin and Kobe, 40 players were drafted by the NBA directly out of high school between 1995 and 2005. Remember: three players in the NBA's first 37 years; then 40 players in the next 11, with 30 of those 40 being selected in the first round.

Some of those prom-to-the-pros types are now the league's highest-profile players: Andrew Bynum of the Lakers, Amar'e Stoudemire of the Knicks, Dwight Howard of the Magic, and, of course, LeBron James of the Heat. Table 11-3 shows who went highest in the NBA draft.

Table 11-3	High Schools Players Who Went Highest in NBA Draft		
Name	*Team*	*Round, Pick Year*	*Yrs in NBA*
Kwame Brown	Washington Wizards	1, 1 2001	10
LeBron James	Cleveland Cavaliers	1, 1 2003	8
Dwight Howard	Orlando Magic	1, 1 2004	7
Tyson Chandler	LA Clippes	1, 2 2001	10
Darius Miles	LA Clippers	1, 3 2000	7

In 2006 the NBA ended this practice for at least the foreseeable future. In its collective bargaining agreement (CBA) with the NBA Players Association, the league and the players agreed that a player must have played at least one year of college basketball or be 19 years old in order to be eligible to be on an NBA roster.

This was done ostensibly with the idea that both the teams and the players would be better served by that player having spent at least one year in college developing both physically and emotionally. At the time too many high-school-aged players who clearly were not ready to play in the NBA were entering the draft. If a high school player signed with an agent, he forfeited any opportunity for a college scholarship. Then, if he did not make an NBA roster, he had nowhere to turn other than to play in a foreign league or developmental league here.

That seemed foolish, and college basketball did not appreciate losing such talent needlessly. Hence, this has come to be known as the "One-and-Done" (as in one year of college basketball and then on to the NBA) rule.

The current CBA expires on July 1, 2011. Whether or not that rule remains in force is yet to be seen.

As for the distaff side of the equation, no girls' high school basketball player has yet jumped from high school directly to the WNBA.

Understanding Hoosier Hysteria

In 1978, Notre Dame played host to the semi-state round (a Sweet 16 regional) of the Indiana high school basketball tournament. We issued more press credentials for those games than we had earlier in the year for our game against top-ranked Marquette. Why do Hoosiers love their high school hoops so much?

✔ **For a long time, it was the only game in town.** No major pro franchise existed in Indiana from the time the Ft. Wayne Pistons moved to Detroit until the ABA Indiana Pacers (now of the NBA) were formed in 1967. High school basketball was the NBA, NFL, and Major League Baseball for sports-starved Hoosiers. The Indianapolis 500 may be the state's signature event, but it only occupies our attention during the month of May. Hoosiers need something else to fill the sports-page void the other 11 months of the year.

✔ **Indiana college teams.** Indiana University, Purdue, Notre Dame, and now Butler have viable programs, further enhancing the basketball aura in the state. Kids in Indiana grow up wanting to play for these teams.

✔ **Hinkle Fieldhouse.** For years, Butler University's cavernous gym on the north side of Indianapolis — as seen in *Hoosiers* — was the site of the state's semifinals and finals. Every Hoosier hoopster dreamed of playing there. A few years back, the state finals were moved to the RCA Dome, the city's then-football stadium that has now been replaced by Lucas Oil Stadium. Thankfully, sanity was restored and the games (more on that later) were moved to Conseco Fieldhouse, home of the Pacers. Still, and especially due to the success of the film *Hoosiers* as well as that of the Butler Bulldogs, I'd love to see it return to Hinkle.

✔ **Facilities are fantastic.** Indiana is home to 13 of the 14 largest high school gyms in the United States. (See what I mean? They're dead serious about high school hoops here.) New Castle Chrysler High School, for example, boasts the world's largest high school gym. The New Castle Fieldhouse, which was built in 1959, seats 9,325 people and always sells out. Table 11-4 shows some of the largest high school gyms.

Table 11-4   Largest High School Gyms in the United States

State	City	High School	Venue	Capacity
Indiana	New Castle	Chrysler	New Castle Fieldhouse	9,325
Indiana	East Chicago	Central	Baratto Athletic Center	8,296
Indiana	Seymour	Seymour	Scott Gymnasium	8,110
Indiana	Richmond	Richmond	Tiernan Center	8,100
Texas	Dallas	multiple	Loos Fieldhouse	7,500
Indiana	Elkhart	multiple	North Side Gymnasium	7,373
Indiana	Michigan City	Michigan City	The Wolves' Den Gym	7,304
Indiana	Gary	West Side	West Side High School Gym	7,217
Indiana	Lafayette	Jefferson	Jefferson High School Gym	7,200

The film *Hoosiers* says it all. Gene Hackman, playing Hickory's new coach, visits the barber shop and is ambushed with strategy by well-intentioned, if not diplomatic, locals. (Boy, I can relate to that.) One of the locals says, "We think you should be playing this zone defense." Hackman says, "I don't like that zone defense. I'll play what I want."

High school hoops film festival

Many film critics put *Hoosiers* atop the list of the best sports films ever made. Those who do not usually rank one of two boxing films, *Rocky* or *Raging Bull*, ahead of it.

Regardless, *Hoosiers* is the Wooden-era UCLA Bruins of basketball films. But it isn't the only one. There are also two excellent documentaries worth your time that use the high school hardwood as its canvas.

The first, *Hoop Dreams*, came out in 1994 and was nominated for an Academy Award. The film follows two Chicago-area boys, Arthur Agee and William Gates, from their freshman year of high school up until their first year of college as they pursue their dreams of becoming the next Michael Jordan or Isiah Thomas.

The second, *More Than a Game*, was released in 2008. It follows the path of LeBron James and his four talented teammates through their high school years in Akron. Both films provide heroes and villains while also illustrating what makes basketball such an incredible game: All the talent in the world will fall flat unless you work together and stay disciplined.

That scene transports me back to Hazelton, Pennsylvania, circa 1964. I recall meeting with some people in town and telling them that I wanted to press more on defense, something different from what the team had been doing. I remember the resistance that I faced. So when I saw that scene in the movie, I cringed. Been there, Gene.

The White Shadow

Finally, while not a film, *The White Shadow* was the greatest television show centered on high school sports until *Friday Night Lights* came along. *The White Shadow* aired for three seasons (54 episodes) from 1978 through 1981. It revolved around a retired Chicago Bull, Ken Reeves, (played by Ken Howard) who was white and took a job coaching a high school team of inner-city kids from south central Los Angeles.

The parade of characters who made up the Carver High School basketball roster were terrific. The storylines were engrossing and unflinchingly real (which was rare back in a television age where your other options were *The Love Boat* or *Mork & Mindy*), and the basketball scenes were credible. No high school team had uglier uniforms and yet more unforgettable players (Coolidge, Salami, Goldstein, and so on).

The best part about *The White Shadow* is that you never felt as if you were watching actors. It always felt as if you were eavesdropping on an actual high school basketball team and its fish-out-of-water and yet street-smart coach. If you are too young to have seen it when it originally aired, do yourself a favor and get a hold of the DVD set of *The White Shadow*.

Wes Leonard

On Friday, March 5, 2011, a pair of rural Michigan high schools, Bridgman and Fennville, played an exciting nip-and-tuck game inside a gym overflowing with fans. Such scenes are common, especially in smaller towns, on Friday nights all across America.

This night would be different, however. Unforgettable, and tragic. With less than a minute to play Fennville's Wes Leonard drove to the basket and scored the game-winning layup. The Blackhawks won 57–55 and Leonard, who scored a team-high 21 points, was hoisted onto the shoulders of his jubilant teammates.

Moments later Leonard collapsed. As stunned fans, friends, and family looked on, Leonard lay on the floor. Attempts to revive the 16-year-old were unsuccessful. Leonard, who had an enlarged heart condition that he was unaware of, died of cardiac arrest.

Leonard's death became national news, and you didn't have to be a basketball fan to glean the stark contrast between a euphoric moment, followed almost immediately by an untimely death. That it was all so public and captured on video and cellphone cameras only exacerbated the tragic elements.

Leonard's teammates bravely carried on with their season, winning three post-season play-off games without their friend before losing the regional semi-final.

AAU Basketball: High School Hoops' 600-Pound Gorilla

The Amateur Athletic Union (AAU) is older than basketball itself. Founded in 1888 under the motto "Sports for all, forever," the AAU has grown into a network of programs across a wide array of sports. Many U.S. Olympians owe their success to the guidance they received in an AAU program associated with their sport or event.

In the last decade, however, the AAU has garnered a lot of attention and scrutiny for its basketball programs. Virtually anyone can start an AAU basketball team — the entry fee for a youth team wanting to host an event in 2011 was $300.

AAU teams can provide a wonderful atmosphere for a boy or girl, especially those who grow up in impoverished areas. On the other hand, some of the adults who coach these teams see the boys and girls as a potential pay day. The same adult may coach an AAU team from the time the boys on that team are 10 years old until they are seniors in high school. Over that time the coach may take on the role of a father figure, particularly if a boy on that team does not have father. Hence, if and when one of those players becomes a top-level high school recruit, that coach may exercise great influence over which school that player chooses. Such coaches, especially on teams that perennially have blue-chip college talent, have enormous leverage when it comes to dealing with college coaches. Some, unfortunately, have used that leverage to gain jobs and/or money for themselves.

From the player's perspective, however, AAU ball offers plenty of opportunity. Let's say you are an elite player in Chicago. Your high school team may be pretty good, but maybe you are the only college-level player on the team. Imagine if you could form a team with some of the city's other terrific players. And imagine if the coach of that team wasn't a high school teacher but maybe your older brother. Or someone who was more like a big brother or an uncle.

Now, imagine that your team could travel to tournaments and play other elite AAU teams from other cities. Suddenly, high school basketball seems like intramurals.

The problem, then, is not the AAU itself. The problem is with the AAU failing to establish a code of ethics for its coaches, or some sort of licensing baseline.

High School All-America Teams

I see very few high school games in a year now that my livelihood no longer depends on it; my hands are usually full following the 345 Division I college teams as an analyst for ESPN. Many news services, such as *USA Today* and *Parade Magazine,* follow the high school game, selecting All-America teams and/or ranking teams on a national basis.

Although these lists and rankings whet fans' appetites — sort of like seeing your favorite store's catalog a month before Christmas — understanding that high school stardom does not guarantee college success is important. In 1974–75, a high school basketball player out of French Lick, Indiana, failed to make an All-State team in this supposedly hoops-enlightened state, never mind an All-America team. But Larry Bird went on to become one of the greatest all-around players in the history of the game and was inducted into the Hall of Fame in his first year of eligibility.

Heater on fire

Cheryl Miller, who recently coached the WNBA Phoenix Mercury, once scored 105 points in a high school basketball game. Her school, Riverside Poly, scored 179 points in that game on January 26, 1982.

However, Miller's tale is not the most incredible one. On January 26, 1960 — exactly 22 years before Miller's marvel — Danny Heater, a senior at Burnsville High School in West Virginia, scored 135 points in a 173–43 victory versus Widen High.

Heater was a prototypical gym rat. The son of an unemployed coal miner, Heater would dribble a basketball between classes and once broke both wrists running into the gym wall.

On the night of the Widen game, Heater's coach, Jack Stalnaker, decided to have Heater gun for the West Virginia single-game scoring record of 74 points. Stalnaker was hoping to garner a scholarship offer for his star player, whose family could not afford to send him to college.

"When the coach told us that, I said, 'No,'" Heater remembers. "But I talked to all my teammates, and they said, 'Go for it.'"

Using a full-court press and passing the ball almost exclusively to Heater, Burnsville led 75–17 at halftime. Heater had 50 points by then. Early in the second half, Heater broke the state record. His teammates urged Coach Stalnaker to keep him in the game and break the national record of 120 points. Recalls Stalnaker, "The boys all got up and said, 'Coach, you made a fool out of yourself already.'"

Heater remained in the game, scoring 55 points in the final ten minutes. His final boxscore reads: 53 of 70 from the field, 29 of 40 from the line, 32 rebounds (!), and even 7 assists.

"I was happy and sad at the same time," says Heater, who never did receive a scholarship offer. "I was embarrassed. I wasn't raised to embarrass people."

Chapter 12

College Basketball

*I*t is naive to say that pro basketball is a business, and college basketball is a game. College hoops is big business, after all. But the games are played and attended by some of the most vivacious, resilient, and just plain fun people I know: college students.

The college game has character, as witnessed by midnight basketball practice to kick off the preseason at many schools around the nation. Or the intensity and atmosphere at any game at Cameron Indoor Stadium at Duke University. In January 2010, ESPN held one of its College Gameday broadcasts at the University of Kentucky's Rupp Arena, and over 23,000 people showed up . . . nine hours before tipoff!

What Makes College Basketball Special?

The biggest difference between the pro game and the college game (besides the amount of income tax the players pay) may be the enthusiasm of the fans. Boisterous Boston Celtics supporters notwithstanding, the enthusiasm at the college level is derived from its amateur nature. Duke students camp out for days in front of Cameron Indoor Stadium — in Krzyzewskiville— in order to secure the best seats in the student section, which happen to be the best seats in the house.

In short, most everyone rooting for a college team has a real connection to it. They might have attended the school, have family members who attend or teach at the school, or know someone with school ties. Most of the fans rooting for a pro team just happen to live nearby.

ESPN College Gameday

ESPN has had an important impact on the college basketball scene since the network began in 1979, and I have been pleased to be a part of that network since 1993. That impact from a color and pageantry standpoint has been in the form of College Gameday. It is a program that travels around the country for eight Saturdays in the heart of the regular season schedule and includes Jay Bilas, Bob Knight, Erin Andrews, Hubert Davis, our host Rece Davis, and me. During our two hours on the air, the show is one part pep rally, one part national college basketball update, and many parts fun. The program took off at Kansas in March of 2008. Thousands attended in Phog Allen Fieldhouse, and the atmosphere was electric.

College Gameday has added to the exposure of the game on a national basis, but also energized basketball in various regions of the nation. In the last few years, we have attempted to visit campuses that are not normally considered to be among the nation's elite. Such pilgrimages have brought exposure to programs like Clemson, Virginia Tech, Baylor, and Kansas State. It is one of the new traditions of college basketball; we do the program right on the court, and it is a show for the entire student body.

It has reached the point where the campus cannot wait for us to arrive. We plan so that each campus knows months ahead of time that we are coming so staff and students can prepare for and promote it.

One of my jobs is to warm up the crowd. I come out and address the students an hour before the broadcast begins. I love it; it feels like I am coaching again. I talk about the upcoming game, the home team's program, and sometimes even do a little dance with the cheerleaders.

March Madness

Many sports fans consider the NCAA tournament the most exciting two-plus weeks of the calendar. Obviously, I agree with them. The NCAA tournament, also known as "March Madness" or "The Big Dance," is unlike any championship in American sport and turns everyone into a college basketball fan as winter turns to spring.

I talk more about March Madness later in the chapter, but one charming element of it each year is the potential for Cinderella stories.

The underdog is known as Cinderella, and the tournament, with 32 first-round (now known as second-round) games, has no shortage of these teams. By now every Cinderella reference this side of Disney has been used in a newspaper lead.

Take a gander at these recent Cinderella stories. This is why so much excitement is generated in the latter half of March:

2006 George Mason University

George Mason was the fourth-place team in the Colonial Conference in 2005–06 and was an 11th seed in the NCAA tournament. But the Patriots, led by Coach Jim Larranaga, had an incredible run in the East Regional, defeating Michigan State, defending NCAA Champion North Carolina, Wichita State, and number 1 seed UCONN to advance to the Final Four.

2010 and 2011 Butler University

Butler became the first school outside the six major conferences to reach the championship in consecutive years since 1958–59. Coach Brad Stevens' team won close game after close game in both seasons. Some remember the 2010 drive as the true Cinderella story, but that team was a number 5 seed. His 2011 team was a number 8 seed and had heart-stopping wins over Old Dominion and Pittsburgh to reach the Final Four. Butler lost in the championship both years, by one point to Duke in 2010 and by a large margin to UCONN in 2011.

2011 Virginia Commonwealth

Shaka Smart's Virginia Commonwealth team had to play five games to reach the 2011 Final Four, the first school in history to do that. Many members of the media disputed their selection to the tournament in the first place. The Rams were one of the final four teams to get a bid and thus had to play in the "First Four" in Dayton to start the tournament.

They defeated the Pac 10's Southern Cal team in Dayton, then defeated teams from the Big East (Georgetown), the Big Ten (Purdue), the ACC (Florida State), and Big 12 (number 1 seed Kansas), to reach the Final Four. Ironically, their run ended when they faced another team from a mid-major conference — Butler.

Diversity in size of players

Since the NCAA adopted the three-point goal on a national basis in 1986–87, there has been a rise in importance of the little man in college basketball. That said, the 2010–11 Wooden All-American team had players of all sizes and positions. There were the dominant big men — Jared Sullinger of Ohio State, JuJuan Johnson of Purdue, and Derrick Williams of Arizona. There was 6'7" forward Kawhi Leonard of San Diego State, and point guards Jacob Pullen of Kansas State and Jimmer Fredette of BYU. Fredette was the National Player of the Year according to the Wooden Award Committee. (Check out Chapter 1 for more information about John Wooden.)

So, if you like to follow a team with a dominant center, a small forward who can score from inside and out, or the quick point guard who can make a 25-foot three-pointer, you can find your favorite player at the college level.

Diversity in player personalities

A high percentage of college basketball fans follow their teams because they went to that school, but some follow teams because they appreciate a particular behind-the-scenes story about a player. And there are many fascinating story lines to follow in the college game. Just take a look at three from the 2010–11 college season.

Delvon Roe of Michigan State somehow found time to perform as a Shakespearean actor at the Pasant Theatre in the school's Wharton Center for Performing Arts. In December of 2010, he played the part of Charles The Wrestler in "As You Like It," a performance that began at 7:30 p.m. Later that night he scored 15 points, and had six rebounds and five assists in one of his best basketball performances in the Spartans victory over South Carolina.

Tanner Smith is in his senior year at Clemson in 2011–12. A starter on three NCAA tournament teams, he is one of the most respected athletes on campus for his work in providing gift baskets for kids fighting cancer. Smith got the idea when he visited his father in the hospital as his father fought the disease. He saw many children his age and thought it would be a good idea to provide some basics for them. His idea, Tanner's Totes, now provides gift baskets for kids in cancer treatment centers all over the nation.

Midnight Madness

Practice for college basketball at the Division I level begins on the first Saturday closest to October 15. It used to begin on October 15.

Prior to the rule change, it had become increasingly chic for teams to stage their first practice of the season at the stroke of midnight on that date. These Midnight Madness sessions are a celebration of hoops, parties disguised as a basketball practice that are open to all students. So the NCAA instituted the "Saturday-after" rule in 1997 so that students would not be up so late on a school night. (Do you get the feeling that the people at the NCAA have never set foot on a college campus?)

What happens at a Midnight Madness session? Some schools have a scrimmage, go through lay-up lines, perform a few dunks, stage a shooting contest or two, and then sign autographs. Midnight Madness has become more effective as a public relations tool for the school than as a legitimate practice. Many programs, such as Kentucky and Kansas, have sold out arenas for Midnight Madness.

Kemba Walker led UCONN to the 2011 NCAA Championship. The Huskies run started with five victories in five nights in Madison Square Garden in the Big East tournament. Walker showed an indomitable spirit with a record 130 points in those contests. The junior who turned professional at the end of the 2011 season first performed in front of crowds as a young dancer at Harlem's famed Apollo Theatre. He graduated in three years from UCONN.

Diversity in style of play

More than 330 Division I teams exist in both men's and women's college basketball (see Table 12-1), which amounts to over 650 different coaches who have not and will never come to a consensus on how the game should be played. The NBA menu reads like a White Castle menu in that there's very little diversity, no matter which two teams are playing. College hoops, on the other hand, is a smorgasbord.

Table 12-1	Four-Year College Basketball Teams by Category	
NCAA	*Men*	*Women*
Division I	345	333
Division II	275	294
Division III	402	441
Total NCAA Teams	1,013	1,068

Note: Totals are for 2010–11 season.

When you hear someone say Princeton, you think back door cuts to the basket. (If you have no idea what I'm talking about, see Chapters 7 and 8 and start watching these teams play.) When you hear Syracuse, you think of a great zone defense. When you hear Maryland, you think flex offense. College coaches can't depend on talent and/or depth year in and year out the way that NBA coaches can because players graduate or turn professional.

Some of the more fascinating stories deal with changing styles of play when there is a coaching change, such as what fans saw when Clemson hired Brad Brownell after Oliver Purnell went to DePaul in 2010–11. Purnell had taken Clemson to three straight NCAA tournaments with a pressing up-tempo style, but Brownell was more half-court oriented from an offense and defense standpoint. The Clemson players bought in to the new system, and at season's end the program was back in the Big Dance for a school-record fourth straight year, much to the delight of the Clemson faithful.

The NCAA tournament — the ultimate goal

The 68 teams are divided into four regions and organized into a single elimination "bracket," which predetermines what team it will face next when a team wins a game. Each team is seeded, or ranked, within its region. After an initial four games between eight lower-seeded teams (first done in 2011), the tournament takes place over the course of three weekends, at pre-selected neutral sites around the United States. Lower-seeded teams are placed in the bracket against higher-seeded teams. Each weekend cuts three-fourths of the teams, from a round of 64 to 16, the first weekend, from the Sweet 16 to the Final Four the next. And from a final four to one of the final two.

The Final Four usually play on the first Saturday in April. These four teams, one from each region, play two semi-finals on that Saturday. Two nights later, the two winners meet to decide the national championship.

Thirty-one teams qualify by winning their conference championship. All but one of them qualify by winning the conference postseason tournament. The Ivy League champion is determined by the regular season. The other 37 teams receive at-large bids, which in effect are invitations tendered to the best teams remaining from the pool of teams that did not win their conference tournaments.

In the history of the NCAA tournament, 20 teams have been offered a bid despite having a losing record. Only once, in 1955, did one of these teams win a game. Bradley, one of the first two teams invited with a losing record, won two games before being bounced. Since 2005 only one school, Coppin State in 2008, has reached the NCAA tournament with a losing record.

If you're new to the game, check out the NCAA statistics in the newspaper or on the Internet. Those stats tell you the high-scoring teams, the teams that shoot the most three-point goals, the teams that play great defense (based on field-goal-percentage defense, not scoring defense), the best shooting teams, and the best rebounding teams — in other words, the teams to watch this season. See Chapter 4 for details on reading stats.

Governing Bodies

The governing bodies for college basketball make the rules of competition, recruiting and many other basics that give structure and organization to the game. Without the NCAA, the NAIA, and junior college governing bodies, there would be chaos.

The NCAA

The National Collegiate Athletic Association (NCAA) is the national governing body of college sports, including basketball. NCAA schools are divided into three levels for college basketball: Division I, Division II, and Division III (non-scholarship). These levels (which are always referred to in Roman numerals) are loosely based on enrollment figures, but schools are allowed to decide at which level they compete.

Most schools are members of the same division for all sports, although some schools compete in Division I in some sports and Division II or III in others. For example, only 120 Division I football schools exist, but 336 play Division I men's basketball (2010–11 totals). Big East schools such as Providence, Seton Hall, and DePaul don't have football teams, but they have all been to the Final Four at some point in their respective basketball histories.

NAIA

But, as they say on the game shows, that's not all. Yet another, smaller-school layer of intercollegiate sports exists: the National Association of Intercollegiate Athletics (NAIA), which represents some 290 member schools that do not adhere to the same academic standards to which the NCAA submits itself.

You may not have heard of NAIA school Southeast Oklahoma State, but you probably know all about its alumnus Dennis Rodman, who was inducted into the Naismith Hall of Fame in 2011. Other alums of NAIA schools include Scottie Pippen, who played with the Chicago Bulls as well as on World Championship teams, and Elgin Baylor, who was voted one of the top 50 NBA players of all time. Pippen played at Central Arkansas, and Baylor started his career at the College of Idaho before finishing at Seattle. Every year the NAIA hosts an outstanding men's tournament consisting of 32 teams in Kansas City. The tournament is played over a one-week period in late February or early March, with games running from 9 a.m. to 10 p.m.

Junior colleges

Junior colleges are two-year schools that constitute yet another layer of backboards and mortarboards. There are roughly 500 junior colleges in the U.S. *Jucos,* as they are known. These schools have become havens for student athletes who have problems qualifying academically as freshmen for four-year schools, or who don't feel they are ready for the Division I college game coming out of high school.

Danielle Adams, the star center for the Texas A&M women's team, attended Missouri Junior College before she transferred to College Station and led the Aggies to the 2011 National Championship.

Conference structure

Conference affiliation within the NCAA structure forms the basic hierarchy of college basketball. A school aligns itself with other schools in a conference for a number of reasons. First, it provides the school with stability in scheduling year in and year out. It also creates amicable rivalries between schools, which amplify interest in the sport. For instance, Duke and North Carolina were charter members of the Atlantic Coast Conference (ACC), and they have been rivals since the 1950s. They are just eight miles apart.

Within Division I college basketball, there are 31 conferences with an average of ten schools each.

Although the NCAA tournament is perhaps the most high profile event in college sports, football is the bread winner for the 120 Division I schools that have big time football. As a result, football drives the conference makeup for college sports and basketball must follow along.

In 2004, the ACC decided to expand from 9 schools to 12 when it added Boston College, Miami, and Virginia Tech. That move created two six-team divisions for the football season so the conference could hold a conference championship game.

How that move has affected ACC basketball is up for debate. In 2011, the conference had just four teams in the NCAA tournament and was ranked fifth by the computer rankings. But, it did come on strong and had 3 of the final 16 teams in the tournament, more than any other conference. And the league had back-to-back NCAA Champions in 2009 (North Carolina) and 2010 (Duke).

The league has lost some of its tradition and a ticket to the ACC tournament is no longer a cherished commodity. ACC fans used to be able to trade ACC tournament tickets for Masters golf tournament tickets, but that is no longer the case.

The Big East will add Texas Christian University (TCU) to its conference in 2012, a move that will make Big East football a stronger national player. But, it will make Big East basketball a 17-team league. Someone is going to have to invent a new computer program to figure out the conference basketball schedule. Good luck to TCU basketball with every road trip being at least 1,000 miles.

Nebraska will join the Big Ten in 2011–12, while Utah and Colorado will go to the Pac 10, also decisions based on football.

The result of all these changes? In 2011–12 the Big Ten Conference will have 12 teams and the Big 12 Conference will have 10.

Team Size

Most men's college teams have between 12 and 14 players on their rosters. Women's teams have up to 15 players. The difference is a result of athletic scholarships. Women's teams are allowed 15 scholarships at the Division I level, and men's teams, just 13 scholarships. (This happens because of a federal law called Title IX that establishes guidelines for equity between the sexes when it comes to athletic participation.)

Some players on a team may not earn athletic scholarships. They are known as *walk-ons* and usually become fan favorites because students identify better with them. Walk-ons rarely, if ever, play — some never even suit up for a game — but they are invaluable during practice sessions.

In 2011, Clemson reached the NCAA tournament thanks in part to the play of walk-on Zavier Anderson. With some transfers, the Tigers had just nine scholarship players for most of that season, and Anderson played 306 pivotal minutes in the schools run to the NCAA tournament.

Coaches

Each Division I college team has a head coach, two full-time assistant coaches, and a part-time assistant coach. Many programs also have a director of basketball operations who handles tasks like team travel, NCAA rules interpretations, and managing the budget. The head coach and two full-time assistants are allowed to recruit off-campus, but the part-time coach is not. He may be involved in all other areas of coaching — scouting, corresponding with recruits, on-floor coaching during practice and games, and so on.

The roles of the college coach

All coaches deal with the media, watch film, prepare for practice, run practice, and coach games. When they get fired, they all go work for ESPN (at least it seems that way). Some, such as my friend Steve Lavin, who was fired from UCLA and then worked for seven years at ESPN, return to coaching. Lavin was hired by St. John's in 2010 and took the Red Storm to the NCAA tournament in his first year.

NBA coaches never have to worry about fund-raising or one of their players failing calculus. One new problem that NBA coaches face that college coaches have long had to deal with: underage players consuming alcohol.

Here are some additional responsibilities that college coaches have:

- ✔ **Monitoring academic performance of players:** Academic affairs are a constant concern for college coaches at all levels. Phil Jackson never has to worry whether Kobe Bryant will be academically eligible to play for the Lakers. In 2009, Ken Mink, the oldest college player in the nation at 73, flunked Spanish and was declared academically ineligible for Roane State Junior College in Tennessee.

- ✔ **Speaking to alumni groups:** Alumni can help a program, but they can create a negative climate as well. Most coaches (especially those who have had a mediocre season) make inroads with alumni during the off-season through various speaking engagements.

- ✔ **Speaking to campus groups:** As with alumni groups, coaches can increase their fan base by putting in efforts with student groups. For example, I used to spend September and April speaking on campus in the lobby of various dorms at Notre Dame. I talked about everything, sometimes even basketball, in a question-and-answer format. If nothing else, getting involved with the students creates campus interest in the program.

- ✔ **Consulting with players:** College coaches often play the role of surrogate father to their players. College is often the first time these young people have lived away from home, and it's only natural that their coach becomes the strongest adult role model in their lives.

  Nolan Smith, the ACC Player of the Year, lost his father, former college and NBA Star Derek Smith, when he died of a heart attack on a cruise with his family. Johnny Dawkins, who was with the Washington Wizards and a teammate of Derek Smith's, became a surrogate father to Nolan. Dawkins later became an assistant coach at Duke and that relationship had a lot to do with Nolan coming to Durham.

> ✔ **Promoting the team:** Most college athletic departments do not have the marketing budgets that NBA franchises do, so athletic departments often enlist coaches to assist. Coaches may be asked to speak to local civic groups, serve as grand marshal at a parade, or make an appearance at the local mall. Tip for reticent coaches: The more you win, the easier it is to say "no" to appearance requests.

The identity of a college basketball team is the school and the coaches. The players change at least every four years — and the headliners, the ones the average fan recognizes, often leave earlier than that. The NBA game, on the other hand, is about the players, not the coaches or the franchise. In fact, when I was a boy, I remember going to Madison Square Garden to see the New York Knicks play the Minneapolis Lakers. The sign on the marquee read, "Knicks face George Mikan tonight at 8:00 p.m." (Mikan was Minneapolis's star center.)

Perhaps for this reason, college coaches enjoy greater job security than NBA coaches. The NBA job mortality rate among coaches is approximately 35 percent annually, whereas college coaches have a 16 percent pink slip rate (54 changes in 345 jobs in 2010).

Games

Each NCAA team, be it Division I, II, or III, is allowed a maximum of 28 regular-season games. Teams wind up playing between 28 and 40 games per season, however. The numbers vary due to postseason success in conference and then national tournaments (you win, you play again; you lose, you don't) and scheduling by each school's athletic director. Some tournaments at the Division I level (such as the preseason National Invitational tournament, or NIT) do not count toward the maximum 28 regular-season games allowed by the NCAA. Don't ask me to explain why. A game is a game, after all.

The Division I men's record for victories in a season is 37, set by Duke in 1985–86 and also in 1998–99, UNLV in 1991–92, and Kansas in 2007–08. Among those teams, only Kansas won the national championship. Note that Memphis won 38 games in 2007–08, but their season was vacated due to the use of an ineligible player.

On the women's side, Tennessee and UCONN each have posted 39–0 seasons over the last 15 years.

Other postseason tournaments

Besides the NCAA tournament, there are three other postseason tournaments in Division I men's college basketball and one for women's.

NIT

The National Invitation Tournament (NIT) is the oldest postseason college basketball tournament, yes even older than the NCAA. The NIT dates to 1938 when there were six teams invited to Madison Square Garden in New York. All NIT games were played in New York until 1977 when early round games were held at on-campus sites.

In the early days, the NIT was actually a bigger event than the NCAA for many years. Prior to 1975, when the NCAA tournament only took one team from a conference, the NIT had some matchups of top 20 teams, throughout the event.

In my second year at Notre Dame we played North Carolina in the semifinals in Madison Square Garden and Dean Smith's team was ranked 11th in the nation on selection Sunday. But they did not win the ACC tournament and thus could not go to the NCAAs. Today, that North Carolina team would probably be a number 3 seed in the NCAA tournament.

The NIT has 32 teams today and is run by the NCAA, something that has been the case since 2007. To qualify, a team must have at least a break-even record on Selection Sunday. Teams are seeded in four different brackets with the four winners advancing to the National semifinals at Madison Square Garden. Wichita State won the tournament over Alabama in 2011.

There is also a women's NIT each year. It is a 64-team tournament.

CBI

The College Basketball Invitational (CBI) began in 2008 and is a 16-team event that is played at on-campus sites. Teams can be selected even though they have a losing record at the end of their conference tournament.

Teams play a single elimination tournament until there are two finalists. The two finalists then play a best two out of three series. Oregon won the 2011 event over Creighton on a last second shot by E. J. Singler, the brother of Duke star Kyle Singler.

CIT

The College Insider.com tournament (CIT) started in 2009. It is a 24-team event that is also played on the home court of one of the teams. It is a single elimination tournament in which four teams receive byes in the first round. Teams with losing records may be selected.

The CIT does not follow a bracket. After the second round, a committee re-pairs the teams in hopes of keeping teams close to each other from a geographic (and cost cutting) standpoint.

Santa Clara won the 2011 CIT over Iona, 76–69.

So why follow games in these tournaments? Many times the teams that are successful in these tournaments have young squads, and they can give you a good indication of who will make strides on the college basketball scene the next season. VCU is a perfect example. In 2010, then first-year head coach Shaka Smart guided that team to the championship of the CBI with five straight wins. That positive experience gave that team confidence for the next year and was a key to its shocking run to the Final Four of the NACC tournament in 2011.

Polls

America has a compulsive need to rank things — just think about David Letterman's *Top Ten List* or Casey Kasem's *American Top 40*. It's a national pastime.

Polls are more important in college football — they determine the national champ from the standpoint that they are a big part of the formula that determines who gets to play for the National Championship of college football — but they play a role in college hoops as well. The polls are a barometer, a pulse rate for teams during the season, right up until the national champion is crowned. For both fans and players, polls heighten interest in games.

Each level of basketball has polls. At the Division I level, two polls exist: Associated Press (AP), which is voted on by the national media, and *USA Today,* which is a compilation of the opinions of college coaches. Each week, from early November until the end of the conference tournaments, these polls provide a ladder for teams to climb — and descend — as fans debate their accuracy. *USA Today* also does a poll after the Final Four.

All-America Teams

You hear less about individual statistics in college ball than you do in the pros, but more about which players deserve to be on an All-America team and win National Player of the Year honors. Unlike the NBA, college basketball does not feature a common ground of opponents — nobody wants to play a 300-game schedule. And that means the quality of opponents on one team's schedule may differ greatly from another's. Thus one player's 28 points per game may mean less than another player's 20 due to the level of competition that he or she faces.

Various services and organizations choose All-America players. You don't have to be an American to win; All-America is just a term for an all-star team. Unlike the NBA, no single All-America team exists. Any organization may choose an All-America team, and depending on its selection procedure, the honor may be tantamount to being elected to public office, or it may mean nothing at all. Basketball All-America teams are either five- or ten-person squads selected by people within an organization. Some organizations select a first and second team.

Player of the Year Awards

Many men's and women's college basketball players can win Player of the Year.

The Wooden Award is selected by a national committee of 1,000 members of the media who select a ten-man All-America team. The Wooden Award has been presented since 1977 for the men and since 2004 for the women. It's named after former UCLA coach John Wooden.

The Naismith Award is presented by the Atlanta Tipoff Club and is named in honor of Dr. James Naismith, the inventor of the game. It has been presented to a male player since 1969 and to a female player since 1983.

The Oscar Robertson trophy is awarded to the player of the year as chosen by 900 journalists of the United States Basketball Writers Association (USBWA). It's been awarded since 1959 when Oscar Robertson, the great University of Cincinnati star, was the first recipient. It was called the United States Basketball Writers Association Player of the Year until 1998 when it was named in honor of Robertson for the first time.

There are also player-of-the-year awards presented by the Associated Press, *Basketball Times*, *Sporting News*, and CBS Sports.

The Wade Trophy goes to the top player of the year in women's college basketball. It's named after former Delta State head coach Margaret Wade, who won three National Championships. It has been presented since 1978. Maya Moore of UCONN, a senior in 2010–11, is the only three-time recipient.

NCAA Women's Basketball

John Wooden was once quoted in *USA Today* as saying, "To me, the best pure basketball I see today . . . is among the better women's teams."

In my first seven years at Notre Dame, we had no varsity women's basketball program. (But you should know that, in my first year there, the college didn't even admit women.) The only competition of note for women on campus was the annual "Jocks versus Girls" pickup basketball game. Seeing Notre Dame's women's team win the national championship in 2001 and reach the national championship game in 2011 reminded me of those games and how far Notre Dame women's basketball in particular, and women's basketball in general, has come in such a short time.

The smaller ball

In 1984–85, the NCAA adopted a smaller ball for women's college basketball. The women's ball is 1 inch smaller in circumference and 2½ ounces lighter than the one used by men. This modification has had a great deal to do with the popularity of the women's game nationwide.

The NCAA thought that the smaller ball would increase scoring and shooting percentages, but that has not been the case; neither statistic has varied greatly. But what has happened is that ballhandling has improved, teams are committing fewer turnovers, and the quality of play is much better. The WNBA realizes the benefit of the smaller ball and also uses it.

One of the positive by-products of the smaller basketball in the women's game is the dunk. Seven women have dunked a basketball in a college game, and six of them have accomplished the feat since the NCAA went to the smaller ball.

The list includes Baylor center Brittney Griner (see Figure 12-1), a junior in 2011–12, who is destined to set many college records (and not just for dunking). She had five dunks through her sophomore season (2010–11), just two off the women's college record of seven by former Tennessee All-American Candace Parker.

There have been many superstar women's college players in recent years, but none like the 6'8" Griner, who wears a size 17 men's shoe and has an 88-inch wing span. She came on the women's basketball scene as a senior at Nimitz High School in Houston, Texas, when she had 52 dunks in 35 games her senior year and was named the top high school player in the nation.

She has taken Baylor to the Final Four and the Elite Eight in each of her first two years in college by averaging over 20 points and 7 rebounds, and shooting 55 percent from the field and 78 percent from the foul line. That free-throw percentage shows what a fine shooting touch she has.

Figure 12-1:
Brittney
Griner.

But her true impact on the game is at the defensive end. She had 232 blocked shots her freshman year, an all-time NCAA record. That included a 14-block game against Georgetown in the NCAA tournament, a single-game record for the postseason

Table 12-2 shows a list of the women's basketball players who have dunked in a Division I college basketball game through the 2011 season. I am sure many more ladies will be added in the coming years.

Table 12-2	Women Who Dunked in the College Game		
Player	*School*	*Years*	*Dunks*
Candace Parker	Tennessee	2005–08	7
Brittney Griner	Baylor	2009–11	5
Michelle Snow	Tennessee	2000–02	3
Georgean Wells*	West Virginia	1984–85	2
Charlotte Smith	North Carolina	1994–95	1
Shaucho Lyttle	Houston	2003–04	1
Sylvia Fowles	LSU	2007–08	1

Wells dunked a men's ball.

Increased media attention

Another reason for the increase in women's basketball interest is media attention. Interest had been growing since the 1980s, but when the media in the East fell in love with the Connecticut women's team in 1995 and its magical 35–0 season, everyone took notice.

When Connecticut won the national championship to consummate only the second undefeated season in women's NCAA history, the media embraced Connecticut star Rebecca Lobo in particular. Lobo appeared on the *CBS Morning News* and *Late Night with David Letterman* and joined her teammates on *Live with Regis & Kathie Lee*. She might be regarded as the Arnold Palmer of women's college basketball.

Attendance at women's college games is also on the rise. The 1997 Final Four in Cincinnati, for example, sold out in four hours. The 1998 Final Four used a lottery system to distribute tickets for the first time in women's history. Dating back to 1993, every Women's Final Four has been a sellout.

UCONN's 90-game winning streak

Connecticut captured the basketball world in November and December of 2010 when it ran a winning streak to 90 games. It was the longest in women's basketball history and extended longer than the men's record of 88 in a row by John Wooden's UCLA teams between 1971 and 1974.

Many members of the media made comparisons between the UCONN streak and the UCLA streak. As the coach of the Notre Dame team that broke UCLA's streak in 1974, I followed the UCONN streak with interest. It was big because it brought attention to women's college basketball, and that is good for the game.

There were some interesting comparisons between the two streaks; the most unusual was seeing that the same school recorded the victory at both ends of the respective streaks. Notre Dame had the last victory over UCLA before we ended the streak in 1974, and Stanford had the last victory over UCONN before the Cardinal ended the streak on December 30, 2010 at Stanford. What makes it so unusual is that they were nonconference opponents in both instances.

Here are some comparisons that show how dominant both teams were during their respective streaks.

Comparison of Streaks	UCONN	UCLA
Win Streak	90	88
Years	2008–10	1971–74
Days Between Losses	998	1,092
Wins vs. Top 25 Teams	31	18
Wins by Double Figures	88	72
Road Wins	30	20
Average Victory	33.4	23.5
Pts Allowed in Game that Ended Streak	71	71
Team that Ended Streak	Stanford	Notre Dame
Games as #1 Team	88	86

Upgrades to the game

A few key factors have prompted the increased excitement surrounding college women's hoops in recent years:

✔ **A national marque matchup.** The UCONN versus Tennessee rivalry has done for the women's game what the Notre Dame versus UCLA rivalry did for the men's game in the 1970s. Our series with UCLA brought regular season college basketball to national television and created interest that spread to the tournament. UCONN and Tennessee have not played in the regular season lately, but that rivalry did a lot for the game in the first decade of this century. In general, there is a willingness of top teams to play each other during the season, much more so than the men's game.

✔ **Higher coach visibility.** Thanks to ESPN and other networks, we are seeing more and more women's college games on television. Many of the women's coaches have shown the type of charisma that fans are attracted to. The avid college fan knows who Pat Summitt, Vivian Stringer, Muffett McGraw, and Geno Auriemma are.

✔ **More summer camps and AAU for women.** The Amateur Athletic Union (AAU) is a national organization for sports that operates outside the constraints of academia. While the men's college game has been hurt by AAU basketball because of the influence of coaches who are in it for monetary gain, I find women's AAU basketball to be a positive learning experience for the players involved. Summer camps are on the rise, and that means that women are playing the game year round.

✔ **Positive influence of international players.** As the women's game has grown, coaches have broadened their horizons when it comes to recruiting.

✔ **The WNBA.** The WNBA has brought renewed interest in basketball to the youth of America. Girls all over the country now can picture themselves playing on NBC on a Saturday or Sunday summer afternoon. They didn't have that dream years ago, and it serves as a motivator for youngsters. That means more and more girls are playing the game all over the world, which will lead to an increase in talented players.

What makes Geno Auriemma a Hall of Fame coach?

Geno Auriemma has won seven NCAA Championships in his career, second only to Pat Summit's eight. He has led UCONN's women's program to a 70-game winning streak and a record 90-game winning streak over the last five years. What is his secret?

He is a tenacious recruiter. A couple of years ago I was flying to Bristol to cover a Gameday at UCONN. The Friday morning before I was at the Cincinnati Airport and ran into Geno. Knowing he had a game on Saturday, I said, "What are you doing here?" He had flown to Middletown, Ohio, on Thursday to see a high school game and now was catching an early morning flight back to get to Storrs in time for practice.

Geno has the ability to get the most out of his young ladies. They believe in him. The women trust him and that gives him the ability to motivate them to reach their potential.

He is a great adjustment coach. He is not afraid to mix defenses and not afraid to make strategy adjustments to the team he is playing. Even though he has the best players, he will still make changes based on who he is playing. From an offensive standpoint, sometime that means getting the ball inside, or sometimes scoring from the perimeter. So many coaches have a system and don't adjust to whom they are playing.

Finally, he plays to his talent. He is not afraid to get his star player the ball. Some years that might be a guard, and other years it might be a center.

Geno and John Wooden have many similarities. The most important is their honesty with their players. That comes across every day. What you see is what you get.

One and Done

An on-going dilemma facing college basketball is the early entry into the NBA draft. College players have been entering the NBA draft before the end of their college eligibility since 1971, when Phil Chenier of the University of California turned professional after his junior year.

Over time, early entry became earlier and earlier, including Moses Malone, who turned professional in 1974 out of high school. No one else did so successfully for about two decades, but then Kevin Garnett heralded a wave of future All-Stars, including Kobe Bryant, LeBron James, and Dwight Howard, who went directly to the NBA from their senior proms.

The NBA instituted a rule in 2006 where a player had to be 19 years old to be eligible for the draft. That has basically forced players to go to college for a year. Either that, or as the Milwaukee Bucks' Brandon Jennings did, sit out for a year. Jennings chose to play professionally in Europe and then returned to be drafted by the Milwaukee Bucks.

The NCAA is in a difficult situation. It is far easier to assess talent in basketball than it is in football, especially in regard to how it will translate to the professional level. If someone such as Kobe Bryant is good enough to play in the NBA without attending college, or someone such as Kevin Love can lead the NBA in rebounding in what should have been his senior season at UCLA (Love left the Bruins after one season), who am I to tell him to turn down millions of dollars?

On the other hand, the college game suffers for it. The traditional powers in the sport, schools such as Kansas, Kentucky, and North Carolina, still attract the best prep players in the nation. However, many of those freshmen are playing in the NBA the following season.

Such turbulent turnover hurts those programs, but it also has an upside. Mid-level schools such as Butler, programs whose players are rarely talented enough to play professionally — and especially not after one season — have closed the gap on the leviathans on the sports. By keeping lesser-talented individuals together for four seasons, they've molded teams that are much closer competitively to the sports' goliaths than they have been in decades.

Chapter 13

Professional Basketball

In 1992 a team of 11 NBA legends (plus Duke University's Christian Laettner) swept into Barcelona, Spain, like rock stars and easily won the Olympic gold medal. It was the first time the U.S.A. had ever used NBA players in the Olympic Games.

More than winning the gold, the "Dream Team" unwittingly incited a revolution. At the time the NBA had only a handful of foreign-born-and-raised players and only one — Hakeem Olujawon of Nigeria — was truly an impact player and perennial All-Star. Also, there were no NBA players — and certainly no All-Stars — who had jumped directly from high school to the NBA.

At the tip-off of the 2010–11 season there were a record 84 foreign-born players on NBA rosters. The NBA All-Star Game included five foreign-born players and an additional five Americans who had never played a minute of college basketball. The league, in terms of from where it culls its most precious resource — the players — has changed dramatically in just two decades.

It's still the NBA, however. The Celtics and Lakers still win more than anyone else, and referees still neglect to call traveling violations on the league's most popular players. The NBA has never been more popular. It's just that now your favorite player is more likely to have a passport or a work visa than a college degree.

National Basketball Association (NBA)

There are 30 teams in the NBA, which is divided into the Eastern and Western conferences. Each conference is divided into three divisions of five teams each. The Eastern Conference contains the Atlantic, Central, and Southeast divisions. The Western Conference has the Northwest, Pacific, and Southwest divisions. Table 13-1 shows all six divisions in both conferences.

Table 13-1	NBA Conference Divisions and Teams	
Eastern Conference		
Atlantic Division	**Central Division**	**Southeast Division**
Boston Celtics	Chicago Bulls	Atlanta Hawks
New Jersey Nets	Cleveland Cavaliers	Charlotte Bobcats
New York Knicks	Detroit Pistons	Miami Heat
Philadelphia 76ers	Indiana Pacers	Orlando Magic
Toronto Raptors	Milwaukee Bucks	Washington Wizards
Western Conference		
Northwest Division	**Pacific Division**	**Southwest Division**
Denver Nuggets	Golden State Warriors	Dallas Mavericks
Minnesota Timberwolves	Los Angeles Clippers	Houston Rockets
Oklahoma Cith Thunder	Los Angeles Lakers	Memphis Grizzlies
Portland Trail Blazers	Phoenix Suns	New Orleans Hornets
Utah Jazz	Sacramento Kings	San Antonio Spurs

Schedule

Since 1968, each NBA team has played an 82-game regular-season schedule. The teams play 41 games at home and 41 on the road — give or take a couple of international games. In 2011, for example, the Nets and Raptors played a pair of games in London.

Each team plays four games (two home and two away) against every team in its division, and two games (one home and one away) against every team in the other conference. If you are good at math, you have already calculated that so far that accounts for 46 games ($4 \times 4 = 16$ and $2 \times 15 = 30$).

For example, Golden State Warriors play four games against each team in the Pacific Division and two games versus each franchise in the Eastern Conference.

That still leaves 36 games. To complete its 82-game schedule, a team plays four games against six other teams in its conference outside its division and three games against the four remaining teams in conference that are not in its division ($6 \times 4 = 24$ and $4 \times 3 = 12$).

The first game

The first game in the history of the National Basketball Association took place at an international site. On November 1, 1946, the New York Knickerbockers defeated the Toronto Huskies, 68–66, at Maple Leaf Gardens. Tickets were priced between 75 cents and $2.50, although the Huskies ran a promotion guaranteeing free admission to anyone taller than 6'8" center George Nostrand. Let the record show that New York's Ozzie Schectman scored the first basket in league history.

Rosters

Each NBA team is allowed a maximum of 12 players on its active roster, which means that 360 players are on opening day rosters. A team also has one player on its inactive roster list. This player practices with the team but does not dress out for games. You can think of him as the "In Case of Emergency, Break Glass" member of the squad. If 1 of the 12 active players is injured and cannot suit up for a game, this player may take his place immediately.

A team can replace players due to injury, retirement, and/or players being *waived* (meaning cut or laid off) during the season. For instance, in 2010–11, the Phoenix Suns had 19 different players suit up for at least one game. A good rule of thumb is that the greater number of players that appear on a team's roster in one season, the lower the chance of success.

A team must have at least eight eligible players dressed and able to play for a game. And sometimes even that is not enough. In January 2010, the Golden State Warriors suited up eight healthy players for a game against the Milwaukee Bucks. In the first half guard Anthony Morrow was lost to a sprained knee. Then in the third quarter power forward Chris Hunter fouled out.

And then there were six.

Center Andres Biedrins fouled out in the fourth quarter, leaving the Warriors with just five players and rendering any ideas that coach Don Nelson might have had about substitution patterns useless.

Finally, with four seconds to play rookie guard Stephen Curry fouled out. Referee Joey Crawford, then in his 33rd season in the league, had never encountered such a situation. Crawford did know what to do, though; he invoked the four-player rule. Curry was allowed to remain in the game, but the Warriors were assessed a technical foul, which resulted in one free throw for the Bucks.

Had the contest continued longer, Golden State would have been assessed a technical foul for each additional foul Curry committed. Frankly, and considering how rarely this would ever happen, it would've been more entertaining to watch Golden State compete four-on-five. They're Warriors, after all.

A team in need of a quick fix may sign a free agent to a ten-day contract to replace an injured or suspended player. The franchise may renew a player's ten-day contract once, but after he has fulfilled two such contracts (that is, 20 days of service) it must either waive or sign the player for the remainder of the season.

Teams may trade players until the trading deadline, which falls on the 16th Thursday of each season. Teams may resume making player trades at the end of the regular season as long as they are not in the playoffs. After a team is eliminated from the postseason, it also may make changes to its roster.

The last 72 hours before the trading deadline are the most anxious of the season for players. Many have heard their names whispered in trade rumors, and why wouldn't they be nervous? A player traded at the deadline not only must change uniforms in midseason, but must also move to a new city and say goodbye to his teammates and coaches, the people with whom he is most likely closest.

It's almost like waiting to see if you've been cut from the team. Most NBA players were never cut from a team in their lives, however. In late February 2011, the league was busier than the trading floor at the New York Stock Exchange. In the final three days before the deadline, 21 of the NBA's 30 teams, or 70 percent, participated in trading a total of 50 players. That's nearly 14 percent of the league being redispersed. In one swap that must have caused a migraine or two at NBA headquarters in New York City (because the league must approve all trades), the Denver Nuggets, Minnesota Timberwolves, and New York Knicks swapped 13 players among the three teams.

Playoffs

Sixteen of the NBA's 30 teams qualify for the NBA playoffs, eight from each conference. The 16 teams are seeded 1 through 8 within each conference. A division winner is guaranteed a spot no lower than fourth, even if four other teams within its conference finish with better regular-season records.

Within those top four spots, however, the seeding follows according to the team's record. Hence, if the Dallas Mavericks finish with the second-best record in the Western Conference, but also finish second in their own division to the San Antonio Spurs, they still are the number 2 seed.

In short, the number 1 seed plays the number 8 seed, the number 2 meets the number 7, number 3 versus number 6, and number 4 faces number 5. Why does it matter to be seeded in the top four? Because the top four teams earn homecourt advantage in the opening seven-game series.

With these rules for seeding teams in the playoffs, the advantage goes to the team with the better record during the regular season, regardless of its standing in the division race. I like this method of seeding teams for the playoffs because it puts more meaning into the regular season.

Each playoff series is best-of-seven games, regardless of the round in which it occurs. There are three elimination rounds per conference (from eight teams to four, four teams to two, two to one) before the NBA Finals. Not too long ago, first-round series used to be best-of-five. I liked that better because there were greater opportunities for an upset. To win an NBA championship now, a team must win 16 games and may wind up playing as many as 28. That equals more than one-third of the regular season.

The NBA Has Come a Long Way

In 1955, the NBA was a very different league. The Syracuse Nationals played the Fort Wayne Pistons in a best-of-seven series that was strikingly different than the spectacles we have become accustomed to seeing.

For beginners, the Pistons were unable to host games 3, 4, and 5 in their own arena, War Memorial Coliseum, because those dates were reserved for an event with the American Bowling Congress. The teams were forced to move to a 13,000-seat arena in Indianapolis, with one game drawing only 3,200 fans.

In game 3, an unruly Pistons fan threw a chair onto the court in anger and then ran on the court himself to argue with officials Mendy Rudolph and Arnie Heft. There was no such thing as NBA security at the time: Not only was the fan not ejected from the premises, but he spent the rest of the game seated behind the Syracuse bench heckling the visiting Nationals (if only Ron Artest had played at the time).

Heft, one of the officials, was so bothered by the mob mentality that he announced he was done refereeing the series. He caught on with the Harlem Globetrotters, who were touring the Midwest at the time. Can you imagine that happening today?

Episodes such as these illustrate the plight of professional basketball in the early days. But proponents of the game have instituted rule changes that were designed to enliven the sport. The following sections describe some of these league-saving changes.

The shot clock: A rule that saved a league

On November 22, 1950, the Fort Wayne Pistons defeated the Minneapolis Lakers 19–18 in the lowest-scoring game in NBA history. Each team made four field goals. In the fourth quarter, Fort Wayne outscored Minneapolis by a score of 3–1. In these early years of the NBA, games were plodding, brutish contests in which teams *stalled* (that is, held the ball and did not shoot), sometimes for many minutes at a time, late in the game. Fortunately, someone recognized that this molasses approach to playing the game was pretty bor-... er, *not lively*.

Every NBA player owes a small percentage of his salary to Danny Biasone (not exactly a name that's on the tip of every NBA fan's tongue). In 1954, Biasone, then the owner of the Syracuse Nationals, invented the 24-second shot clock and altered the game of basketball forever — and for the better.

How did Biasone come up with his magic number? First, he determined that the average number of shots two teams take during a game is 120. He then divided the length of a game — 48 minutes or 2,880 seconds — by the average number of shots and came up with 24.

The 24-second shot clock rule made its debut on October 30, 1954. During its first season, it produced dramatic results:

✔ In the debut game, the Rochester Royals defeated the Boston Celtics 98–95. That would have been the seventh highest scoring game of the previous season.

> ✔ The year the rule was instituted, NBA teams averaged 93.1 points per game. This average showed an increase of 13.6 points per game from the previous year.
>
> ✔ That season, the Celtics became the first team in NBA history to average more than 100 points per contest.

No team may have been more grateful for Biasone's impact in the game that first year than his own, the Nationals. In the seventh game of the NBA Finals, Syracuse trailed Fort Wayne 41–24. A year earlier the Pistons would have gone into a stall with that comfortable 17-point lead. Now, thanks to their owner, the Nationals had a chance to come back, and they did, winning the game and the NBA championship.

In 2000, basketball historians recognized Biasone's contributions to the game, inducting him posthumously into the Basketball Hall of Fame.

Illegal defense: What is it?

Zone defense — the idea of defending an area instead of a person — was once a strict no-no in the NBA. (See Chapter 7 to find out more about zone defenses.) The NBA disallowed zone defenses because they took away from scoring, which took away from entertainment.

Sports are always evolving, however. In the late 1990s coaches figured out that they could isolate their two best offensive players on one-half of the court and place the other three far from the ball. The result was a glorified half-court game of two-on-two while six other players stood and watched. The other three defenders were obligated to guard their men, even though those three were deliberately placed as far from the ball, and often basket, as possible.

Well, that was just silly. In 2001 the league tweaked the rule, instituting what is known as the *defensive three-second violation*. Teams are now allowed to play zone, but a defender may not remain in the lane for more than three seconds unless he is actively guarding someone. To be considered actively guarding someone, the defender must be within arm's reach of an offensive player.

Failure to comply with the rule results in a one-shot technical foul. Referees rarely call this penalty, and if they do, it's usually done in the first half of a game, almost as a warning to that team's coach.

Kobe Bryant versus Michael Jordan

Before the day Michael Jordan even retired, the NBA was looking to see if the next generation would produce such an ethereal talent. In fact, one poor player who showed early Jordan-like skills in his career, Harold Miner, was dubbed "Baby Jordan." That was unfair. His college coach at USC, George Raveling, said, "I always felt the worst thing to happen to Harold was the Baby Jordan tag."

Miner played five seasons in the NBA and won the NBA Slam Dunk Contest twice — he was a spectacular leaper — but his career was otherwise unspectacular. Living up to Michael Jordan's legacy is a burden that no player should shoulder. Well, almost no player.

Ever since he entered the league at age 18, Kobe Bryant has not only welcomed the Jordan comparisons, he has aspired to them. Bryant, who is about the same size as MJ, is without a doubt the league's best all-around player to come along since Jordan retired in 2003. Whereas MJ won six NBA championships, Kobe has won five. Whereas Jordan once scored 69 points in a game, Kobe scored 81 (only Wilt Chamberlain's epic 100-point game tops that).

But those are just numbers. What stands out about these two men is that, while they were playing, there was simply no one else in the NBA who approached their degree of competitiveness. And the NBA is not exactly a place that harbors passive people. These two were the most competitive of the ultra-competitive.

In each player's respective era, there was no one else whom you'd rather see take the last shot with the game on the line (that is, unless Michael or Kobe was playing against your favorite team).

	Kobe	Jordan
Nickname	Black Mamba	Air Jordan
Height	6'6"	6'6"
Weight	205	215
Draft pick	1st round 13th pick	1st round 3rd pick
Slam Dunk Champion	1997	1987, 1988
NBA MVP	1 time	5 times
NBA scoring champ	2 times	10 times
All-Star games	13	14
All-Star game MVP	4 times	3 times
NBA championships*	5	6
NBA finals MVP	2 times	6 times
Career scoring average	25.3 points per game	30.1 points per game**

* All of their 11 championships were won under the guidance of coach Phil Jackson.

** Jordan is Number 1 all-time in career scoring average, just a fraction of a point ahead of Wilt Chamberlain.

Although teams are now allowed to play zone defense, rarely will you see it. If you do, it may only be for a possession or two in hopes of catching the offense unprepared.

Foreign Infusion

It all began with a dream. Actually, it all began with The Dream, as in Hakeem "The Dream" Olajuwon. A native of Nigeria, the seven-footer found his way to the University of Houston in the early 1980s. Olajuwon played as if he not only was born on another continent, but another planet.

Olajuwon was sleeker, swifter, and taller than any man his size, but he also had excellent footwork. As a child in Lagos, he had primarily played soccer and it showed in his game and to his advantage.

Before Olajuwon entered the league, the idea of foreigners being good enough to play in the NBA was laughable. Then again, it was a foreigner, Canadian native James Naismith, who had invented the game.

The Dream entered the league in 1984 and was named a starter in the All-Star game eight times during his 18-season Hall of Fame career. Olajuwon was not the first foreign-born NBA player, but he was the first dominant one.

In the two decades since, NBA scouts have learned the values of scouting across the border. In the past decade alone, five different MVP awards have gone to three players born and raised outside the United States: Dirk Nowitzki (Germany), Steve Nash (Canada, who won twice), and Tim Duncan (Virgin Islands, twice).

Nine of the past ten All-Star games have featured at least two foreign-born starters. The 2006 West squad included five green-card studs: Duncan, Nash, Nowitzki, Pau Gasol of Spain, and Yao Ming of China.

The San Antonio Spurs, who have won four NBA titles since 1999, have built their team around a trio of gifted foreigners: Duncan, point guard Tony Parker from France, and guard Manu Ginobili of Argentina. In 2006, the Toronto Raptors, a franchise located beyond American borders, made Italian Andrea Bargnani the first overall pick in the NBA draft.

What amazes me about all of these players is how fundamentally skilled they are. Too many American players, weaned on SportsCenter, are either all about dunks or three-point plays. Watch the foreigners, however. They shoot beautifully and seem to play, for lack of a better word, more artistically. The only possible drawback I see is that, like their soccer-playing countrymen, international players are notorious for flopping (pretending to be fouled when they were not). I'm looking directly at you, Vlade Divac and Manu Ginobili.

The foreign infusion has been a shot in the arm for the NBA, just as immigration has always helped reshape and revitalize America. "Give us your tired, your poor . . . " has been replaced by "Give us your tall and your sleek-shooting . . . "

NBA Economics

Cap space is not a keyboard command. It's one of many fiscal terms that, for better or worse, the knowledgeable NBA fan has been compelled to learn in the last decade. If you want to keep stats, such terms as *rebounds* and *turnovers* probably have less to do with your favorite team's chances of success than do the numbers involving cap space and luxury tax.

Since the 1984–85 season, the league has had a salary cap that represents the total payroll a team is allowed to spend on its roster. Why? Because large-market franchises, such as New York and Los Angeles, earn more revenue than small-market teams such as Milwaukee and Utah. By holding every team to the same spending standard, the theory is that the larger-market teams will not be able to stockpile all the best players.

Cap space, therefore, refers to the amount of available dollars any team has below their salary cap. Just as many trades are made in the NBA with the intent to free up cap space as to obtain a better player. In 2010–11, for example, the Phoenix Suns acquired veteran Vince Carter, who may have been the most overpaid player in the NBA (Carter earned $17.5 million, making him the league's 10th highest-paid player).

Why did the Suns want Carter, also known as Vinsanity, who despite his gargantuan salary had not made an All-Star roster in four years? Because he was in the final year of his contract. When the season ended, the Suns did not re-sign Carter and thus had $17.5 million of available cap space in which to sign a free agent.

Ten best foreign-born players in NBA history

10. Detlef Schrempf (Germany): Nowadays the sight of a 6'9" international player draining three-pointers is commonplace (ever watch a Utah Jazz game?), but in the 1980s and 1990s, Schrempf's heyday, it was bizarre. A three-time All-Star, the Teutonic terror with the blonde buzzcut was a two-time NBA Sixth Man of the Year.

9. Tony Parker (France): Quicker than the storming of the Bastille, Parker makes some of the world's swiftest athletes appear as if they are moving in honey. The quarterback of the Spurs, the most successful team not coached by Phil Jackson (see below) the league has seen the past twenty years.

8. Manu Ginobili (Argentina): The epitome of a guy whom you hate if he's on the other team yet love if he is on yours, the lefty has a slashing, unorthodox style. His court intelligence is off the charts, and he does everything well.

7. Pau Gasol (Spain): The 7'0" Spaniard passed up medical school to play in the NBA. With his elongated wingspan, Gasol plays as if he is a 14-year-old on a Nerf hoop in his bedroom. The Lakers were unable to win an NBA championship with only Kobe Bryant, but then won two in a row after trading for Gasol.

6. Yao Ming (China): The first Asian player to make an All-Star team, the 7'6" Yao might be among the top three on this list if not for an injury-plagued career. An eight-time All-Star, although the introduction of online voting coupled with China's population contributed to that.

5. Dikembe Mutombo (Congo): The 7'2" Mutombo led the league in blocks for five consecutive seasons and is second all-time in that category. An eight-time All-Star, Mutombo's trademark finger-wag after rejecting a shot belongs in the Hall of Fame. Full name: Dikembe Mutombo Mpolondo Mukamba Jean-Jacques Wamutombo.

4. Steve Nash (Canada): Born in South Africa, Nash belongs in highly elite company (names such as Larry Bird, Michael Jordan, Magic Johnson, LeBron James, and so on) as a multiple-league MVP. Barely 6'2", Nash has led the NBA in assists five times and will likely retire as the most accurate free throw shooter in league history.

3. Dirk Nowitzki (Germany): No seven-footer has ever been more unstoppable on offense outside the paint. The ten-time All-Star and 2007 MVP has a 22.9 points per game career average

2. Tim Duncan (Virgin Islands): Many consider "The Big Fundamental" to be the greatest power forward the league has ever seen, although Karl Malone fans are welcome to disagree. A 13-time All-Star and 2-time MVP, Duncan's most essential attribute is that he is a winner, having led the San Antonio Spurs to four NBA titles.

1. Hakeem Olajuwon (Nigeria): The league's all-time leader in blocked shots led the Houston Rockets to a pair of NBA championship in the mid-Nineties. He ranks 11th all-time in scoring, 12th in rebounding, and belongs in any conversation about the top ten centers of all time.

Here are some facts about the NBA salary cap:

- The salary cap was $58.04 million per team for the 2010–2011 season. That was nearly a 20 percent increase over the salary cap ($49.5 million) just five years earlier. In the first season of the salary cap, 1984–85, the cap was $3.6 million. In the 2010–11 season, 182 individual players earned more than that.

- Under the Collective Bargaining Agreement (CBA), the contract between the owners and the NBA Players Association, the salary cap represents 51 percent of the league's total revenue. The CBA was set to expire, however, as of July 1, 2011, and as of this writing no new agreement is in place.

- What is a luxury tax? If a team exceeds the salary cap in making its player payroll, it must pay the league a tax based upon how much money it has overspent. It's not that simple — nothing ever is when it comes to pro sports finances — but you get the idea.

- There are exceptions to the salary cap. Exemptions allow a team to exceed the cap. For example, a team may exceed the salary cap in order to re-sign its own player who has just become a free agent. The Cleveland Cavaliers, for example, were able to spend more money in the summer of 2010 in order to keep LeBron James than any team that was courting him. When LeBron, who was a free agent at the end of the 2010 season, chose to sign with the Miami Heat instead of remaining with Cleveland, he opted to play for less money — but still a lot of money — than he could have earned with the Cavs.

- Finally, and I can feel your eyes glazing over, you may have heard the term *sign-and-trade*. Using the previous example, the Cavaliers could have signed LeBron for more money than anyone else and then traded him to another team. Why would a team do that? Let's say that LeBron had told the Cavs that there was no way he would remain in Cleveland but that he was willing to play in, for example, Minnesota (stop laughing). The Timberwolves might have been willing to overspend for LeBron because it would be the only way to acquire him. And the Cavs would've at least gotten some players in return for him.

The salary cap deals on a per-season basis. When you hear about players signing a $100 million contract, that contract is for multiple years. Kevin Garnett of the Minnesota Timberwolves signed a $126 million contract in 1998, but it is spread over a ten-year period.

One for the money, two for the show: Player salaries and league rankings

The Los Angeles Lakers got the most for their money on a team and star basis during the 2009–10 season. The Lakers won the NBA championship despite being ranked 13th in terms of the size of their payroll ($77 million to be exact). That was approximately $40 million less than the Cleveland Cavaliers, the NBA's highest-paid team, who did not even advance to the Eastern Conference finals.

Player salaries do not always correspond to player value. For example, during the 2010–11 NBA season, Kevin Durant of Oklahoma City led the league in scoring, Kevin Love of Minnesota led the league in rebounding, Steve Nash of Phoenix led the league in assists, and Matt Bonner of San Antonio led in three-point shooting percentage. And yet, because some of them are so new to the league and another (Nash) chose to remain in Phoenix rather than sign for more money elsewhere, none of those players ranked among the top 50 in the league in player salaries.

Some teams are notorious for spending foolishly. Since the dawn of the new millennium the New York Knicks have been among the league leaders in spending, and in that time had yet to win a single playoff series. In 2009–10, for example, the Knicks had the league's second-largest payroll ($114 million) and finished 29–53.

In many ways, then, a team's most important figure is not its leading scorer but its general manager, or GM. The GM is the person who decided which players to pursue, whom to trade or whom to draft, and how much a franchise is willing to spend on someone.

Bargains and busts, 2010–11

Here's a peek at some salary numbers for the most recently completed NBA season. The highest paid player is Kobe Bryant of the Los Angeles Lakers at $24.8 million for one year. Hard to argue with that. The Lakers have won two consecutive NBA championships with Kobe leading them.

And who is the lowest paid player? Well, multiple players earn the league minimum of $473,604.

Hands down, the best bargain had to be Kevin Love of the Minnesota Timberwolves. The third-year player led the league in rebounding (15.2, the highest average in eight years) while earning just $3.6 million for the year. Sure, that's a lot of loot, but more than 150 players made more than Love in 2010–11.

What was the worst fleecing? Rashard Lewis, who played 31 games each with the Orlando Magic and Washington Wizards, was the league's second-highest paid player ($19.6 million for one year). Lewis missed nearly one-fourth of the season, 20 games. When he did play, the 12-year veteran averaged a solid but unspectacular 16.3 points and 5.6 rebounds per game, but not stats for the second-highest-paid player in the NBA.

The greatest basketball achievement

Many basketball historians point to Wilt Chamberlain's 100-point game in 1962 as a great achievement, a record that will never be broken. That may be true; Chamberlain's achievement may be up there with DiMaggio's 56-game hitting streak in baseball. But when it comes to the greatest achievement in basketball, I have to vote for Oscar Robertson averaging a triple double per game for the course of an entire season.

A triple double is achieved when a player records at least double figures in scoring; rebounding; and assists, blocks, or steals. This statistic is a true measure of a player's all-around abilities.

During the 1999–2000 season, Jason Kidd of the Phoenix Suns and Chris Webber of the Sacramento Kings had five triples doubles to lead the entire league. During the 1961–62 season (the same year that Wilt had his 100-point game and averaged a record 50.4 points a game), Robertson averaged a triple double for the course of an entire season. Now just think about that!

The then-Cincinnati Royal averaged 30.8 points, 12.5 rebounds, and 11.4 assists that year. He's still the only player in NBA history to achieve that feat. Two years later, he averaged 31.4 points, 11.0 assists, and 9.9 rebounds a game, so he nearly did it again. Robertson actually averaged a triple double over his first 308 career NBA games.

Robertson showed these all-around abilities early in his college career. Playing for the University of Cincinnati in his first college game in 1959, Robertson scored 45 points, grabbed 25 rebounds, and handed out 10 assists in a victory over Indiana State. He finished his college career with 10 triple doubles.

During his pro career, Robertson accumulated 181 triple doubles, 43 more than Magic Johnson of the Los Angeles Lakers, the man for whom the statistic was invented.

Following are the NBA career leaders in triple doubles:

Oscar Robertson	181
Magic Johnson	138
Jason Kidd	107*
Wilt Chamberlain	78
Larry Bird	59

* Kidd is still active

Coaching in the NBA

The San Antonio Spurs have won four NBA titles since 1999, all of them with future Hall of Famer Tim Duncan at center and coach Gregg Popovich seated on the bench. Popovich is one of the most respected men in the NBA, but he is fond of saying, "At the end of every season I thank Tim Duncan for allowing me to coach him."

The NBA is a players' league. When future Hall of Famer Dennis Rodman signed with the Dallas Mavericks near the end of his career in 1999, he had it written into his contract that practices would be optional. (Dallas was a bizarre team. When then-assistant coach Donn Nelson told rookie Leon Smith to run laps during Smith's very first day of practice, Smith sassed back, "Run 'em yourself!")

In 2001, Allen Iverson was named the league's MVP. The following season his coach, Larry Brown, criticized Iverson for being chronically late for practices. "We're sitting here, I'm supposed to be the franchise player, and we're in here talking about practice," ranted Iverson in what would become a notorious YouTube clip. In the rant Iverson used the term "practice" more than 20 times.

For all the problems that a star player may cause, if he can flat-out play, chances are that he will remain and the coach will be jettisoned. In 2011, Utah Jazz coach Jerry Sloan got into a locker room tiff with the team's best player, Deron Williams. No one knows for certain what happened next, but it appeared that behind the scenes the team's management questioned Sloan's authority in disciplining Williams.

The next day Sloan resigned, right in the middle of the season. At the time Jerry Sloan had been the longest-tenured coach in any of the three major professional sports, having spent 23 seasons coaching the Jazz. Oddly enough, two weeks later the Jazz traded Williams. That's coaching in the NBA.

Deal of the century

In 1976, the NBA, covetous of such talents as Julius Erving and George Gervin, agreed to merge with the American Basketball Association (ABA), which had been considered a pariah by the more established league throughout its ten years of existence. The NBA agreed to adopt four of the six existing ABA teams: the Denver Nuggets, the Indiana Pacers, the New Jersey Nets, and the San Antonio Spurs.

Two other ABA franchises — the Kentucky Colonels and the Spirits of St. Louis — were offered financial packages but were not permitted to enter the league. In exchange for agreeing not to contest the merger, the Spirits' owners struck a deal that, at the time, did not seem too beneficial: They would collect one-seventh of the national television revenue from the four teams (Denver Nuggets, Indiana Pacers, New Jersey Nets, and San Antonio Spurs) that were taken into the NBA. Under the terms of the agreement, the NBA agreed that this deal would run in perpetuity — in other words, forever.

In the first year of the deal, the Spirits' owners split only $273,000. But the league soon became home to Magic Johnson and Larry Bird, and it began to prosper. To date, the owners have collected $46 million — with not a dollar spent on overhead.

The Colonels' owners, by the way, accepted a $3 million settlement. In retrospect, by investing in the NBA's future, the Spirits made a far wiser decision.

Great coaches command respect from their players, which makes those players perform with a purpose. In the NBA, that is difficult to accomplish for two reasons: The season is very long, and it is difficult to get respect from players who earn millions more dollars per year than the coach does. The average NBA coach makes $3.5 million per year, which would usually put him below any of his five starters on the team's salary scale.

Phil Jackson, who retired at the conclusion of the 2010–11 season, was a master of the art of communicating with his players. One of the reasons is that he never sought the limelight. When he coached the Chicago Bulls, as soon as the season ended (usually with a championship), he was off on his motorcycle to Montana. He is not afraid to be himself, and above all his other outstanding characteristics, he is honest with his players. Being honest allows him to be a great communicator. He sells pure water, not magic medicine.

In the last two decades Jackson was the most successful coach in professional sports. He led his teams to 11 world championships. No coach has ever won more NBA titles; only three have won more games. No coach has a higher winning percentage in the regular season or in the playoffs, either.

Jackson would be the first to agree that he had the tremendously good fortune of coaching three of the greatest players ever to lace up shoes, Michael Jackson with the Chicago Bulls and then Shaquille O'Neal and Kobe Bryant with the Los Angeles Lakers. But he might also remind you that it takes a certain talent to earn those players' trust and respect.

In his later years, Jackson seemed to wear a perpetually wry grin on his face, this Montana backwoods type amused by sharing the same courtside view with celebrities such as Jack Nicholson. He never seemed to be overly upset. When his Lakers lost to the league's worst team, the Cleveland Cavaliers, in their final game before the 2011 All-Star Break, Jackson did not fume. He simply said, "I think our guys started their All-Star break early."

As Laker fans panicked — that loss was the team's third straight — Jackson remained calm. After the All-Star break Los Angeles won 15 of its first 16 games.

It is no coincidence that neither Michael Jordan (Figure 13-1) nor Shaquille O'Neal won an NBA Championship in their first seven years in the league. Then each won a title, with Jackson as their coach, in their eighth seasons.

O'Neal had such respect for Jackson from the beginning that he went to Montana in the summer of 1999 to meet with him about the coming season. Jackson was straight up. He told O'Neal that he had to get in better shape and make some adjustments to his game.

This quote by O'Neal that appeared in the October 14, 1999, edition of *USA Today* summarizes what I mean about player respect leading to a championship: "He's a white version of my father. Big guy. Bad back. Knows the game. Played the game. Understands the game. He expects a lot out of me and isn't afraid to tell me. They're so much alike it's kind of scary. People always say there's somebody that looks like you and acts like you out there. That's like my father and him (Jackson)."

Figure 13-1:
Basketball
great
Michael
Jordan.

Most victories, NBA coaches

1. Don Nelson, 1,335 (four teams). Nelson never won an NBA championship as a coach, although he won five as a Hall of Fame member of the Boston Celtics.

2. Lenny Wilkens, 1,332 (six teams). Led the Seattle Supersonics to the 1979 NBA championship. His 1,155 losses are the most in NBA history, but he still won more than two-thirds of his games.

3. Jerry Sloan, 1,221 (Utah Jazz). No coach ever won more games with one team, but Sloan never led the Jazz to a championship.

Twice his team lost in the NBA Finals to Michael Jordan's Chicago Bulls.

4. Pat Riley, 1,210 (three teams). Riley led the Los Angeles Lakers to four championships and the Miami Heat to a fifth. He coined the term "three-peat" as a challenge to his Lakers to win a third straight championship — which they did.

5. Phil Jackson, 1,154 (Chicago Bulls, Los Angeles Lakers). Eleven NBA championship rings says it all.

Gone but Not Forgotten: The ABA

You could write an entire book about the now-defunct American Basketball Association; in fact, Terry Pluto wrote an outstanding and hilarious one entitled "Loose Balls." I highly recommend it.

Between 1967 and 1976, the ABA existed from paycheck to paycheck — many of which bounced — as it attempted to take on the far more established NBA. The league's cast of characters included the likes of future Hall of Famers Artis Gilmore, George Gervin, and Julius Erving.

The ABA was the counter-culture league for a counter-culture era. It used a red, white, and blue basketball and tried many gimmicks that the NBA has since adopted as its own: the three-point shot, cheerleaders or dancers, and the All-Star Game slam-dunk contest, just to name a few.

Bob Costas got his start announcing games for the Spirits of St. Louis; the late Morton Downey, Jr., former talk-show host, owned part of the league's inaugural champions, the New Orleans Buccaneers.

Between its colorful characters and its penchant for playing above the rim, you were far more likely to see a dunk in 1970 watching an ABA game than an NBA game — the ABA might have survived if cable TV had been around at the time. If you were lucky enough to see an ABA game, or have ever watched footage, you will notice that today's NBA is much more similar to the ABA than to the NBA of that era.

No One Like Wilt

Befitting his stature on the basketball court — and off it — Wilt Chamberlain's statistical feats remain larger than life nearly 40 years since his retirement. The 7'1" Chamberlain, who played for the Philadelphia Warriors, Philadelphia 76ers, and Los Angeles Lakers, was as dominant a force as the NBA has ever seen.

Consider just these five statistics associated with his name, besides the well-known 100-point game, figures that are mythic in scale:

✔ Most Rebounds, One Game: 55, Philadelphia Warriors (vs. Boston Celtics), Nov. 24, 1960.

✔ Most Free Throws Made, One Game: 28, Warriors (vs. New York Knicks), March 2, 1962.

✔ Highest Scoring Average, One Season: 50.4, Warriors, 1961–62.

✔ Highest Rebounding Average, One Season: 27.2, Warriors, 1960–61.

✔ Most Minutes Per Game, One Season: 48.5, Warriors, 1961–62. (Imagine that! A regulation game without overtime is only 48 minutes.)

Women's Pro Hoops: The WNBA

Women's basketball may never be as popular as the men's game, but in recent years the sport has made strides, especially on the collegiate level. The WNBA, the women's professional league, has tapered off in popularity after its initial few seasons.

Starts and stops

Women's leagues have been started in the past, but all have failed. The Women's Basketball League (WBL) lasted from 1979 to 1981, followed by the Women's American Basketball Association (WABA), which held out from October to December 1984. The National Women's Basketball Association (NWBA) was in existence from October 1986 to February 1987, but no games were played. The Liberty Basketball Association (LBA), which outfitted its players in Lycra unitards and set the rims 9'2" above the court, opened shop in the winter of 1991 before folding after one exhibition game.

When we published the first edition of *Basketball For Dummies,* two women's professional leagues existed: the American Basketball League (ABL) and the WNBA. I said in that book that two leagues would not last. The ABL lasted two years until the WNBA, with the NBA's financial and marketing backing, overpowered the ABL.

The WNBA's evolution has been a series of fits and starts. Only three franchises — the New York Liberty, Phoenix Mercury, and Los Angeles Sparks — remain both intact and in the same cities from the time the league made its debut in the summer of 1997. To be fair, only two NBA franchises (the New York Knicks and the Boston Celtics) can make the same claim from the league's inaugural season in 1946–1947. 'Anyone remember the Providence Steamrollers?

Still, it is unfortunate that the Houston Comets, who won the league's first four championships behind the dominant trio of Cynthia Cooper, Sheryl Swoopes, and Tina Thompson, no longer exists. The Detroit Shock won three titles and then moved to Tulsa.

Twenty different franchises have existed in the league's 15 seasons, an era that has been marked by constant upheaval. The current roster of teams is shown in Table 13-2.

Table 13-2	WNBA Teams 2011
Eastern Conference	*Western Conference*
Atlanta Dream	Minnesota Lynx
Connecticut Sun	Los Angeles Sparks
Chicago Sky	Phoenix Mercury
Indiana Fever	San Antonio Silver Stars
New York Liberty	Seattle Storm
Washington Mystics	Tulsa Shock

Cynthia Cooper

Who is the only professional basketball player to be league MVP, lead the league in scoring, and play on the championship team each year between 1997 and 1999? It is Houston Comets guard Cynthia Cooper.

When the WNBA began in the summer of 1997, Cooper was an unknown entity. The league's PR machine did not use Cooper in the forefront of its campaigns until the final week of the season, when they realized her star quality.

What she accomplished was truly incredible, because Cooper was no young lady when the league began. She had played on two NCAA Championship teams at Southern California with Cheryl Miller in 1983 and 1984. She was a role player on those teams; even the McGee twins (Paula and Pam) received more attention. Later, Cooper took her game to Spain, where she led the league in scoring at 45 points per game. She also played on the United States Gold Medal team at the '88 Seoul Olympics. Other scoring championships followed in various foreign lands, but we never heard much about it. Not until, in her thirties, she became the best player in the WNBA over its first four seasons.

The D-League

Men's professional minor league basketball leagues come and go in the United States You may recall the USBL or the CBA. Currently, the only minor league of note is the NBA Developmental League, or D-League. Unlike the aforementioned leagues, the D-League is owned and operated by the NBA and serves as a de facto minor league to the NBA.

The D-League launched in autumn of 2001 with eight teams. Currently it has 16 teams with entertaining handles such as the Fort Wayne Mad Ants and the Rio Grande Valley Vipers.

Unlike major league baseball, more than one NBA team may be affiliated with a single D-League franchise. For example, a member of the Sioux Falls SkyForce is just as likely to be called up by the Miami Heat as the Minnesota Timberwolves. Those two teams are affiliated with Sioux Falls.

The D-League offers players hoping to make it in the NBA an option without having to relocate overseas. That said, many young players have spent a season or two abroad and been enriched by their cultural education. Still, the D-League allows up-and-comers to stay home.

In 2009–2010, a record 27 players were called up at some point of the NBA season. Most were offered no more than a ten-day contract or two, but some, such as Sundiata Gaines of the Utah Jazz, remained on the roster the rest of the season. In his first week with the Jazz, Gaines hit a game-winning three-pointer against the Cleveland Cavaliers, who had the league's best record that season.

The Harlem Globetrotters

The Harlem Globetrotters, who have been around for 70 years, once walked a fine line between pro basketball and pure Vaudeville. The Harlem Globetrotters have changed their style of play since we wrote the first edition of *Basketball For Dummies.* They still put on a show before and after the game and during time-outs, but for the most part, the games are more conventional contests against legitimate teams.

Their new style received the most attention at the 2000 Final Four in Indianapolis when they played and defeated a team of college all-stars.

Historically, the Globetrotters have been America's Goodwill Ambassadors of basketball, playing exhibition games around the world. The shows were structured like a basketball game; however, the team played by its own rules. The opponents on any given night were simply straight men for the team's antics. Players have been known to drop-kick half-court shots, hide the ball under their jerseys, or climb on each other's backs for lob dunks. But their style of play was (and still is) true family entertainment — and the greatest basketball show on earth.

Highlights in the history of this unique team include playing in front of the largest crowd ever to see a basketball game — 75,000 fans in 1951 in Berlin's Olympic Stadium. In 1954, the team played the first night event in the history of Wrigley Field; they brought in their own portable light system for a summer evening's exhibition. In the 1940s, the Globetrotters arrived in Peru while a Civil War raged. The Peruvians were so anxious to see the Globetrotters play that a cease-fire was declared for a few days until the team left town.

While the Globetrotters' play has been exhibition in style, other teams have developed strategies from it. The Globetrotters were the first team to use a fast-break offense, and they also developed the weave offenses you see some teams run today.

Three Globetrotters players stand out:

- ✔ Former guard Marques Haynes was a virtuoso of ballhandling. To this day, you still hear television announcers refer to a good dribbler as doing "a Marques Haynes imitation."

- ✔ Goose Tatum joined the team in 1942 and was a legendary comedian who brought many routines to the team's exhibition.

- ✔ Meadowlark Lemon joined the team in 1954 and was the "Clown Prince of Basketball," bringing unprecedented interest to the team.

Today, the Globetrotters are still going strong, playing a schedule of events that includes up to 20 games/performances a month.

Chapter 14

International Basketball

In January of 2010, Troy Justice, an NBA executive, emigrated to India to spread the good word of basketball in the world's second-largest country. India, a nation of 1.2 billion people, has never produced an NBA or WNBA player. Not even close.

Justice's primary mission was to cultivate the game across the heavily populated but, outside of cricket, largely sports-oblivious country. One month after his arrival, however, he came upon a 14-year-old boy who already stood seven-feet tall. That lad, Satnam Singh Bhamara, has since been given a full scholarship to a sports academy in Florida with the intent of developing enough to at least earn a college scholarship. In this chapter, I explore the synergy between American basketball and the international game. In the past 20 years, the United States has aggressively exported its game, especially to Europe, and in return, the rest of the world has developed players at a rate that would have seemed absurd beforehand. Twenty-five years ago, the idea of a foreigner earning a roster spot, much less starting, on an NBA team appeared far-fetched. In the past decade three foreign-born players (Tim Duncan, Steve Nash, and Dirk Nowitzki) have won the league's Most Valuable Player award, and Nowitzki led the Dallas Mavericks to the 2011 NBA title.

The exchange is a two-way street. Professional leagues abroad, most notably in Europe, are a haven of modest wealth for American players who find themselves one rung below the NBA talent level. The NBA, on the flip side, has provided jobs for players from all over the world. The infusion of such talent will only accelerate as the children being raised in the homelands of these players — pioneers, really — are inspired to duplicate their feats.

How Hoops Took Over the World

Archeologists claim that the Mayans of Mexico played a crude form of basketball centuries ago. The game was crude not so much because the "basket" had no net but because members of the losing team were sometimes beheaded. In the last half-century, however, James Naismith's invention has mushroomed into a vast empire. Basketball poles are planted in the ground all over the globe, their backboards and rims stationary flags claiming yet another land as hoops territory. This section explains how basketball took over the world.

We would be remiss if we did not remind you that Naismith himself was born and raised in Canada. The game has always had international seasoning.

Winning at the 1960 Olympics

The 1960 Olympics in Rome provided the initial spark for interest in basketball beyond American shores. The United States Olympic team, whose backcourt (that is, the duo of guards) was composed of Jerry West and Oscar Robertson, was one of the best squads ever assembled — the first "dream team," if you will.

That summer the United States won its Olympic contests by an *average* of 42.4 points per game. No game ended by less than a 27-point margin, and that was the gold medal game in which the United States beat Brazil, 90–63. In a preliminary round game versus Japan, the United States won 125–66.

The Japanese attempted to guard low-post player Jerry Lucas, who stood 6'8", with a 6'3" player. To the credit of Lucas, a brilliant man who is an internationally renowned memory expert, he memorized phrases in Japanese and other languages so as to converse with his opponents throughout the tournament.

Many of the sport's true believers consider the 1960 Olympic team, coached by Hall of Famer Pete Newell and shown in Table 14-1, to be the best amateur squad of all time. In 2010, in fact, they were inducted into the Basketball Hall of Fame as a single entity.

Table 14-1		1960 U.S. Olympic Team Roster		
Name	*Position*	*School*	*NBA Years*	*Hall of Fame*
Jay Arnett	F	Texas	2	No
Walt Bellamy	C	Indiana	13	Yes

Name	Position	School	NBA Years	Hall of Fame
Bob Boozer	F	Kansas State	11	No
Terry Dischinger	F	Purdue	9	No
Burdette Haldorson	F	Colorado	--	No
Darrel Imhoff	C	California	12	No
Allen Kelley	G	Kansas	--	No
Lester Lane	G	Oklahoma	--	No
Jerry Lucas	F	Ohio State	13	Yes
Oscar Robertson	F	Cincinnati	14	Yes
Adrian Smith	G	Kentucky	11	No
Jerry West	G	West Virginia	14	Yes

The Rome Olympics were the first to be televised on a significant global scale, and as with the 1992 Dream Team, people were captivated by this club's excellence. Winning was a foregone conclusion, but you don't get to witness utter mastery in sports very often.

Losing at the 1972 Olympics

The 1972 Olympic final between the United States and the Soviet Union in Munich remains the most controversial international game ever played. That game ended an American streak of 36 years of international Olympic competition without a loss. Until then, making the U.S. Olympic squad was equivalent to earning a gold medal.

The controversy centered around the game's final three seconds. The Soviets trailed by one with three seconds left and had to in-bound the ball from under its own basket. A series of incredible misunderstandings between the officials, the timekeeper, and the coaches allowed the U.S.S.R. three attempts at the last play. On the final try, Alexander Belov scored to give the U.S.S.R. a 52–51 lead. The Americans, outraged by the officiating, refused to accept their silver medals.

Yugoslavia defeating the Soviets

At the 1976 Olympics, the Yugoslavians spoiled a much-anticipated Cold War rematch between the United States and the U.S.S.R. by defeating the Soviets in the semi-final game. Everyone stateside wanted to see an American team coached by Dean Smith of North Carolina and led by Adrian Dantley of Notre Dame exact revenge on the Russians. Despite the fact that the United States won in the gold medal game, Yugoslavia's success gave that country and others that were not considered "world powers" hope, and it stimulated worldwide interest in basketball.

Touring American college teams

In the 1970s, college teams began touring Europe; the NCAA adopted legislation that allowed college teams to make a foreign tour once every four years. Touring was a cultural exchange, hoops style, and everybody benefited. College teams were afforded a unique bonding experience, a chance to play in front of some truly hostile crowds, and a fantastic getaway. The Europeans were in essence taking a Berlitz course in basketball from the very best tutors around.

DIGGER SAYS

My trip with the Notre Dame team in 1979 was memorable. We traveled to Yugoslavia for a two-week tour in late May. The Yugoslavians at that time had just won the European Championships and had won 14 straight games against the previously indomitable Soviets. We beat the Yugoslavs on our first night in Belgrade, leaving the country in shock. Bill Hanzlik hit a shot to win at the buzzer. Judging by the fan reaction, you'd have thought that Archduke Ferdinand had been shot all over again and that World War I was about to be relived.

The great Drazen Petrovic

In 1980, I was teaching at a clinic in Sibenek and came upon what seemed to be a 16-year-old European Pete Maravich. This guy just shot and shot and shot and seemed to swish every attempt effortlessly. An interpreter told me, "That's Drazen Petrovic, the next great international player."

I knew from the first time I saw Drazen shoot that I wanted him at Notre Dame. In the fall of 1984, Notre Dame played host to the Yugoslavian national team. After the game, Petrovic indicated that he'd be coming to Notre Dame as a student the following fall. I was ecstatic. David Rivers and Drazen Petrovic would have given us the best amateur backcourt in the world, never mind the NCAA.

Alas, Petrovic signed with a professional team in Spain, Real Madrid, which paid him something in the neighborhood of $350,000 a year — $350,000 more than I could pay him. I was heartbroken.

Petrovic did eventually cross the pond, playing five years in the NBA with the Portland Trail Blazers and New Jersey Nets. On June 7, 1993, however, he was tragically killed when his car skidded off rain-slick pavement on the German autobahn.

Petrovic's death was a national tragedy. On the day of his burial in his hometown of Zagreb, more than 100,000 people gathered in the town square. His entire country, which was at the time embroiled in a bitter civil war, stopped fighting for one day to mourn the untimely death of Europe's most gifted basketball player.

Dream Team 1

The 1992 U.S. Olympic basketball team — the first American entry to the Olympic Games to be composed of professional players — took the game to new heights worldwide. The portal to such an ethereal assemblage of talent was opened three years earlier by FIBA (the International Federation for the Sport of Basketball), when a 56–13 vote allowed "open competition" in Olympic basketball. That score (56–13) was also the average margin at half-time of a typical Dream Team I game, or so it seemed.

Coach Chuck Daly's team was perhaps the most talented and famous group of athletes assembled in the history of sport. Of the dozen players who wore the red, white, and blue in Barcelona, ten were named to the NBA's list of the 50 Greatest Players, which was announced in 1996. The team averaged 117 points per 40-minute game, which is the equivalent of 140 points per NBA game (which lasts 48 minutes).

Table 14-2 shows the roster, including each player's scoring average, for the best American-only team ever assembled.

Table 14-2		1992 Dream Team	
Player	*Position*	*NBA Team*	*Points per Olympic Game*
*Charles Barkley	F	Phoenix Suns	18.0
*Larry Bird	F	Boston Celtics	8.4
*Clyde Drexler	G	Portland Trail Blazers	10.5
*Patrick Ewing	C	New York Knicks	9.5
*Magic Johnson	G	LA Lakers	8.0
*Michael Jordan	G	Chicago Bulls	14.9
Christian Laettner	F	Duke University	4.8
*Karl Malone	F	Utah Jazz	13.0
Chris Mullin	F	Golden State Warriors	12.9
*Scottie Pippen	F	Chicago Bulls	9.0
*David Robinson	C	San Antonio Spurs	9.0
*John Stockton	G	Utah Jazz	2.9

* Named to NBA's list of 50 Greatest Players

HALL OF FAME

The NBA goes international

The 1995–96 Chicago Bulls, a club that won an NBA-record 72 games in one regular season, was deservedly called the best basketball team in the world. It was also the best basketball team of the world.

Chicago's top eight players that year represented four countries and three continents. Center Bill Wennington was Canadian (he still is, but you know what I mean). Toni Kukoc, winner of the NBA's Sixth Man Award for the 1995–96 season, was Croatian. Center Luc Longley was Australian. Only Scottie Pippen, Michael Jordan, Dennis Rodman, Ron Harper, and Steve Kerr (who is American but was born in Lebanon) were Yankee Doodle Dandies.

International Players Infuse the U.S. College Ranks

An increasing number of international players are also making their mark — and three-pointers — at U.S. colleges. In 1984, the last time an all-amateur U.S. team won an Olympic gold medal, only 25 foreign-born players competed in NCAA Division I basketball. In 2010–11, at least 500 foreign-born players were on D-I men's basketball rosters. (A similar number of foreign-born females played for D-I women's teams.)

The 2011 National Champion Connecticut Huskies featured a 7'0" center, Charles Okwandu, from Lagos, Nigeria, and a forward, Niels Giffey, from Berlin, Germany. Neither started, but both were two of the first three players off the bench for Jim Calhoun's NCAA champs.

Beginning in 1997, when Tim Duncan, a native of the Virgin Islands, was selected first overall in the NBA draft by the San Antonio Spurs, five foreign-born players have been selected No. 1 overall. They are Michael Olowakandi (1998) from Nigeria, Yao Ming (2002) from China (see Figure 14-1), Andrew Bogut (2005) from Australia, and Andrea Bargnani (2006) from Italy.

Did you notice in that list that no two players were from the same continent? Not "same country," but same continent? Basketball is not just extending its scope in certain pockets of the world, but rather anywhere that the sun rises. Sure, hoops is more popular in regions where height and athleticism are more prevalent (such as in Eastern Europe and central Africa), but it is ecumenical. Anywhere there is a hoop there is potential for someone to grow up and play in the NBA.

Figure 14-1:
Yao Ming.

Lost in translation: The Enes Kanter saga

Enes Kanter is a native of Turkey and stands 6'11". Born in 1992, Kanter will likely be a prominent rookie or second-year player at least by the time you read this. Unlike most international NBA stars, Kanter emigrated to the United States in high school and hoped to play college basketball. It's just that the NCAA would not let him.

Kanter's talent is off the charts. At the Nike Hoop Summit in 2010, where the world's best pre-college talent assembled, Kanter scored 34 points and had 13 rebounds against a U.S. squad of blue-chip talent that included Kyrie Irving, Jared Sullinger, and Harrison Barnes. Kanter had signed a letter-of-intent to enroll at Kentucky for the 2010–11 season on scholarship.

The problem? A few years earlier Kanter had played limited minutes for a professional team, Fenerbahce Ulker, in his native Turkey. His expressed plan was to simply play to gain experience, and his family only accepted enough money — about $33,000 in U.S. dollars — to cover his travel expenses. Enes turned down much larger offers from more prominent clubs because he did not want to put his NCAA eligibility in peril.

Kanter still enrolled at Kentucky and spent the 2010–2011 academic year in Lexington as a student assistant coach. He worked out with the Wildcats but of course never appeared in a game. Kentucky advanced to the Final Four but lost to eventual national champion UCONN in a semi-final. I'm sure Kentucky coach John Calipari will forever wonder how things might have gone differently in that game if the NCAA had not ruled Kanter ineligible.

Kanter was the #3 pick of the 2011 draft by the Utah Jazz.

The world is gaining on the United States, basketball-wise. Although that may be bad for American nationalism, it's great for the sport. During the 2010 NCAA tournament, charismatic players such as Venezuela native Greivis Vasquez of Maryland and Australian Matthew Dellavedova of St. Mary's were memorable for their high-energy and slightly unorthodox styles. Both played brilliantly as well. The tallest player in that tournament was 7'3" Greg Somogyi, a Hungarian who played for UC-Santa Barbara. The man who hit the biggest shot of the tourney, Ali Farokhmanesh of Northern Iowa (his three-pointer buried number 1 seed Kansas) is the son of an Iranian Olympic volleyball player.

The infusion of international players, both male and female, into the U.S. college game will only continue to increase. With the stricter academic entrance requirements now set by the NCAA, the number of academically eligible players in the United States is shrinking. Meanwhile, the global popularity of NBA stars has accelerated the growth of the sport abroad. The talent gap between United States and international teams will continue to narrow with each Olympics.

It's a different game

The international game is not played exactly the same way as the American game. During the Olympics, international rules apply, which are used everywhere but in the United States. Here's a list of the major differences between the American game and the international game.

- ✔ **The trapezoidal lane:** The international game uses a three-second lane that is trapezoidal instead of rectangular. (The wider end of the trapezoid is at the baseline.) The idea behind the trapezoid is that the lower an offensive post player sets up near the basket, the farther away she has to place herself from the basket — unless she wants to be whistled for a three-second lane violation. The trapezoid is actually a clever shape to use.

- ✔ **Three-point distance:** In the international game, the three-point distance is 6.75 meters, or 22'2". It's a tougher shot than college ball's 20'9", but easier than the NBA's 23'9" from the arc (and 22' in the corners)

- ✔ **The shot clock:** In international games, the shot clock is 30 seconds, skirting the middle between college (35) and the NBA (24).

- ✔ **The game period:** In international play, a game consists of two 20-minute halves — same as college, but shorter than the NBA's four 12-minute quarters.

- ✔ **Offensive goal-tending:** Offensive goal-tending is now legal.

Hoops Cultural Exchange: International Influence on the American Game

For years, Africans, Asians, and Europeans played the game without undue American influence. The game developed differently as players from those countries gave it their own flavor. Thus the international game has some glaring differences in style from the American game.

Offense, for example, rules. The French played better defense against Germany in WWII than you're likely to see them play today in a European Championships outing. International games remind me of Arena Football: Whoever scores last usually wins.

Watch an NBA or college game now. If you compared it to a game in the mid-1970s, for example, you'd see a few of the newfangled sights that I discuss in this section. All of these owe a little credit to the influence of international hoops, international players, and their ideas.

Outside shooting by big men

More and more frontcourt players in the NBA and on college teams are deft outside shooters. Big men abroad — as in wide *and* overseas — are not known to revel in banging elbows inside. As a result, tall players from abroad are more fond of shooting the three-pointer in international play and now do so in the NBA.

Two great examples of this in the NBA in recent years are Dirk Nowitzki of the Dallas Mavericks and Mehmet Okur of the Utah Jazz. Both are seven-foot-tall Europeans. Nowitzki is from Germany and Okur from Turkey. Both have had five seasons in which they've made at least 80 three-pointers (roughly one per game) and both are approximately 38 percent shooters from beyond the arc. That's a terrific percentage for a player of any size, and an all but unheard of accuracy mark for a seven-footer.

By comparison Kevin Garnett, an American-born seven-footer who also likes to play from the wing as opposed to the low post, has never made more than 37 threes in a season and is a career 28 percent shooter from outside the arc.

Skip passing

The skip pass is a wing-to-wing pass that skips one of the passes normally used — such as a pass to the point guard at the top of the key — to get the ball to the other side of the court quickly.

The international style of play, where the three-point shot and zone defenses are the norm, features the skip pass (so that the offense can shoot three-pointers against a zone defense). The skip pass is an effective way to move the ball around the perimeter, because the defense can't move as fast as the ball. An open wing shot is usually the result.

Better passing

International players grew up in countries where soccer was the dominant sport. Players who have a soccer background have a greater appreciation for spacing and passing in order to move the ball and find an open shot. Kobe Bryant may be able to go one-on-two in the NBA, but he'd never be able to do that with long-term success in the English Premier League.

The three-point shot

The trey was a major contributor to the downfall of the United States in international competition in the mid-1980s. The United States lost international games in 1986 and 1987 and then in the 1988 Olympics because they did not have outside shooters who could match the precision of their international opponents. Not coincidentally, U.S. colleges did not adopt the three-point shot until 1987. (The NBA had adopted it in 1979.) The three-point shot proved to be a great equalizer. I wonder if the NCAA would have adopted the shot if foreign teams had not been humbling college teams with such regularity during that era?

A more perimeter-oriented game

The trapezoid-shaped lane has made for a more perimeter-oriented game at the international level. Thus, when international frontcourt players come to the United States, their perimeter skills are superior. They know how to play facing the basket (in other words, they can rely on more than just their pivot moves).

The myriad talents and superior footwork of athletes such as Pau Gasol of the Los Angeles Lakers and Dirk Nowitzki of the Mavs — players who don't try to out-bang the defender but rather out-finesse them — has made the game more aesthetically pleasing.

Dribble penetration, then kick out for the three-pointer

When a guard dribbles into the lane, she draws a crowd. Two and sometimes three defenders converge on her, making it hard to attempt a shot. But what if the guard acts as a decoy? What if the goal of her penetration is to draw the defenders her way, thus freeing up a teammate outside the three-point circle? All the guard must do is pass the ball to her teammate, who shoots an uncontested three. International players had this ploy down cold long before Americans began copying it.

A 1986 exhibition game between the Providence Friars and the former Soviet Union changed the face of basketball in this country. In that game, held at Providence, the Soviets introduced the dribble penetration ploy. When the defense collapsed upon the dribbler, he kicked the ball out to a teammate — usually on the wing — who would find himself with an open three-pointer. The tactic was quite literally a foreign notion to American hoops purists at the time.

Although the Friars won the game 91–88, the U.S.S.R. shot 30 of its 46 shots from beyond the arc. If the Soviets had made more than just 7 of 30 treys, they probably would have won.

Then-Providence coach Rick Pitino was smart enough to copy the ploy. The Friars led the nation in three-point shooting that year (with an average of 8.24 treys per game) and marched all the way to the Final Four.

Hoops Cultural Exchange: American Influence on the International Game

Basketball was invented in America; how's that for influence? So was McDonald's, which seems to be a daily staple of the international hoopster's diet. Here are a few more American traits that have rubbed off on international hoops.

Improved ballhandling

Between the 1936 and 1972 Olympics, Soviet guards had trouble handling pressure defense. Their coaches saw that they had to improve ballhandling to the level of American guards. In 1988, the Soviets won the gold in part because the Americans were unable to pressure them into committing turnovers.

Improved perimeter defense

For a long time, international players never seemed to deny the pass to the wing or pressure outside shots. International players were rough when the ball was passed inside — around the three-second lane — but they never devoted much effort to denying the initial penetration. Now, having been burned often enough by quicker American guards, they have begun playing tough defense outside.

Development of the inside game

Although the larger (because it's trapezoid-shaped) three-second lane makes it next to impossible for a center to set up close to the hoop, the lane can work to his advantage if he's quick. Tim Duncan, for example, dominates in international play because he has more room to maneuver after he gets into the lane. International players are going to have to become quicker on the inside to contend with him.

Why the rest of the world has caught up with the United States

The challenge to American dominance by foreign imports is not restricted to auto sales; basketball has witnessed international players close the gap on Americans in the last decade as well. That direction is only natural. The learning curve was steeper for players abroad — they were so far down that they had more room for dramatic improvement. The following factors contributed to the improvement:

- ✔ **Television:** Even in India, which sits halfway around the globe and where cricket is the sport of choice, NBA games are televised most every night.

- ✔ **Foreign imports:** Since 1986, when the Prop 48 rule increased the academic entrance requirements for freshmen in college basketball, foreign players have been gaining recognition as a talent source. By and large, international players are older, more mature, and ready to make an impact right away.

- ✔ **American exports:** Because the money was there early, many United States players who failed to make NBA rosters emigrated to European leagues, especially in Italy, Greece, and Israel. This phenomenon became especially popular in the 1970s and still happens frequently today. The American players were exciting to watch, so the locals went to see them play and became more and more interested in the game. Not only that, but the locals began copying their American hoops heroes.

Worldwide Hoops: Top Pro Leagues

Basketball has spread as quickly across Europe in the last quarter century as the Latin language once did nearly two millennia ago. Virtually every European nation has one or more professional leagues, as does Israel, Australia and China.

Take a look at a few nations where pro hoops is flourishing.

✔ **England:** The British Basketball League (BBL) was launched in 1987. The league consists of 12 teams located throughout England and Scotland. The season runs from early September through early April. The league's all-time leading scorer is a man whose name would please any anglophile: Peter Scantlebury. He now coaches the Sheffield Sharks.

✔ **France:** The LNB (Lique Nationale de Basket) also staged its inaugural season in 1987–88. The LNB has an A division and B division, each of which has 18 teams. The A division features the upper echelon teams. At the end of the season the two lowest A division teams are relegated to the B division while the top two B teams are promoted. Alumni of the LNB include Tony Parker of the San Antonio Spurs and Nicholas Batum of the Portland Trail Blazers.

✔ **Germany:** The Basketball Bundesliga (BBL) consists of 18 teams; the season runs from October through April. The league began in 1966, though predecessor pro leagues in Deutschland go back all the way to 1939. TSV Bayer Leverkusen is the perennial powerhouse of the German league, winning 14 championships, but ALBA Berlin has won eight titles since 1997.

✔ **Greece:** In Greece, unlike most of Europe, basketball outranks soccer in popularity. The HEBA A1 or Greek Basketball League was founded, believe it or not, back in 1927. Over the years, Olympiakos and Panathinaikos have maintained a rivalry not seen in the Mediterranean since the tilts involving Greece and Troy. The 14-team league competes from late September to mid-May.

✔ **Israel:** Pro basketball is well represented in Israel, where the Ligat HaAl has 12 teams and was founded in 1954. The Maccabi Tel Aviv team is the near-perennial champion, having won 48 titles since the league's inception, including 23 straight from 1970–92. In 2005, Maccabi Tel Aviv defeated the Toronto Raptors in an exhibition game played in Toronto 105–103.

✔ **Italy:** LEGA Serie A of Italy, founded in 1920, is one of European basketball's more formidable pro leagues. Cities throughout Italy are represented in the 16-team A League, which also has a B series league (lower in stature). The LEGA Serie A season runs from mid-September to May, when a champion is crowned.

✔ **Spain:** The Liga ACB (the Asociacion de Clubs de Baloncesot) has a rich history of basketball. Eighteen teams are in the league, which was founded in 1956 as Liga Nacional, and the season runs from mid-September through May. Real Madrid and FC Barcelona, two clubs with a strong soccer rivalry, have nearly as strong a rivalry in basketball. Liga ACB may be the best of the international basketball leagues.

International Basketball Tournaments

FIBA (the International Federation for the Sport of Basketball) is basketball's international governing body. Currently, 214 national member federations belong to FIBA. (The acronym FIBA is derived from the French *Federation International de Basketball Amateur.* The word *amateur* was dropped in 1989, but the A remained. Who wants to belong to an organization named *FIB?*)

FIBA consists of five zones: Africa, the Americas, Asia, Europe and Oceania. (Oceania represents Australia and the islands of the South Pacific.) This section discusses major FIBA basketball tournaments played internationally.

The Olympic Games

Twelve countries compete in Olympic basketball every four years. The host country automatically qualifies, as does the winner of the most recent World Championship game (assuming that the winner is not the host country). Each of FIBA's five geographic zones receives one spot for the Olympics. The remaining five or six spots (depending on whether the host country qualifies anyway by winning the prior World Championships) are awarded to the top five or six finishers at the most recent World Championships.

The Olympic tournament represents the top international competition in the world and is held every four years as part of the Summer Olympic Games. Each region of the world (Africa, Asia, Pan America, Europe, and Oceania) is represented. Upon qualification, the 12 competing nations are divided into two six-team pools.

National teams compete against others within the same pool in a round-robin format, meaning that each team plays one another once. Hence, each team within a pool plays five games.

The top four teams within each pool, based upon their record, advance to the medal round. The medal round is single elimination, so in effect you have eight teams playing quarterfinals, then semi-finals, then a final. The two losers of the semi-final games square off to see who will win the bronze medal. The two winners meet in the gold medal game, with the losing team earning the silver medal.

The United States men's team has dominated Olympic competition and is 123–5 all-time. Check out Table 14-3 for details.

Table 14-3	Past Olympic Medalists in Men's Basketball		
Year	*Gold*	*Silver*	*Bronze*
1936	United States	Canada	Mexico
1948	United States	France	Brazil
1952	United States	Soviet Union	Uruguay
1956	United States	Soviet Union	Uruguay
1960	United States	Soviet Union	Brazil
1964	United States	Soviet Union	Brazil
1968	United States	Yugoslavia	Soviet Union
1972	Soviet Union	United States	Cuba
1976	United States	Yugoslavia	Soviet Union
1980	Yugoslavia	Italy	Soviet Union*
1984	United States	Spain	Yugoslavia
1988	Soviet Union	Yugoslavia	United States
1992	United States	Croatia	Lithuania
1996	United States	Yugoslavia	Lithuania
2000	United States	France	Lithuania
2004	Argentina	Italy	United States
2008	United States	Spain	Argentina

*The United States did not compete in the 1980 games in Russia because the entire U.S. Olympic contingent was participating in a boycott. Likewise, the Russian teams did not compete in 1984.

The European Championships

The European Championships, also known as EuroBasket is perhaps the most prestigious basketball tournament held outside the United States. Europeans are rabid hoops fans, and NBA stars such as Dirk Nowitzki, Pau Gasol, and Peja Stojakovic all first distinguished themselves at this tournament. Twenty-four teams compete, and five advance to the World Championships.

The first European Championships were staged in 1935 in Geneva, Switzerland. Latvia defeated Spain, 24–18, in the gold medal game. Since 1947, the tournament has been held biennially in odd-numbered years. The Soviet Union, which is now defunct, has won the most EuroBasket titles with 14. Spain, which was the runner-up in that 1935 gold medal game, won its first EuroBasket in 2009 behind MVP Pau Gasol, who also won an NBA championship with the Los Angeles Lakers that year.

A modern-day Maravich?

In 2005, at the age of 14, Ricky Rubio became the youngest player in Spain's ACB League, one of the top professional leagues in Europe. At 17, he started for Spain against the United States in the Olympic Gold Medal Game. In 2009, he became the first player born in the 1990s to be selected in the NBA draft, when he was selected as the fifth overall pick by the Minnesota Timberwolves.

Rubio has not appeared on the radar of most American basketball fans because he has continued to play professionally in Europe, but he is expected to play for Minnesota in the NBA in 2011-12. He helped F.C. Barcelona win the EuroLeague championship in 2010 and was in the second year of a six-year contract with that club in 2011.

His style of play captivates those who watch him. At 6'4", he has an aggressive slashing style that includes trick shots and moves and innovative passes that remind many of Pete Maravich. His boyish good looks resemble a basketball version of Justin Bieber.

One of the biggest reasons I think Rubio will be a star in the NBA some day is that he plays defense.With a 6'9" wingspan, he has already been named Defensive Player of the Year in the EuroLeague (2008–09) and led the league in steals

"He's an amazing defender," said Kevin Durant, who played against Rubio in the FIBA World Games of 2010. "I think one thing that stood out to me was how he pressured the ball."

The Pan American Games

NBA players often take part in the World Championships and the Olympics, but not in the Pan American (Pan Am) Games, which are held every four years and feature nations from the Western hemisphere (i.e., the Americas). Usually, the Pan American Games are staged the year prior to the Olympics, though they have no bearing on who competes in the Olympics.

Some of the more memorable moments involving the United States and international hoops have been the province of the Pan Am Games. In Indianapolis in 1987, for example, Oskar Schmidt, one of the best long-range shooters any country has ever produced, led Brazil to an unbelievable 120–115 backyard upset of the United States. That game was a watershed moment in international hoops because a U.S. national team had never lost a game to a foreign team in the United States — let alone in Indiana, America's holy land of hoops. Schmidt scored 46 points. I woke up early the next day to see if the sun would rise. It did, but nothing is a given anymore after that loss.

The FIBA World Championship of Basketball

This major international tournament involves national teams from 24 countries throughout the world. The tournament has been held every four years since 1950 for men and since 1953 for women.

Like the Olympics, each region of the world is represented. Both the men's and the women's World Championship are staged every four years at a different site.

National teams compete in four six-team pools, with the top four teams in each pool advancing to a 16-team knockout (i.e., single-elimination) round. It's like the NCAA's Sweet Sixteen from that point on until the championship game.

The 2002 FIBA World Championships were held in Indianapolis, Indiana, and much like the 1987 Pan American Games I noted earlier (also held in Indy), they provided a wake-up call for USA Basketball, the national governing body for the sport. Despite hosting the tournament, the United States finished a disappointing sixth. It marked the first time that a U.S. team composed exclusively of NBA players lost a game in international competition.

Part of the problem was the roster. Many of the NBA's top players, such as Kobe Bryant and Shaquille O'Neal, declined to participate.

The 2002 FIBA World Championships was the advent of a U.S. decline in international hoops that would last for the better part of the decade. The 2004 U.S. Olympic team failed to medal in Athens, despite being made up entirely of NBA players.

The humiliation of Athens woke up USA Basketball. It appointed long-time Phoenix Suns CEO Jerry Colangelo to select the team for the 2006 FIBA World Championships. Colangelo appointed Duke's Mike Krzyzewski as head coach and told players that if they wanted to play in the 2008 Olympics in Beijing, they'd need to play in the 2006 FIBA World Championships. Although the team finished with the bronze at the FIBA Worlds, they ultimately won the gold medal in Beijing.

What caused the change in attitude among the NBA's top-tier players? Maybe it was the experience of competing against foreign-born players in the NBA night in and night out over the previous six or so years. The 2002 debacle might have seemed like an anomaly back in the last days of the Michael Jordan era.

The NBA's first Cuban player

Although the year 2000 will long be remembered for the Elian Gonzalez controversy, it was also the first year a Cuban played in the NBA.

Lazaro Borrell, a 26-year-old rookie, defected to the United States during the Pre-Olympic Qualifying Tournament in San Juan, Puerto Rico, in July, 1999. A 21-point per game scorer in the Argentina Basketball League the previous year, he was the top player on the Cuban National Team.

But Borrell's dream was to play in the NBA, so he defected to the United States with the help of the Miami-based Cuban American Foundation, which arranged for a van to steal him away during the tournament from his hotel in Puerto Rico.

Borrell (full name: Lazaro Manuel Borrell Hernandez) worked out for many teams over the summer and was signed by the Seattle SuperSonics. He took English classes three times a week in the fall of 1999, and he eventually made the team. He played in 17 games in 2000 and averaged 3.6 points per game for his 167 minutes of play.

Although Borrell missed his family, he said his freedom makes the sacrifice worthwhile: "Even though I'm alone, I'm free to conduct my life as I want to," he says. "I'm surprised how open the opportunities are (in this country)."

The following year Borrell played in the Continental Basketball Association (CBA), a now-defunct minor league in the U.S., before joining pro leagues in Puerto Rico and Argentina. He retired in 2007.

By 2008, however, what with foreign-born players such as Tim Duncan, Steve Nash, and Dirk Nowitzki winning NBA MVP hardware, the level of respect for international players was finally where it belonged. Ironically, only when American-born NBA players were able to accept that foreign-born players were their equals were they able to defeat them again on the international stage.

Part IV
And You Don't Have to Pick Up a Ball

"Just how much do you think you can embarrass me? If you think I'm going to the basketball game with you wearing those ridiculous socks, you're sadly mistaken!"

In this part . . .

This part is your ticket to understanding how to focus on the game . . . on television, in a stadium, on the radio, or on the Internet. I tell you everything I look for when I'm watching a game, from checking out the defense to monitoring the tempo. I also clue you in to some great magazines and publications, give you the 4-1-1 about fantasy games, and suggest places to visit where you can get your basketball fix.

This part also details the phenomenon of March Madness. I explain the all-important NCAA tournament bracket, and how to pick the winning teams!

Chapter 15

You Don't Need to Play to Be a Fan

The title of this chapter may be the all-time understatement in roundball. No sport, not even football, is as widely and enthusiastically embraced by television as basketball. ESPN, ESPN2, ESPNU, ESPN3, TNT, TBS, ABC, Fox, and CBS all televise college or pro games; ESPN televises multiple high school basketball all-star games. And I haven't even broached the topic of other special packages on DirecTV.

A typical season runs from early November to — thanks to the creation of the WNBA — after Labor Day. During that time, a typical viewer has access to more than 1,000 men's and women's games if she has DirecTV. Watching all 1,000 games would be impossible. (Then again, there is the miracle of TiVO.) But for some folks, 1,000 games is a fervent goal.

For the last 17 years, I've been a basketball studio analyst at ESPN. This job has rekindled my fandom for hoops. Also, because I'm paid not only to sit there and look spiffy (complete with matching tie and highlighter) but also to discuss what I see, I have honed my skills as a couch-potato connoisseur of the game. You can do it, too — as long as you promise not to take my job.

Following a Game on TV

You'll get a lot more out of watching a basketball game on TV — or even live — if you do more than watch the ball go into the hoop. This section gives some insider tips for catching the *real* action and increasing your enjoyment of the sport.

Anticipate the next pass

Try to think like the players. When you can anticipate the next pass, you are as connected to the players as you can be from your living room. You're thinking like the players.

Where a player passes the ball depends on a few factors: what type of ball handler he is, which teammates are on the floor, what type of offense the team is running, and what type of defense the opposition is running. See, you have to know what's happening on the court.

Pretend that you're the point guard. Analyze the defense and then make decisions about how you would react. Did the point guard on television act accordingly? Disregard this tip if you're watching old highlights of Magic Johnson. Nobody could predict what he was going to do with the ball.

Watch the action away from the ball

While you're watching, don't be afraid to stray away from the ball. Follow the action away from the ball on the *weakside* (the side of the court opposite the ball), or watch the *post* action (down near the basket). Of course, the television camera's eye is yours, and it usually follows the ball; but most cameras show the court from the side and give a decent half-court view of the proceedings.

Here are some things to look for:

- ✔ Pushing and shoving underneath the hoop
- ✔ Weakside screens (picks that players set on the side of the court away from the ball)
- ✔ Rick Pitino's white suit for special games at Louisville

All are entertaining sideshows to the main event.

By watching action away from the ball, you can answer your own questions as well as other viewers' questions. For example, if Dwayne Wade of the Miami Heat is such a terrific shooter, why doesn't the defense do a better job of denying him the ball? Answer: Watch Wade while the Heat are running their offense. Nobody in the NBA is better than him at using picks set by teammates to get an open shot. You can argue that Wade earns his buckets not so much when he shoots the ball but when he leaves his defender behind a pick.

The inveterate hoops fan is one who uses the Previous Channel button on her remote only if both ESPN and CBS are broadcasting college hoops simultaneously on a Saturday afternoon. This kind of fan can spot the alley-oop play before the pass is ever thrown. She follows the weakside and notices the *backpick* (a weakside pick that frees a player who's cutting toward the basket) being set on the alley-ooper's defender.

When to avoid James-vision

Watch the other players on the court besides the star. LeBron James is fun to watch, but don't keep your eyes on him all the time. Many great players are in each game, and you may miss something. Miami Heat teammate Chris Bosh is just as fun to watch maneuver underneath or how he goes after an offensive rebound. Or, focus on an unsung player for five or six straight trips down the court, and you'll find out a lot about him. DeJuan Blair of the San Antonio Spurs was a rookie in 2011 who had a big impact on the Spurs success. Does he hustle back on defense? Does he "take a series off" (that is, fail to hustle on a trip down the court) on defense once in a while? If you watch Blair, you will see the answer is no.

When to get James-vision

Whether the star of the game is LeBron James or your local high school phenom, watch his every move in crunch time. Chances are with the game on the line, he is going to be the focal point. He is an outstanding passer and rebounder, but chances are the winning play will start with LeBron.

Sometimes the game's star is not the team's best player, but the guy with the hot hand that evening. Keep an eye on him. Then during the next game, when he reverts to the form of a mere mortal, try to see whether he's doing anything differently.

Follow stats

You can keep stats yourself as you watch, or you can rely on the television statisticians to follow more than the score. Some of the less discussed but fun stats to track are offensive rebounding, points off turnovers, points in the paint, and bench scoring.

You can also follow this online while the game is in progress. A lot of basketball junkies will follow the boxscore of a game they are watching. On ESPN. com you can follow just about all college boxscores through the live stat link. They also update the team's cumulative stats after the game.

If you look at the 2011 final regular season game between Duke and North Carolina in Chapel Hill, a game that decided the ACC regular season title, you see that North Carolina won points off turnovers 15–11 and made four three-point goals, four for the Blue Devils. But the key to North Carolina's 81–67 win was points in the paint. The Tar Heels dominated inside with a 44–20 margin in points in the paint. And while North Carolina didn't shoot a lot of threes, they were 4–9 compared to just 6–27 for Duke.

Watch the officials

Officials can dictate the pace of the game. If they're whistle-happy, they can slow the pace. Neither team can find a rhythm when the officials are calling a foul on every possession. If an official makes a *grandstand call* (a call that draws attention to the official) by running into another official's area to make a call, this is a bad sign. If an official overrules another official, this may mean that the first official thinks he is bigger than the game.

Officials can also take a team out of its offense or defense by calling a game too tight (whistling too many fouls) or too loose (seldom blowing the whistle). Some teams play more physically than others, and their success can hinge on how much contact the officials will allow.

The best officials are the ones you don't know or don't remember. When an official does the extra little things on a call, like throwing in a little extra body English, he draws too much attention to himself. That's bad. Conversely, officials must keep a game from getting out of hand. They can do so by communicating with the players and then, if necessary, calling a technical foul or two.

Who are the top officials? All officials are evaluated at every game in college and the NBA. You can tell who the top ones are by who gets the best games to call, like the Final Four. Table 15-1 shows the officials who have called the most Final Fours and thus would be considered the best officials over the last 50 years.

Table 15-1   Top Officials: Most Final Fours Worked Through 2011

Rank	Official	Time Span	Number
1.	Jim Burr	1985–06	15
2.	John Clougherty	1985–00	12
3.	Ed Hightower	1988–08	10
4.	Tim Higgins	1988–04	9
	John Cahill	1995–11	9
5.	Ted Valentine	1992–10	8
6.	David Libbey	1994–03	7
	Hank Nichols	1975–86	7

Rank	Official	Time Span	Number
7.	Tony Greene	2001–09	6
	Irv Brown	1969–77	6
	Ed Corbett	2001–08	6
	Dick Paparo	1984–95	6
	Curtis Shaw	1999–10	6
	Lenny Wirtz	1961–79	6

What I Watch For

Having coached for as many years as I did, I may watch a basketball game differently than you do. For example, I still have to remind myself that no matter how much I scream at the TV, the refs can't eject me. That's a nice change. Here's what I look for:

Check out the defense of both teams. Whenever Bill Raftery of ESPN broadcasts a game, he establishes the first defensive set from the opening tip. In his staccato voice, Raftery says something like, "Duke opens man-to-man."

As you sit there, ask yourself, "Are they playing man-to-man? Matchup zone? Two-three zone?" The defense acts as a harbinger for what type of game it will be. If one team has a great one-on-one player and the opponents are playing man-to-man, you're in for a show. It also means the team playing man-to-man defense is not afraid of that star player. Perhaps the team has a defensive stopper to contend with the great offensive threat.

See who is controlling the offensive rebounding. The team that controls the boards (rebounds) usually controls the game. Keep an eye on which specific players are grabbing the boards, too. Look for tendencies. Are the guards getting the offensive rebounds? If so, that team is taking quite a few outside shots, because long shots lead to long rebounds.

Pay attention to tempo. If you are watching the New York Knicks play the New Orleans Jazz, tempo will be huge in determining the outcome. The Knicks are one of the highest scoring teams in the league and want to get the ball out on the break with Carmelo Anthony on the team.

The New Orleans Hornets, coached by one of my former players, Monte Williams, is closer to a half-court team that wants a slower tempo. Both teams were successful in 2011, but went about it in contrasting ways.

Watch what happens after a time-out. Has the coach changed defenses or a specific man-to-man assignment? Is the offense running a set play for one particular player?

When a team scores on its first possession after a time-out, that's a sign of a good coach. The coach can see a flaw in the opponent's defense and can take advantage of the flaw with a special play that leads to a matchup and a score.

Are a lot of turnovers occurring early in a game? Is either team capitalizing on them? Those turnovers are in effect extra possessions. Forcing turnovers is one thing, but scoring off them is another. You have to score off turnovers to make them worthwhile.

Who's got the hot hand from the free throw line? Free throw shooting is usually contagious. If you shoot free throws well early in the game, you may gain confidence late in the game at crunch time. In the opposite direction, missed free throws earlier in the game (like so many variables in a basketball game) often foreshadow what will transpire at the end.

How is an injury influencing the game? Whether suffered before or during the game, an injury to a key player can dramatically alter his team's style of play.

What adjustments did the teams make at halftime? The first five minutes of the second half often dictate the rest of the game. During that time, each coach wants to make adjustments in strategy or lineups to take control of the game or get back in the game — whatever the case may be. For example, if you are ahead by ten at the half, you want to withstand the first five minutes of the second half because the opposing coach is going to try out her adjustments. If you are behind by ten, you want to insert all your half-time adjustments in the first five minutes of the second half. You want to make the adjustments work early so that you can build your team's confidence. Cut that ten-point deficit to five by the first media timeout in the second half and you are in business.

Notice substitution patterns and scoring by players who come off the bench. A team that substitutes often tells the viewer one of the following:

- ✔ Our bench is deep.
- ✔ Our starters are not that much better than our bench players.
- ✔ We plan on running a lot and hope to wear out our opponent.

Observe what's happening and then deduce *why* it's happening, and soon you'll be the guru of your sports bar (if you should aspire to such lofty heights).

You don't keep score in hoops by tallying bench points, but — like offensive rebounding — they usually dictate who wins. When I had a good bench, I always felt that the job of my subs was to increase the lead (assuming we had it) by five to seven points. In 1977–78, the year Notre Dame went to the Final Four, our bench had three future NBA players: Bill Hanzlik, Bill Laimbeer, and Tracy Jackson. I knew that those three subs were going to be better than my opponent's subs. So I set goals for those subs to increase the lead when they were in the game for their four-minute interval. I charted the points like a plus-minus statistic in hockey (See *Hockey For Dummies*).

To get a *plus-minus statistic,* you simply keep track of each team's scoring while a player is in the game. For example, Jackson would have a +6 figure if our lead increased by six points while he was on the floor. You can chart this statistic for each player.

Which team went on a scoring run and why? A *run* (which I used to call "spurt time" when I coached) occurs when one team outscores the other by a significant margin in a certain period, such as a 12–2 run in the first four minutes of the second half. A run normally is the by-product of good defense by one team and turnovers by the other. Runs seem to be more dramatic and occur more often in college ball, perhaps because one team gets too tight and begins to worry about the opponent's run, which only makes the situation worse. The same thing often happens with football in the Super Bowl.

Who will be tired down the stretch? Because of the plethora of TV and game time-outs (in NCAA tournament games, each media time-out lasts 2½ minutes), combined with better-conditioned athletes, player fatigue is not as large a factor at the end of a game as it once was. The best way to spot fatigue is to watch for players bending over and grabbing their shorts during free throws. These are the players who are starting to run out of gas.

Watch for the key matchups. Watching for the key matchups is probably more important in the pro game because those teams play man to man a high percentage of the time.

When the Chicago Bulls played the Miami Heat in the 2011 NBA playoffs the matchup between the Heat's Dwyane Wade and the Bulls' Derrick Rose was very important in determining the outcome.

What is the field goal percentage differential? It's halftime and the stats flash on your TV screen. Say that Miami (FL) is shooting 16 percent better from the field than its opponent, Clemson, but Miami (FL) has only a two-point lead. What does that tell you?

Answer: Miami (FL) is in trouble. Shooting usually evens out during the course of a game due to a coach's halftime adjustments. But Clemson is probably rebounding better or scoring more points off turnovers. The general rule: A team should have a lead equal to half its field goal percentage differential. In other words, Miami (FL) should be up 8 points, not 2.

Televising basketball

Believe it or not, in 1972 college basketball was only televised regionally. As for the NBA, you need only to travel back in time to 1981 to find an NBA championship game between the Boston Celtics and Houston Rockets that was not televised live. (CBS aired the game on tape delay after the local news.)

The NBA had a national television contract as far back as the 1960s, but most of those games were joined in progress because the stations left only a two-hour window on Sunday afternoon. The average NBA game lasted 2 hours and 10 minutes, so tipoff would be at 1:50 p.m. Eastern time. Ten minutes later, ABC would come on the air with the score something like 10–8.

TVS's Eddie Einhorn is responsible for the two most crucial national broadcasts in college basketball history. Fittingly, he was inducted into the Naismith Basketball Hall of Fame in 2011 for his contributions to the game. In 1968, Houston upset UCLA, 71–69, in the first made-for-TV regular-season contest at the Astrodome. Einhorn's TVS syndicated the game nationally, and the results proved to the networks that college hoops was a viable product. Televising college hoops may not seem revolutionary now, but consider that, at the time, even the NCAA semifinals were not televised. When Houston and UCLA met in a Final Four semifinal for a rematch later that season, few people got to see the game. Six years later, the TVS cameras were in South Bend for Notre Dame's regular-season victory that ended UCLA's 88-game winning streak.

Two years later (in 1975–76), NBC purchased rights to a weekly national college basketball package. Notre Dame, I'm proud to say, was the most-televised team in that package.

Following a Game on the Radio

Sometimes radio is the only way to follow your favorite team, especially when it is playing on the road. Listening can be even more captivating than watching on TV, because your imagination replaces your eyes. And there's more suspense, too, because if you don't see the play developing, you are more susceptible to being surprised. The crowd reaction time to a play versus the announcer describing it to you is akin to seeing lightning first and then hearing thunder. The crowd roar always slightly precedes the announcer's explanation, which creates — you guessed it — electrifying moments.

Good play-by-play announcers are descriptive and tell you what's happening; good analysts tell you why. The play-by-play person is information; the analyst is theory. The play-by-play person tells you how a player floats in for the dunk; the analyst tells you how the player got open for the dunk.

Even though many people keep stats when watching a game on television, keeping stats is more appropriate when listening to a game on the radio. Your eyes are free to look down at the paper without missing anything, and you can become more involved with what's happening. You just can't see Dwight Howard's Superman tattoo.

Following Your Team on the Internet (a.k.a. "Cyberspace Jam")

The Internet is a great source of information about particular teams and even the sport itself. You can follow your team on the Internet in three ways:

- ✔ **Listen to Internet broadcasts.** Most college and pro teams broadcast their games on the Internet. So if you're a Minnesota Timberwolves fan and you're out of town, you can bring your computer and listen to the game over your laptop. To locate the Internet site, call the team's or school's public relations (PR) department. (Information about NBA Internet broadcasts is available at the league's web site. Or just Google it and the link will come up.

- ✔ **Look at in-game Internet reports.** More and more teams are becoming sophisticated with their Internet sites, including the use of video. Some organizations have one person at their press table transcribing the play-by-play over the Internet, while other people shoot photos of the game and transmit them to the site. Duke University was one of the first schools to use photos over the Internet. Today, many colleges and NBA teams post postgame video interviews with players and coaches on their websites. The NBA's website provides live stat updates for every game.

- ✔ **Download Internet releases.** Every college and certainly every pro team — as well as the NBA office and some college conferences — has an Internet site. Expect to find such items as team rosters, statistics, bios of top players, and coaches' notes available for downloading. Teams usually update these facts on a game-by-game basis. So if you want to know who's starting, who's healthy, or who's leading the squad in steals per minute played, head to cyberspace for the most up-to-date info.

Subscribing to Magazines and Other Publications

Every hoops junkie needs to read about the sport in addition to watching games on TV — what else are you going to do when no game is on? Here are my top publications for following hoops:

✔ *USA Today:* "The Nation's Newspaper" provides daily updates of scores and stats, along with features and commentaries.

✔ *Sports Illustrated:* A feature-oriented weekly magazine that provides insight into players, coaches, and teams. People read it for the features and in-depth reporting on issues bigger than simply the games.

✔ *The Sporting News:* Also has features, but it's more statistics-oriented than *Sports Illustrated.* More acclaimed as a baseball publication, this weekly covers hoops from December through the NBA playoffs.

✔ **In-house publications:** Most college and pro teams produce a weekly publication during the season devoted to that team. For example, Kentucky has *CatsPaws,* which covers Kentucky athletics from cover to cover. The reporting in these publications is biased because most of them are owned by the school or franchise, but they're a good way to keep up with your team.

✔ *Basketball Times:* A national publication produced weekly during the season and monthly in the off-season. It has the largest compilation of basketball-oriented columns in the country. This publication, originally produced by the late basketball writer Larry Donald, is one of the best for keeping up with hot hoops topics.

✔ *Blue Ribbon Basketball Yearbook:* The most complete of the pre-season college basketball yearbooks. This is a truly impressive and exhaustive resource year in and year out that will, if you really love college hoops, be dog-eared by mid-January. *Blue Ribbon* gives a neat one-page summary on every team, complete with roster, schedule, and outlook. This publication comes out late (usually December 1), so it won't whet your appetite in the preseason, but it can serve as an in-season bible.

✔ *Basketball Almanac, Publications International Ltd.:* A yearly publication that's handy for the basketball fanatic. This publication provides a full-page bio with complete career stats on every veteran NBA player, bios on the top NBA rookies, a two-page feature on each team, and the NBA schedule. For the college game, it offers a one-page outlook on the top 64 teams and a page summary of the top 100 players. It's also the only publication I've found with a short bio on everyone in the Basketball Hall of Fame.

Watching Your Child Play

Although you may not be in shape to play, or you may not be a fan of any school or pro team, you can certainly be your own child's fan. This duty comes with being a good parent.

The number-one fan

The title of this chapter is "You don't have to play to be a fan." Barack Obama, the 44th president of the United States, is a big fan, but he also still plays the game.

It was a relatively uneventful Thanksgiving week in 2010, so the President had some time to play his favorite game with some friends at Fort McNair, Washington, D.C. In the course of this game, he was elbowed by Rey Decerega, the director of programs for the Congressional Hispanic Caucus Institute. Blood flowed and the president received 12 stitches to his lip. The injury required a statement from press secretary Robert Gibbs, a former NC State soccer player in his own right.

Hoops has always been a big part of Obama's life, and his love of the game has only enhanced the game's reputation nationwide. His personal assistant, (well, his bodyguard) is former Duke basketball captain Reggie Love, who was also a top receiver on the Blue Devils football team in the mid 2000s.

On election day, 2008, President Obama had a midday game of hoops with a roster of players that included ESPN.com's Andy Katz. You can go on the White House website and see an Obama interview with Marv Albert of TBS. The interview takes place on the full outdoor basketball court at the White House. In 2011 he presented former Boston Celtics legend Bill Russell with the Medal of Freedom, the first NBA player to receive the honor.

There are other basketball connections in his family as well. His brother in-law, Craig Robinson, was in his third year as head coach at Oregon State in 2011.

And best of all, each year he fills out his complete NCAA Tournament bracket with Katz on ESPN. The first year he did it, he correctly picked North Carolina as the winner.

All politicians talk about creating good family values. What could be more basic than attending one of your child's games, or better yet, taking her to a local court to play the game with her yourself?

Don't relive your youthful dreams through your kids. Let them decide that they like the game, let them play for fun, and give them nothing but encouragement. Sure, that includes giving them some hints based on mistakes you may have made when you played, but always remember that it's just a game.

Participating in Fantasy Leagues

You want to own your own basketball team, but you don't have millions of dollars to spend? No problem! These days, becoming the owner and general manager of your own basketball franchise is easy. Welcome to the world of fantasy basketball.

More and more fans are enjoying basketball by participating in fantasy (or *rotisserie*) leagues. These imaginary leagues are popping up all over the United States. Some have money or other prizes at stake, and others are simply a competition for pride.

Participating in a fantasy league can be an enjoyable way to watch basketball and to get more out of it. The competition can be both fun and challenging — and in some cases, profitable.

Setting up a fantasy league

To form a league, you can gather friends in your community, at your office, or in your college dorm. (They don't even have to be friends.) The size of the league can vary, but if you're putting together an NBA fantasy league, you don't want it to be too large because there are only 30 teams from which you can choose players.

Many fantasy league teams resemble all-star teams. A good, challenging league forces its participants to do their homework and make intelligent picks — that is, you probably won't end up with Dwight Howard, LeBron James, Tim Duncan, and Blake Griffin on the same team.

You can put together the team rosters in a few different ways. One way is *open bidding* (an auction of players), which usually involves a salary cap. For example, each participant may have a maximum of $200 to spend on a roster of 12 players. Of those 12 players, only ten are active in the competition at one time, with four forwards, four guards, and two centers. Again, this is just a simple example, and different leagues use different ideas.

Another way to put together a roster is to hold a *draft*. The league commissioner determines a draft order (by drawing numbers from a hat, for example), and then participants choose players in order for the first round. Usually, you flip-flop the draft order for the second round and all even-numbered rounds after that. (Drafts usually have 12 rounds total.)

You can also make up your own league rules for picking up, cutting, or trading players during the season. Some leagues charge a fee every time you change your roster; others allow trades and roster changes free of charge. The more complex the league, the more likely you'll need a secretary or statistical service to handle the standings and player transactions.

Putting together your fantasy team

Before bidding or drafting, you must know the rules that clearly affect your strategy. For example, say that ten teams are competing, and that team standings are based on overall player performance in seven statistical categories — total points, total rebounds, field goal percentage, free throw percentage, assists, three-point field goal percentage, and steals. You want to pick players who are strong in those categories.

A league can use many different categories, including percentages and ratios. The scoring in this example would go from ten points for the leader in each category down to one point for the last-place team in the category. Then each team's total points from the seven categories would determine the league standings.

You don't want players who are good in one category but struggle in others. For example, a player like Marcus Canby of the Portland Trailblazers can help you in rebounding (over ten per game in 2011), but he scores less than six points per game.

Some of the more valuable players are those who score in double figures and excel in other areas as well. Kevin Love of the Minnesota Timberwolves has turned into a fantasy league star because of his ability to record double-doubles at a record rate.

You also need to think about the player-allotment process when choosing your team. A straight draft involves some strategy. Bidding involves a lot of strategy — you may want to escalate the bidding on a big-name player, just so you can deplete your competitors' bank account. Saving money for the later rounds could lead to bargains. A lot depends on the savvy of your competitors.

In preparing for the draft, stay on top of injuries and off-season transactions. A player who is traded may not have as great an impact on his new team. Also keep an eye on the top rookies and newcomers because they can have value in the right situation. Keep track of players *during* the season as well, because potential trades in your league could affect the standings.

Visiting the Halls of Fame

A visit to any basketball Hall of Fame is a great way to improve your knowledge of the sport. There are three major Halls of Fame — the Naismith Hall of

Fame in Springfield, Massachusetts (the birthplace of basketball); the College Basketball Hall of Fame in Kansas City, Missouri; and the Women's Basketball Hall of Fame in Knoxville, Tennessee.

The modern day halls of fame are great experiences for fans of all ages. They are very kids friendly and can be an excellent initial basketball experience for a youngster. All three facilities have theatres that feature the great games, teams, players, and coaches, documenting the history of the game. All three basketball halls of fame have interactive areas where kids can shoot free throws or jumpshots. There is even a full court in the College Basketball Hall of Fame.

Each hall of fame has a college tournament in November or December at a coliseum that is near each facility. It's a great holiday trip for a family with young fans because you can take in some great college basketball and experience a hall of fame.

Naismith Hall of Fame

Located in Springfield, Massachusetts, the birthplace of basketball, the Naismith Memorial Basketball Hall of Fame promotes and preserves the game of basketball at every level — professional and collegiate, men and women.

Over 100 former players, coaches, referees and contributors to the game are nominated each year. Prior to 2011, there were three basic nominating committees — North American, Women's International, and Veterans. In 2011, an American Basketball Association Committee and Early African-American Pioneers Game Committee were added to the voting process.

This is the oldest of the basketball halls of fame. The Naismith Hall of Fame was formed in 1959 and the first building opened in 1968. Another facility opened in downtown Springfield in 1985, and in 2002 the current 80,000 square foot facility opened.

College Basketball Hall of Fame

The National Collegiate Basketball Hall of Fame, located in Kansas City, Missouri, is a hall of fame and museum dedicated to college basketball. The museum is an integral portion of the college basketball experience. The hall is meant as a complement to the Basketball Hall of Fame with a focus strictly on those who have contributed greatly to college basketball.

The facility opened in 2006 and has all the modern facilities to make this a full-day experience. You can sit at the ESPNU desk and call a SportsCenter Highlight. Kids can compare their physical attributes with those of some of the college greats of the past.

Women's Basketball Hall of Fame

The Women's Basketball Hall of Fame opened in June 1999 in Knoxville, Tennessee. It is the only facility of its kind dedicated to all levels of women's basketball. So whether you are looking for inspiration, education or just plain fun, the Women's Basketball Hall of Fame is the place to find it.

The outside of the striking 32,000 square foot hall of fame is encompassed by two amazing basketballs. The world's largest basketball is located on the north end of the hall, weighs 10 tons, and sits on top of a glass staircase that resembles a basketball net. A brick courtyard, shaped like a basketball, is located on the southern end of the facility. Many of the bricks are engraved to honor guests, inductees, and a host of others who have chosen to leave their legacy at this Hall of Fame.

Chapter 16

Filling Out Your NCAA Tournament Bracket

. . . .

In This Chapter

▶ Following the NCAA tournament from Selection Sunday to the Final Four

▶ Finding sources of information about teams when making your picks

▶ Which factors are really important in picking winning teams

. . . .

So you think there is interest in the NCAA Tournament? When UCONN played Butler for the National Championship on the first Monday in April of 2011, the game had a rating of 20.1. CBS's Sunday Night staple of programming, *60 Minutes*, had a 13.4 rating the night before.

People who don't follow sports year round follow March Madness. Why? Probably because someone at work got them hooked on the excitement of filling out a bracket before the tournament. So they follow the progress of the tournament to see if they have a chance to win a prize at the tournament's conclusion, or just have office bragging rights.

March Madness is all about filling out the bracket. Can you pick the right upsets in the 68-team, 67-game affair that dominates the sports pages, Internet sites, and SportsCenter reports for three solid weeks from mid March to the first Saturday and Monday in April?

Following the Chronology of the NCAA Tournament

Division I college basketball teams begin playing games in November, but for the best two to three dozen schools, the regular season is a lot like the first two-thirds of the Kentucky Derby. There's a lot of jockeying for position, but nothing of real consequence is at stake.

Everything changes on Selection Sunday. That, for many fans, is the real first day of the college basketball season. Take the 22-day journey from the NCAA tournament Selection Sunday to One Shining Moment.

Selection Sunday: On either the second or the third Sunday in March, at 6:00 p.m. EST (eastern standard time), the tournament draw is announced. All 68 teams, along with where and whom each one will play in the opening round, are announced on television. That is the first time the schools find out as well; there is no advanced notice provided to coaches or athletic directors.

CBS has the rights to the tournament, which it has held since 1982. The CBS network also has proprietary access to release the bracket on television before any other network (read: ESPN) may do so, which it does during a special one-hour live telecast. ESPN also has a show and I am proud to be a part of it. Our program runs for two hours, and countless other programs on the ESPN family of networks continue to break down the tournament through the wee hours of the morning.

During the announcement it used to be standard practice among fans to acquire a blank copy of the bracket and fill in the teams as the announcement progresses. Nowadays, you can print out a copy of the bracket on any number of websites within a few minutes after the conclusion of the Selection Sunday program. Old-timers still prefer to copy down the names into the brackets as they are being announced, however. Some habits die hard.

Figure 16-1 shows a sample bracket.

There were changes made to the bracket in 2011 as the tournament was expanded to 68 teams. There are now four first-round games played each year. In 2011, the games were played in Dayton, Ohio (and they will be there again in 2012). The schedule included two games on Tuesday night and two on Wednesday night. Each night there was a battle of 16-seed teams with the winner moving on to play a number 1 seed in the second round. The second game on Tuesday featured two 12th seeded teams, whereas the last game on Wednesday featured two 11th seeded teams. The winner of the game between 12th seeded teams faces a well-rested 5th seeded team at another site, whereas Wednesday's winner of the battle of 11th seeded teams faced a 6th seeded team at another site.

It is not an easy task for the winners of those four first-round games. For instance, in 2011, Clemson beat the University of Alabama-Birmingham (UAB) in the second game on Tuesday night, a contest that ended at 11:55 p.m. The Tigers reached their hotel in Tampa at 4:50 a.m., then had to play fifth seeded West Virginia just 31 hours later. Clemson had just one hour of on-court practice for that game, which was their most critical game of the season, as each succeeding NCAA tournament game is by definition. West Virginia, the far fresher team, pulled away in the second half to win.

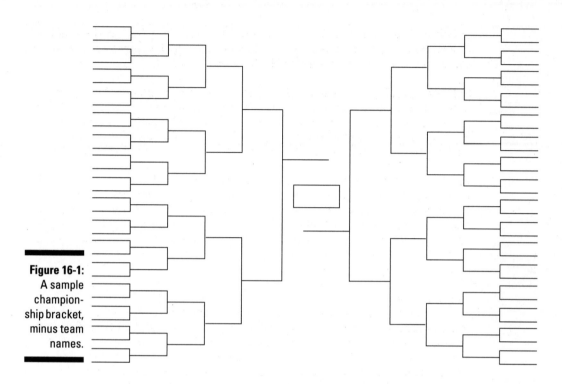

Figure 16-1:
A sample champion-
ship bracket, minus team names.

Monday: Office pool sheets are distributed. Most pools do not require an entrant to return her sheet until just before the first game of the tourney, which is now Tuesday at 7:00 p.m., eastern time. Don't forget to make a copy of your picks for yourself to peruse during the tourney.

With the new wrinkle of four first-round games, as opposed to just one, many office pool poobahs have chosen to ignore the results of that first round. Your own office pool should think about doing the same. In other words, you still do not need to turn in a completed bracket until noon eastern time on Thursday morning. As for the results of the first four games, everyone starts on the same page, and the four winners advance.

The thinking behind this gesture? An office pool is more likely to lose poten-tial participants if it demands that they hand in their completed brackets by Tuesday afternoon as opposed to Thursday morning. The more entrants in an office pool, the greater the excitement.

In a sense, you can say that these office pool directors are doing the same thing for their participants as the selection committee is doing for the first 60 teams they select for the tournament — giving them a first-round bye.

The game that expanded the field

As you can see by the following numbers, the NCAA tournament began with just eight teams in 1939. The number of teams increased slowly but surely over the years, with the number varying based on the number of conferences that had automatic qualifiers.

Prior to 1975, only one team from each conference could be selected for the NCAA tournament, which meant the conference champion (as long as it was not on probation) would go. This was a big advantage for independents like Notre Dame, Marquette, Dayton, and DePaul, because they did not have to win a conference title to get selected. They just had to win a beauty contest.

The one-team-per-conference rule changed before the 1975 tournament, and one game can be traced to the rule change. In the 1974 ACC tournament championship game, North Carolina State faced Maryland. Both teams were ranked in the top five of both wire service polls, but because of the existing rule, only one team would advance to the NCAA tournament.

Maryland had three All-Americans in guard John Lucas, seven-footer Len Elmore, and Tom McMillen. Elmore and McMillen both were chosen in the first round of the 1974 NBA draft. Four more Terrapin teammates were eventually drafted.

North Carolina State won the game 103–100 in overtime, then went on to win the NCAA tournament. At the end of the season there was such an outcry that Maryland should have at least been tendered an invite to the NCAA tournament: the Terrapins were easily one of the country's top 24 teams that year. In fact, they were probably one of the top four.

The NCAA listened and altered the rule later that spring. By today's standards, Maryland could have been a number one seed, yet didn't get into the NCAA tournament.

It was such a frustrating loss for the Terps that coach Lefty Driesell turned down a bid to the National Invitational Tournament (NIT) the following Monday, thus ending the careers of both Elmore and McMillan without playing in any postseason event as seniors.

History of Number of Teams in NCAA Tournament

Year	Teams
1939–50	8
1951–52	16
1953–74	22, 23, 24, or 25
1975–78	32
1979	40
1980–82	48
1983	52
1984	53
1985–2000	64
2000–10	65
2011–Present	68

Yes, I understand that in 2011 Virginia Commonwealth was sent to Dayton and advanced all the way to the Final Four, and for that the Rams deserve a hand. That said, these are games that we would ordinarily relegate to ESPN2 or ESPNU if they were taking place in January or February.

Thursday and Friday: Bring the TV to work or call in sick. This is wall-to-wall basketball from noon eastern to nearly midnight, and those first two days feel as if they are — or at least that they should be — a national holiday. Remember, the Super Bowl is on a Sunday. The second round of the tournament — I still cannot get used to calling it that — has elements of playing hooky and Christmas morning rolled into one.

Thirty-two games feature all 64 remaining teams. Within a 36-hour span, the tournament field is pared in half. Surprises, shocks, and upsets are to be expected. You just never know where they will come from.

Saturday and Sunday: Cinderella must prove she can dance. Any team can get lucky for 40 minutes; to survive the first weekend, however, a team must prove its mettle. These 16 games again cut the field in two, from 32 to 16. Most coaches won't admit it publicly, but if you advance past this round you can pronounce your tournament performance as, at worst, satisfactory.

Picking Your Teams Wisely

Before filling out your bracket, you can inform yourself by doing a little research. Fortunately (or maybe unfortunately), as much literature pertaining to college hoops is published each season as is literature pertaining to the economy. I draw that comparison as a reminder that no matter how much you read about either topic, you'll never solve the mystery. You will always find an exception to every bracket pickin' rule.

In-season publications and Internet sites

Following the game *during* the season is important, especially in November and December when nonconference games are more common.

Basketball Internet

When preparing to fill out your bracket, there are countless websites you can follow. You want a good combination of stats and articles to use in your preparation. The articles can fill you in on intangibles that are going on within a program (Tennessee's 2011 NCAA investigation, for example, had an effect on their outlook heading into the tournament), while the stats can also help you in matchups of teams.

Heading into the 2011 tournament, Virginia Commonwealth was the only team in the nation with six players having made at least 30 three-point field goals. That fact may have at least helped you pick them over Southern California in the first round. (Who would have predicted they could win four additional games and reach the Final Four.)

- **Warrennolan.com:** I don't know Warren Nolan, but he has a great website when it comes to statistics . . . and it is free. If you want a quick reference for every Division I team's overall record, conference mark, record against the ratings percentage index (RPI) top 50, the strength of schedule, record in the last ten games — I can go on and on — go to warrennolan.com.

  What I like the most about this site is that it updates the RPI in real time. So, if it is February 15, and your favorite team just beat a ranked team on the road, you can go to that site just 30 minutes after the game and check your team's updated RPI. That kind of road win can jump your team 15 spots and you won't have to wait until the next day to find out.

- **ESPN.com:** ESPN.com has the data, the articles, and Bracketology with Joe Lunardi. Joe picks the entire field with matchups and seeds throughout the year. It can help you pick your own bracket on pool due day by keeping you posted throughout the year as to who should be a 2 seed or a 10 seed.

  No one keeps up with college basketball throughout the year better than ESPN through data and articles. There is also a page on each team with complete stats, roster, articles and results. And I mean every team, so when it is time to get up to speed on some teams with whom you are not familiar, this is the place to go.

- **Cbssportsline.com:** CBS and its partners at Turner Sports do a comprehensive job covering the tournament, and its corresponding website keeps you up-to-date throughout the year. This site also picks the bracket late in the year and it is fun to compare the people at CBS and ESPN when it comes to who is in and who is out. This site also has an outstanding roster of writers who follow the latest stories in college basketball.

- **Basketball-Reference.com:** This site is the best when it comes to historical data on college basketball. It comes in handy when you want to determine the rate of success for a program or a coach in the tournament. You can get every Division I team's record year-by-year and historical performance in the tournament. The data is also broken down by coach.

  There are also interesting statistical dissertations on over-achieving teams and coaches over the years in the tournament.

Types of pools

The objective of any NCAA pool is the same: to correctly pick as many of the Final Four teams as possible. The most common type of pool is also the most mathematically complex. The entrant must pick the winner of each of the 67 games, all the way to the championship game. *Point system* pools — that is, how many points you receive for each winner correctly picked — vary. Check out the following four types:

✔ **Graduated point system:** A correct pick in the first round, which has 4 games, is worth 2 points apiece. A second-round pick, which has 32 games is worth 4 points; a third round, which has 16 games, is worth 8; a Sweet Sixteen game is worth 16; a regional final is worth 24; and a Final Four (that is, a national semifinal game) is worth 32 points. Correctly picking the champion is worth 50 points. This puts a premium on picking the Final Four teams correctly and does not penalize you for missing a few of the first-round upsets, which is inevitable.

✔ **One point for every game selected correctly:** Your maximum possible score is 67 points. Here, the drama tends to be at its peak during the early rounds, because 52 of the 67 games are played during the tournament's opening six days.

✔ **NCAA auction:** You bid on each team in the tourney. Obviously, a top seed commands a higher price than a number 16 seed. After you "buy" that team, it's yours for the tourney. After all the teams have been auctioned off, the auction fees go into a hat (or other safe place; I'm not married to the hat idea). The champion collects 40 percent of the pot, while the remaining 60 percent is divvied up equally among the "owners" of the other three Final Four teams.

✔ **Random draw:** The names of all 67 teams are placed in a hat (you may use a sombrero if you so choose, or even a box), and participants pick a name at random. If you want to choose more than once, you contribute double to the pot. The drawback of this game is that you can't use any of your hoops wisdom, accumulated over a season of watching games. That's half the fun of playing.

Newspapers are also helpful. Among the best are *USA Today, The Atlanta Journal-Constitution, The Washington Post, The Boston Globe, The Chicago Tribune,* and *The Dallas Morning News.* Look for newspapers that have a national college basketball beat reporter; those weekly notes columns that cover the entire country will keep you informed come March.

But don't overload that most personal of computers, your brain. Too much info can only confuse you — and how much do you plan on spending on all these journals, anyway? Will your investment exceed the return you reap if you win the office pool?

Selection Sunday shows on CBS and ESPN

At the present time, CBS and ESPN are the leading networks in college basketball coverage. They assess the game all winter, and by the time Selection Sunday arrives, they are eager (no, foaming at the mouth) to tell you about such obtuse matters as RPI (Rating Percentage Index) rankings or a school's record against teams in the Top 50 or a particular conference's power rating (how strong one conference's teams are versus another conference's).

I'm partial, but I think the ESPN selection show is better. By airtime, we have been doing nothing for the previous ten days but watching all of the conference tournaments play out. We know who's hot, and we have a ton of singularly dedicated on-air experts who are ex-players and ex-coaches, whose passion and knowledge is above reproach. But I'm not asking you to form an allegiance. If you're a complete basketball junkie, tape one show while watching the other.

Filling Out Your Bracket

I present these factors without considering whether you have a gambling problem or how many times you can stomach hearing the term "Big Dance."

Ratings

When you evaluate your bracket, consider these four major ratings:

- ✔ **RPI (Rating Percentage Index).** The RPI considers a team's strength of schedule and the strength of the schedules of that team's opponents. It has a rating and strength of schedule rating. This rating has been used by the NCAA Committee since 1981 in evaluating teams.

- ✔ **Jeff Sagarin index.** Published through the USA Today website, it gives another statistical rating of each team. It also has a strength of schedule component. The biggest difference between the Sagarin ranking and the RPI is that Sagarin takes into account victory margin.

- ✔ **Associated Press (AP) poll.** A human analysis, this poll reflects the collective opinion of members of the media from around the country. There's nothing scientific about it. How accurate is the AP poll? Well, don't use it as a guide for picking the national champion. The top-ranked team in the final AP poll entering the NCAA Tournament has gone on to win the national title just twice since 1995.

History of the term "Final Four"

The first recorded use of the term "Final Four" was listed in the 1975 NCAA Official Collegiate Basketball Guide. On page 5 in the national Preview-Review section written by Ed Chay of the Cleveland Plain Dealer, Chay wrote, "Outspoken Al McGuire of Marquette, whose team was one of the final four in Greensboro (in 1974), was among several coaches who said it was a good day for college basketball when UCLA was finally beaten.

The first time "Final Four" was capitalized was in the 1978 NCAA Official Collegiate Basketball Guide.

✔ *USA Today* **poll.** This is similar to the AP poll, except that the votes are cast by 60 head coaches nationwide. As with the AP poll, each voter picks the top 25 teams, with the number-one team receiving 25 points, the number-two team receiving 24 points, and so on down the line to the number-25 team, which receives one point. Then the numbers are added, with the highest score being ranked number one.

Strength of schedule

The NCAA Tournament Selection Committee, those enlightened ten people who select the 68 teams, do not pick the field based solely upon each school's win-loss record. Neither should you. A wide range of opponents are in Division I — remember, some 336 schools are in the lot — and you have to look at whether a school's record is artificially inflated with a slew of patsy opponents.

How do you examine schedules? Look at the strength of schedule rankings according to the RPI and Sagarin.

You can assess a difficult schedule in two opposite ways: The regular-season rigors prepare a team well for the hazards of March Madness, and the tough schedule leaves a team with battle fatigue. Alas, both theories have proven correct every year. There were examples within the Big East in 2011 because the league had a record 11 teams selected. Only two teams made the Sweet Sixteen so nine were exhausted from the rigors of the conference schedule. But UCONN won the national championship after playing 18 Big East regular-season games and 5 more conference tournament games. They were battle tested.

Player experience

You can play in all the tough gyms in the nation against all the great teams with the nastiest, most obnoxious fans, but if you haven't been to the Big Dance you haven't seen anything yet.

Consider the Butler Bulldogs in 2011. They were a number 8 seed entering the event, and were underdogs in many peoples' minds in the first round against Old Dominion. But Butler had many players remaining from the previous season's unlikely run to the NCAA championship game. The Bulldogs had tournament experience and not only beat Old Dominion, they advanced to the championship game for the second straight year.

Conversely, Louisville had an outstanding season thanks to the development of two freshmen and a sophomore who were new to the starting lineup. But those players didn't have a lot of NCAA tournament experience, and they were upset as a number 4 seed by number 13 seed Morehead State in the first round. The Cardinals were the only top four seed to lose in their first game in 2011.

Coaching experience

Coaching in the Big Dance (there is that term again) is a whole new experience as well. Only three coaches have won the NCAA tournament in their first year with a program: Steve Fisher at Michigan in 1989, Ed Jucker at Cincinnati in 1961, and Tubby Smith at Kentucky in 1998. In 2011, Brad Brownell of Clemson was the only first-year coach to win an NCAA tournament game.

Furthermore, no coach under the age of 40 has won the national championship since 1984, but three times a coach at least 60 years of age has won the title in the last decade. That includes 68-year-old Jim Calhoun in 2011.

Why is preparing a team for the NCAA tournament such a challenge?

- ✔ Teams often play other teams that they've never played before and do not have much time to scout.
- ✔ Games are played in surroundings unfamiliar to the players.
- ✔ The hysteria is unlike anything the players have seen. All three times Calhoun won the national championship with Connecticut, the Huskies were shipped far from home to the West regional. Calhoun actually considers that as an advantage because his players have a three time-zone buffer from friends and campus (not to mention the rabid East Coast media).

In general, the more experience a coach has in the tournament, the better his team's chances in the Big Dance. (See Table 16-1 for a list of the winningest active coaches in NCAA tournament games.) Duke automatically advances to the Sweet Sixteen each year on my bracket just on the strength of having Mike Krzyzewski as coach.

Table 16-1	Best Winning Percentage, Active Coaches in NCAA Play (Minimum 15 Games; through 2011 Tournament)			
Coach	*School*	*Years*	*Win/Loss*	*Percentage*
Mike Krzyzewski	Duke	1984–2011	79–23	.775
Roy Williams	Kansas, UNC	1990–2011	58–19	.753
Jim Calhoun	Northeastern, UCONN	1981–2011	51–18	.739
Billy Donovan	Florida	1999–2011	25–9	.735
Brad Stevens	Butler	2010–11	11–4	.733
Tom Izzo	Michigan State	1998–2011	35–13	.729
Rick Pitino	BU, PC, Kent, Louis	1983–2011	38–15	.717
John Calipari	UMASS, Mem, KY	1992–2011	32–13	.711
Bill Self	Tulsa, Illinois, Kansas	1999–2011	28–12	.700

Conference tourney success

Winning a conference tournament may be a harbinger of a team on a roll — but not always. Beware of teams that win their conference tournament in an upset or win the tournament for the first time in school history or for the first time in a number of years.

Over the last 27 years, the eventual NCAA Champion has won the NCAA tournament 15 times after having won its conference postseason tournament. So, it's about 56 percent, hardly a strong factor in identifying a potential national champion. In short, it's a coin toss.

Often, a team is motivated by a loss in a conference tournament (because the coach rips the players and gets their attention). Also, the practice time and rest gained from an early exit from conference tournament play can be used to fix glaring problems. Pre-tournament time is probably the most time the team has had to practice since Christmas break.

Each of the last two times North Carolina has won the National Championship, in 2005 and 2009, the Tar Heels were beaten in the ACC tournament. Roy Williams had his team's attention, and they rebounded to win six straight in dominating fashion to win the title each year.

Conference ratings

You can evaluate the toughness of a conference in two ways: *top-heavy* and *top-to-bottom*. Conferences that are top-heavy, or have four or five teams that stand out and have a top-20 ranking, usually do better in the NCAA tournament than conferences that are tough from top to bottom.

In a top-heavy conference, four or five softies are on the schedule. Play each of them twice a year, and that's eight to ten games during which you can catch a breather. The emotional strain of playing is harder than the physical strain. No coach can have his team at top intensity each game. Emotional lulls are inevitable, and a seasoned coach makes sure his team's lulls coincide with the easy games.

In a conference that's tough from top to bottom, teams often get burned out. Yes, they're battle-tested come March Madness, but they may be shell-shocked, too.

Successful programs

The cream usually rises to the top, and that can be the case when picking your bracket. Although there are upsets every year and special Cinderella stories (check the 2011 Final Four), most of the time the eventual National Champion has been there before.

Since 1999, eight schools have combined to win the last 13 National Championships, including three by UCONN, two by Duke, and two by Florida. A school from one of the six major conferences (ACC, Big East, Big 12, Big 10, PAC 12, and SEC) has won every NCAA Tournament since 1991. UNLV in 1990 was the last school from a smaller conference to win the title. In the last 20 years there have been just 5irst-time National Champions.

So, it might be a good idea to give credence for an NCAA tournament run to schools that have done well in the tournament before. Table 16-2 shows the schools with the most wins in the history of the tournament.

Table 16-2	Most NCAA Tournament Wins	
Wins	*School*	*Years*
105	North Carolina	1941–2011
105	Kentucky	1942–2011
96	Duke	1955–2011
95	UCLA	1950-2011
88	Kansas	1940–2011
60	Indiana	1940–2008
60	Louisville	1951–2011
53	Syracuse	1957–2011
52	Michigan State	1957–2011
46	Georgetown	1943–2011

UCLA's 38-game streak in the tournament

UCLA received much acclaim for its 88-game winning streak between 1971 and 1974. That attention was rekindled in 2010 when Connecticut's women's team achieved a 90-game winning streak.

But the streak that deserves more attention, perhaps even more than the 88-game record, is the Bruins' 38-game winning streak under John Wooden over a ten-year period in the NCAA tournament. I never thought that much about it until ESPN did a special on various sports dynasties when they launched the ESPN Sports Century series. In that piece Dick Enberg, noted broadcaster for NBC and CBS as well as the voice of UCLA basketball during that era, exclaimed that the 38-game winning streak "in the tournament" is among the more incredible streaks in sports history.

A look at the NCAA record book shows that the second-longest streak for consecutive wins in NCAA tournament play is 13 games by Duke from 1991 to 1993. Let me repeat, 38 is first and 13 is second. Tell me how many records have exceeded the previous mark by nearly 300 percent. That would be like someone breaking Joe DiMaggio's 56-game Major League Baseball hitting streak with a 163-game hitting streak.

It is true that the NCAA tournament of the 1960s and early 1970s was more regional in its approach. John Wooden's Bruins played only west coast teams before the Final Four with one exception (Dayton 1974) between 1964 and 1974, and 8 of the 38 games were played in Los Angeles. Also, his Bruins never had to win six games in a row in one tournament.

But, UCLA won the 38 consecutive games by a total margin of 619 points, 16.3 points per game. And 28 of the 38 games were decided by 10 points or more, including 12 wins by at least 20 points. Only five of the games were decided by five points or less and just one overtime — a triple overtime win against Dayton.

It takes six wins . . . or seven

There aren't many absolutes in making selections for your NCAA tournament bracket, but one that comes close is a six-game winning streak at some point in the season for your eventual champion. That makes sense when you think about it: it takes six (or seven, if you have to play in the First Four as Virginia Commonwealth did in 2011) straight wins to capture the championship.

Because the NCAA tournament went to 64 teams in 1985 (and now 68), only two teams have won the NCAA tournament without having a winning streak of at least six games on their regular season resume. The two schools to do it were Arizona in 1997 and Michigan State in 2000. Both had winning streaks of five games during the regular season. So, when you are picking your champion, check those results and make sure that team has had a winning streak of at least six games at some point in the season.

Who's hot, who's not

When the 2011 calendar turned to March, UCONN's women's basketball team was expected to be a virtual lock to win a third straight NCAA championship whereas the school's men's team had lost four of its last five regular season games.

But by the end of the month, Notre Dame's women's team had eliminated the Huskies women from the NCAA women's tournament, and the Huskies men's team had won 11 straight postseason games to capture the NCAA men's championship.

The Husky men were just 9–9 in the regular season in the rugged Big East and were the number nine seed in the Big East tournament. The ninth place ranking meant the Huskies had to win five games in five nights to win the Big East Championship, something no other team in any conference has ever accomplished. But, they did it, then won six straight in the NCAA tournament over three weeks, giving Jim Calhoun's team 11 postseason victories, more than any other team in NCAA history.

The point of this discussion, if not the entire chapter: If you use hindsight, you can make a case for and against just about any line of reasoning. That's not exactly a heartening thought as you prepare to fill out a bracket, but it's the truth. If there were a formula that was foolproof, someone would have figured it out long ago.

Consider this: In 2011 Connecticut men won the national championship and in retrospect we can provide all sorts of reasons to buttress their status as the tournament's best team. Having said that, UCONN won six games; in two of those six (versus Arizona and Kentucky), however, the opposing team missed a potential game-winning three-point shot with less than six seconds to play.

Luck matters in the NCAA tournament. And there's no way to discern beforehand who will be the luckier team.

Who has the guards?

The most important position in the NCAA tournament is not center; having an experienced guard who can control the tempo of a game is more important. Even the great UCLA teams in the 1960s and '70s had great guards in addition to Kareem Abdul-Jabbar and Bill Walton. Someone had to get them the ball and control the flow of the game after all.

You may remember early 1990s Duke center Christian Laettner. Not only was he the Blue Devils' on-court leader, but he also set a tournament career scoring record that still stands. But where would Duke have been without diminutive but scrappy point guard Bobby Hurley? The media recognized this in the 1992 tournament when it named Hurley, not Laettner, Most Outstanding Player (MOP). In fact, 13 of the last 22 MOPs of the NCAA tournament have been guards, including UCONN's Kemba Walker, who willed the Huskies to the 2011 national title with a 24-point average in the tournament.

Winning close games

One of the keys to success in the NCAA tournament is the ability to grind out some tough games. If you look at the NCAA tournament champions the last few years it is apparent that you have to win close games.

The four Final Four teams of 2011 all had close victories during their drive to Houston and they had a record of winning games by five points or less during the regular season that gave them confidence in the tournament. Butler won four games by five points or less during the regular season, then won three by three points or less during the NCAA tournament.

Connecticut had an incredible 9–3 record in games decided by five points or less on Selection Sunday, including three in the Big East tournament. The Huskies then defeated Arizona 65–63 in the Regional Championship, then defeated Kentucky by 56–55 in the national semifinal.

So, when you are filling out your bracket, pick teams that have done well in close games.

Season records: Stubbing your toe isn't all that bad

Don't be enticed into picking a school just because the team heads into the tourney undefeated or with only one loss. College basketball is not like college football: Losing once in a while is good. Sure, you want to be on a roll entering the tournament, but if you're undefeated or have just one loss heading into the tournament, the pressure rises.

In the last 35 years, 23 teams entered the NCAA tournament with one or no losses, and none of them won the national championship. The last team to go undefeated in the regular season and win the national championship was Indiana in 1975–76, a perfect 32–0. Why?

- ✔ Too much pressure. Teams start playing not to lose instead of playing to win.

- ✔ Losing is good once in a while. It allows you to take an honest look at where you need improvement. Coaches can preach what needs to be improved — but if the team didn't lose the preceding game, their preaching may not sink in.

If you're looking for an ideal number of losses, I suggest four. Four of the last ten national champs entered the NCAA tournament with four losses: Duke in 2001, Maryland in 2002, North Carolina in 2005, and North Carolina in 2009. Note that all four are ACC teams.

The importance of seeding

Follow the seeds when you make your selections. Although you can't pick every game according to seeds, you'll be right more often than not. In fact, in 2011, the higher seed won 25 of the 32 second round games. That's why it's the higher seed, after all. Give the NCAA tournament selection committee some credit; they work long and hard on seeding the teams.

Although every rule I mention in this chapter has its converse side, one rule has never yet been broken: *A number-one seed has never lost its first game.* Top seeds are a perfect 108–0 entering the 2012 tournament in the first round since the NCAA first started seeding teams for the 1985 tournament. You can take the number two seed (104–4) to the bank for their first game, 96 percent of the time as well.

The eight-seed versus nine-seed game is supposed to be even, and it has been the most even matchup since 1985. Since then, the number 9 seed has won 57 and the number 8 seed has won 51. The seven versus ten games have seen the number 7 seed win 65 times, compared to 43 for the number 10 seed.

Here are some other facts to remember about seeds.

- ✔ A number 1 seed has won the NCAA Tournament 18 of the last 33 years, or since seeding began in 1979.

- ✔ A number 12 seed has upset a number 5 seed at least once in 10 of the last 11 years. The 2007 tournament was the only year an upset of a seed did not take place.

- ✔ Twenty times in the last two years a team seeded at least five spots lower (worse) than its opponent has pulled off the upset victory, including a record tying 11 times in the 2011 event. VCU had three of those upset victories in 2011.

- ✔ Villanova has won more games as the lower seed (underdog) than any other school.

- ✔ A number 1 seed has reached the Final Four 45 of the 108 opportunities since 1985, the year the field reached 64 teams. Only three times since 1979 has there been a Final Four without a number 1 seed — 1980, 2006, and 2011. The 2011 tournament is the only one without a 1 or 2 seed in the Final Four.

- ✔ A team seeded third or better has won 29 of the last 33 NCAA tournaments. As many upsets as there were in the 2011 event, it was won by number 3 seed UCONN.

- ✔ Number 11 seed is the lowest seed to reach the Final Four, having happened just three times — LSU in 1986, George Mason in 2006, and Virginia Commonwealth in 2011.

- ✔ All four number 1 seeds reached the Final Four in 2008, but no number 1 seeds reached the Final Four in 2006 or 2011.

The following shows the overall records of NCAA tournament teams in the round of 64 since 1985.

#1 vs. #16	108–0
#2 vs. #15	104–4
#3 vs. #14	92–16
#4 vs. #13	85–23
#5 vs. #12	72–36
#6 vs. #11	72–36
#7 vs. #10	65–43
#8 vs. #9	51–57

Physical teams

Bob Huggins, the coach at West Virginia, told me that there really is a difference in the way the game is officiated in the NCAA tournament. The attitude among the refs is to let the teams decide for themselves on the court. (In other words, the refs will be loathe to call as many fouls, especially late in the game.) To go a long way in the NCAA, teams had better not rely totally on finesse. They'd better play some defense and rebound and scrap for every loose ball. Rebound margin (see Chapter 8) is a good indicator of a team's penchant for physical play.

In the 2010 tournament, West Virginia reached the Final Four. They did that thanks to a +6.4 rebound margin, the 14th best average in the nation.

Injuries and distractions

Late-season distractions, usually centering on an NCAA violation or academic suspension, can have a devastating effect on a team. In 2011, Tennessee was involved in an NCAA investigation, and speculation was rampant about the future of Head Coach Bruce Pearl. It was a distraction entering the tournament. Even though Tennessee was the higher seed and had a much better RPI than opponent Michigan, most thought this would be an easy win for the Wolverines. And, it was by a 75–45 score.

Teams on a mission

Be aware of special motivating factors for teams. In 1995–96, for example, Pete Carril was coaching Princeton in his final NCAA tournament. The result: an upset of defending national champion UCLA in the first round.

In 1990, Loyola Marymount had just lost its star player Hank Gathers, who died on the court in the conference tournament just days prior to the start of the NCAA tournament. Marymount beat defending champion Michigan in the first round in one of the greatest team shooting performances in tournament history. Loyola Marymount advanced to the Elite Eight before succumbing to eventual champ UNLV.

The charismatic leader factor

Every NCAA tournament has a most valuable player, but some players hoist their team on their backs more than others. In recent years, Danny Manning of Kansas (1988), Glen Rice of Michigan (1989), and Mateen Cleaves of Michigan State (2000) carried their teams to the title on what often seemed like sheer willpower. That was the case with UCONN in 2011 as Kemba Walker carried a very young Husky team to the title.

Each year, someone makes a run behind a great junior or senior player who's motivated by the fact that this is his last go-round. Who will it be this year?

Charting it out

If you want to do an in-depth analysis of a key match-up, say an 8 versus 9 game, it might be beneficial to size up the teams in various categories. How much you weigh each category is up to you, but if you get one team with a lot more check marks than the other, you better give strong consideration to advancing that team in your bracket.

The following is an example from an 8 versus 9 game in the 2011 NCAA Tournament.

Category	George Mason	Villanova
Seed	X8	9
Player NCAA experience	X	
Coach NCAA experience	X	
Geography	Wash	Wash
RPI	X24	38
RPI schedule strength	91	X33
Overall record	X26-6	21-11
Conference record	X16-2	9-9
Record away from home	X13-7	8-8
Common opponents	X2-0	1-0
Top 50 RPI wins	3	X7
Games decided by 5 or less	1-2	X5-6
Last 10 games	X9-1	3-7
3-point shooting percentage	X.395	.348
Rebound margin	+2.1	X+4.5

George Mason has eight check marks and Villanova has six. George Mason won the game.

Note: Geography means that the team will have a fan support advantage at the game site.

The Rodney Dangerfield theory

There has been no better use of the Rodney Dangerfield theory ("I don't get no respect") in the last 30 years of the NCAA tournament than the motivation techniques of Virginia Commonwealth University (VCU) coach Shaka Smart. Of course Smart had some help, courtesy of many members of the media, including my good friend Jay Bilas of ESPN.

On Selection Sunday programs many experts said that VCU had no business in the NCAA Tournament. Bilas said he didn't even have VCU on the bubble. Time and again in pregame talks Smart referred to the media and their lack of respect for the VCU program.

Well, VCU shocked the world with an opening victory over a favored Southern California team, then proceeded to make a run over favored teams from power conferences that had not been seen previously in the NCAA tournament. The list included a win over number 1 seed Pittsburgh. The number 11 seed VCU team reached the Final Four, just the third number 11 seed to make it in history.

Haven't we met before?

NCAA tournament games are almost always non-conference contests. The tournament committee works the bracket so that teams in the same conference do not meet until Sweet Sixteen at the earliest (unless a league gets more than eight bids). So when you pick games, be aware of how a team played against its non-conference competition. Granted, a lot of games have been played since December, and teams can improve or get worse, but don't discount these contests.

But also be aware that sometimes there are rematches and what happened in the first game can be a barometer. In November of 2010, UCONN beat Kentucky in the Maui Classic by 17 points. The teams were then paired again in the Final Four. UCONN won the rematch — by just one point, but they won.

The importance of being ignorant

Even if facts and figures bore you, and you'd rather read the NASDAQ stock quotes than the Sagarin ratings any day of the week, you may still want to enter the office pool. If so, you may want some other basis on which to select your winners. Try school colors or mascots.

If you use the color method, go with blue. Each of the last 8, and 19 of the last 24 NCAA champions have had blue in their school colors. All four teams in the 2011 Final Four had some shade of blue. Stay away from green because Michigan State is the only school with green in its school colors to win the NCAA championship since the 64-team field began in 1984.

The princess of pick-em

There are many theories to follow when filling out your NCAA tournament bracket. None are more strange but more successful than the path followed by Diana Inch, a librarian at Jefferson High School in Salem, Oregon, for the 2011 tournament.

Inch turned in one of over 3 million brackets on Yahoo.com and was the only person to successfully select all four Final Four teams for the 2011 tournament (Virginia Commonwealth, Butler, UCONN, and Kentucky).

In interviews with media after it was publicized that she was the only person on the website to pick all the Final Four teams correctly, she stated that she followed two theories: Play the numbers 7 and 11, and pick teams who have dogs and cats as mascots.

Following that theory meant selections for the Butler Bulldogs, the UCONN Huskies, and the Kentucky Wildcats. She went with VCU because the Patriots were a number 11 seed. She also pointed out that Butler was a popular pick for her because Brad Stevens has 7 letters in his last name and 11 letters in his first and last name combined.

Before you think Diana is a basketball genius, she did pick two 16 seeds to beat number 1 seeds in the first or second rounds. Of course, no 16 has ever beaten a number 1 seed, and it did not happen in 2011. There is an easy explanation because the 16 seed Boston University Terriers and the 16 seed UNC-Asheville Bulldogs have dogs in their nickname.

Other teams eventually upset all four number 1 seeds and the four number 2 seeds before the Final Four, leaving Inch with all four teams selected correctly.

In the Final Four, she correctly picked UCONN and Butler to reach the finals, and then correctly picked UCONN to win the national championship. Why did she pick the Huskies to go all the way? She has a 13-year-old dog that resembles the UCONN Huskies mascot.

Part V
The Part of Tens

The 5th Wave By Rich Tennant

"Glen Rice made his 9th rebound, Kobe Bryant just hit for 3 points, and Jack Nicholson's on his 2nd soft drink."

In this part . . .

Jump to this part if you need a quick breather. Here you can join me on my reminiscent journey of games that changed the course of basketball history, the greatest NBA players of all time, the coolest websites, and the most important dates in the game.

Chapter 17

Ten Games That Changed the Course of Basketball History

- -

In This Chapter

▶ The first game — and the football icon who played in it

▶ Games that sparked widespread interest in the college game

▶ Women's basketball's coming-out party

▶ The dawning of the NBA's Bird and Magic era

- -

So many games, so many stories. Literally thousands of basketball games occur each day, from the televised prime-time NBA Finals to a kid playing against make-believe opponents on his driveway. Here are ten games that, in my opinion, have had the most resonance.

Springfield YMCA 5, Springfield Teachers 1

When: March 12, 1892

Where: Springfield YMCA (Springfield, Massachusetts)

What would a list of this nature be without including the first game? This game was played in front of 200 spectators and is considered to be the first public display of basketball.

The students won the game, but the most incredible note on the contest concerns the person who scored the only point for the teachers — none other than Amos Alonzo Stagg, the Hall of Fame college football coach of the era. According to the *Republican,* "The most conspicuous figure on the floor was Stagg, in the blue Yale uniform, who managed to have a hand in every scrimmage play. His football training hampered him, and he was perpetually making fouls by shoving the opponents."

Texas Western 72, Kentucky 65

When: March 19, 1966 (NCAA championship game)

Where: College Park, Maryland

Texas Western, now known as the University of Texas at El Paso (UTEP), became the first school to start five African-American players in an NCAA Final. Meanwhile, Kentucky, the bastion of the old guard, started five white players, among them future NBA coach Pat Riley. Texas Western's win opened the gates for the racial integration of American college teams, especially in the South. Just three years earlier, Mississippi State coach Babe McCarthy defied a school policy prohibiting the Bulldogs from playing integrated teams and snuck away in order to play Loyola (Illinois), which started a few black players, in a first-round tourney game. The complexion of the game never looked the same afterward.

Houston 71, UCLA 69

When: January 20, 1968

Where: Houston Astrodome (Houston, Texas)

This game foreshadowed the present-day Final Four: a domed stadium and a nationally televised, prime-time college basketball game. This was the first made-for-TV matchup that was marketed around the country (150 stations in 49 states carried the telecast). When these two teams met again later that year in the Final Four (although that term was not born until 1975), the rematch wasn't televised nationally.

Fortunately, this contest lived up to its billing, as Elvin Hayes of Houston scored 39 points and held UCLA's Lew Alcindor (later Kareem Abdul-Jabbar) to only 15 points and 12 rebounds. Alcindor made just 4 of 18 shots from the field, his effectiveness limited by an eye injury that required him to wear a patch over his left eye. As if depth perception inside a dome wasn't already a problem — there were no floor seats, so it looked as if they were playing in the middle of a vast abyss. UCLA had entered that game on a 47-game winning streak.

North Carolina 54, Kansas 53 (three overtimes)

When: March 23, 1957 (NCAA championship game)

Where: Kansas City, Missouri

This is the only national championship game that ever went into triple over-time. This game is not in this chapter because it was a big upset, but rather because it was an exciting game for 55 minutes. North Carolina's Joe Quigg connected on a pair of free throws with six seconds left to score the winning points.

People remember this as a landmark game because North Carolina, which entered the game undefeated, beat the team that featured Wilt Chamberlain, a dominant presence in basketball for many years. Chamberlain scored 23 points and had 14 rebounds in the game, but that contribution was not enough.

Adding to the drama was the fact that, in the national semifinal, North Carolina needed three overtimes to defeat Michigan State. Imagine winning two triple-overtime games on consecutive days to win the national championship!

Notre Dame 71, UCLA 70

When: January 19, 1974

Where: South Bend, Indiana

I'm obviously biased on this one, but when ESPN selected the ten greatest games in college basketball history, this was one of them. Beating a UCLA team that had won seven straight national championships and 88 straight games (surpassing the all-time national record by 28 games) was big enough.

As much as anything, the thrill was in the way we won. Imagine how UCLA must have felt when we called time-out with 3:22 left, trailing 70–59. Bill Walton, the Bruins' star center, had not lost at UCLA and had never lost in high school. He must have believed that this one was over.

We then scored the last 12 points to win the game — which created doubts about the UCLA dynasty. UCLA then lost two more regular-season games, at Oregon and at Oregon State, and then lost to North Carolina State in the national semifinals. The Notre Dame victory helped to crumble the UCLA empire and launch a new era of parity in college hoops.

Michigan State 75, Indiana State 64

When: March 26, 1979 (NCAA championship game)

Where: Salt Lake City, Utah

This remains the highest-rated college basketball game in television history. The attraction: Larry Bird of undefeated Indiana State against Magic Johnson of Michigan State. This matchup was the beginning of one of the sport's great and amicable rivalries between two players.

Johnson won this matchup, scoring 24 points and grabbing 7 rebounds. Bird had 19 points and 13 rebounds, but shot just 7 of 21 from the field due to a hand injury.

This game turned the country on to college basketball. The future success of Bird and Johnson in the NBA only enhanced interest in the college game.

Soviet Union 51, United States 50

When: September 10, 1972

Where: Munich, West Germany

The United States' 63-game Olympic winning streak ended controversially when the Soviets were allowed to make a last-second inbounds pass three times in the championship final. After the USA's Doug Collins made two free throws with three seconds left, the Americans led 50–49. International rules prohibited calling a time-out after a made free throw, but the Soviet team's bench spilled onto the court after it in-bounded the ball. The referee called his own time-out to halt the chaos and allowed a second inbounds pass, this time with one second remaining. That inbounds pass was deflected out of bounds, and Team USA players rejoiced in victory.

Or so they thought. An Olympic official — not a game official — ruled that the referee should have allowed the Soviets to in-bound the ball with three seconds on the clock. On the third attempt, Aleksander Belov received a length-of-the-court pass between two USA players and made a game-winning layup.

That loss was the United States' first loss in Olympic play; *Sports Illustrated* called it "the greatest injustice in Olympic history." Adding insult to injury, someone stole USA coach Hank Iba's wallet (with $370 inside) during the frenzy immediately after the final buzzer. The members of the USA squad, protesting the outcome of the game, refused to accept their silver medals.

Connecticut 77, Tennessee 66

When: January 16, 1995

Where: Storrs, Connecticut

This was, excuse the expression, the debutante ball game of women's hoops. Number 1-anked Tennessee, 16–0, played against Number 2-ranked Connecticut, 12–0. ESPN cablecast the game nationally, and a rowdy crowd packed the sold-out arena on the University of Connecticut's (UCONN's) Storrs campus. The UCONN Huskies went on to post a 35–0 record and beat Tennessee to win the national championship. But this regular-season game, played in the afternoon on Martin Luther King Day, ignited Huskiemania and has contributed to the increased interest in women's hoops in recent years.

Boston Celtics 135, Chicago Bulls 131, 2OT

When: April 20, 1986

Where: Boston Garden

Michael Jordan had missed 49 games of his second NBA season with a foot injury, but there was no way that he was going to miss the Chicago Bulls' first-round playoff series versus the Boston Celtics. In a Game 1 loss at Boston Garden, Jordan scored 49 points. Here, in Game 2, his brilliance found a new summit as he scored a single-game playoff-record 63 points while being covered by Dennis Johnson, the best defensive guard of that era. The 63-point outburst remains unsurpassed today. The Bulls lost the game (Boston entered the afternoon with a 41–1 record on their parquet home floor), but the era of Michael Jordan unofficially began on that afternoon. Number 23 was, as fellow NBA legend Larry Bird described it, "God disguised as Michael Jordan."

New York Knicks 113, Los Angeles Lakers 99

When: May 8, 1970 (Game 7 of the 1970 NBA championships)

Where: New York, New York

Never has an NBA Game 7 been played on a bigger stage — Madison Square Garden may be basketball's most august — or with more courage. Willis Reed, the New York Knicks' star center, had a thigh injury and could barely walk. Reed had missed Game 6 in Los Angeles, and Laker center Wilt Chamberlain toyed with New York's frontcourt (that is, its forwards and substitute center), scoring 45 points. Reed took a cortisone shot in the locker room and then limped out onto the floor near the end of the pregame warm-ups.

Reed made the game's first shot, a jumper from the elbow, and if a game ever ended with the score at 2–0, this was it. (He made only one other shot all night.) The Knicks rode Reed's leadership to their first world championship. Often overlooked are the efforts of Knicks guard Walt Frazier, whose 36 points and 19 assists marked one of the greatest performances ever by a guard at any level, and backup center Nate Bowman, who had to cover Chamberlain most of the evening.

This championship was the watershed moment at which New York officially made the transition from being a college hoops city to a pro hoops city. With the Big Apple decidedly in its corner, the NBA — which is headquartered there — had fortified the most important media stronghold.

Los Angeles Lakers 123, Philadelphia 76ers 107

When: May 16, 1980 (Game 6 of the 1980 NBA championships)

Where: Philadelphia, Pennsylvania

Only a year earlier, Magic Johnson had mesmerized the college basketball realm. Then he bolted for the NBA with two years of eligibility remaining. Had he left too soon? Larry Bird, after all, would defeat him in the Rookie of the Year Award balloting.

Normally, the 6'9" Johnson moved from starting point guard to center when regular center Kareem Abdul-Jabbar had to miss some action with an injury. That in itself is incredible because no two positions on the court could have less in common (by now, we know that you have learned that much).

How did the rookie react to playing a new position in Game 6, on the road, in the NBA Finals? Magic scored 42 points and put the title on ice. His performance set a standard for greatness that would endure a decade, but it also turned the page into the modern era of the NBA.

The NBA had a serious image problem in the late 1970s. The NBA style of play — as popularized by stars such as George Gervin, Bob McAdoo, and David Thompson — had evolved into one-on-one playground ball with little emphasis on teamwork. It was not a pretty game to watch, nor were any of the league's stars — with the exception of the Philadelphia 76ers' Julius Erving — particularly charismatic. The arrival of Bird and Magic put the NBA back on course. Suddenly, passing and teamwork were in vogue again. The game became fun to watch. If any one contest symbolizes this dramatic turn-around that may very well have saved the league, this is it.

Chapter 18

Ten Best Basketball Websites

*I*s it even possible to watch a basketball game now without also being online? If Duke is playing North Carolina, for example, you want to follow along with live, updated stats on cbssportsline.com. But you also want to be on Twitter in case @JayBilas unleashes a particularly pithy tweet. And you may be tempted to YouTube a classic past finish from college basketball's greatest rivalry.

In the last decade of the 20th century, basketball went global. In the first decade of the 21st century, the game has gone digital. The major sports sites (yahoosports.com, espn.com, foxsports.com, and si.com) will always have excellent coverage of basketball, both college and pro. Those sites, however, are charged with covering all sports, not just hoops.

In this chapter, I provide ten basketball-specific sites that you should bookmark as soon as you close this book.

Basketball-Reference.com

This site provides everything you will ever need to know, statistically, about any season, any team and anyone in NBA — and, for that matter, ABA — history (I put it first for a reason). Are you curious about who is the NBA's all-time leader in turnovers, and would it interest you to learn that that top two men in that category are, respectively, former Utah Jazz teammates Karl Malone (4,524) and John Stockton (4,244)? You can find that within 24 seconds on this site.

Rushthecourt.net

Is it possible to be too enamored with college basketball? This site, which bills itself as "The Ubiquitous College Basketblog," thinks not. Dive into news, blogs, and updates at the beginning of the season, and you may not resurface until the Big East tournament.

Collegeinsider.com

Here I am reading a story from this site: "Wow, I didn't know that; I'll have to tell Jay Bilas and Hubert Davis before we go on the air tonight. Better yet, maybe I won't." Great info here.

Truehoop.com

This award-winning blog, founded by journalist Henry Abbott in 2005 and featuring a panel of experts, has been folded into the ESPN.com umbrella. Just type in the truehoop.com URL, and you will be sent to it directly.

Hoopshype.com

This is a site that lives up to its name and is so much more. If you're an NBA diehard, this needs to be a part of your daily regimen. An exhaustive array of links provides all you'd ever want to know in terms of player salaries, free agents, rumors, interviews and even sneakers. Excellent!

Allbrackets.com

Yes, but are you sure Oklahoma A&M beat Oregon State in the 1949 national semi-final? Every bracket of every NCAA tournament dating back to the inaugural year, 1939, can be found here. This site also lists location of the championship game, the game's most outstanding player, and winning coach.

NBAhoopsonline.com

How dedicated is this site to all things NBA? There's a link that shows the ten tallest players in league history (anyone remember 7'4" Priest Lauderdale?). Another shows every NBA logo ever created and used. This is definitely another fun site in which you can happily lose yourself for hours.

KenPom.com

NCAA geeks who want to evaluate their favorite school's chances of making the tournament find Ken Pomeroy's (hence, KenPom) site indispensable. If you are an actuary or accountant, you'll probably enjoy it more than the rest of us.

Slamonline.com

Slam magazine was the original crossroads of hip-hop and hoop. This site follows the sport with the passion of a street 'baller. And for your reading pleasure, it includes more than 30 blogs.

Hoopsworld.com

This site is as satisfying, if not more so, than any of the major sports sites' NBA homepage. This is a daily must-glance for an NBA acolyte.

Chapter 19

Ten NBA Legends

Before the Internet, before YouTube, before SportsCenter's "Top Ten Plays," amazing stuff was happening in the NBA. It was difficult enough to trim this list to ten players (I cheated and used 11), and I still have to apologize for cutting the likes of Rick Barry, John Havlicek, Pistol Pete Maravich, and Bob Pettit from this squad. This chapter gives you, if not the 11 greatest NBA players of all time (though they may just be), then certainly those whose feats predate the ubiquity of both the World Wide Web and ESPN.

Kareem Abdul-Jabbar

Kareem Abdul-Jabbar is the league's all-time leader in points scored (38,387) and ranks third in rebounds (17,440). He averaged 24.6 points per game for 18 seasons. He was the NBA MVP six times — more than any other player — and his team won the NBA championship six times. During his career, Kareem's sky hook was the single greatest offensive weapon in the game.

Elgin Baylor

DIGGER SAYS

Elgin Baylor was the original hangtime player. Michael Jordan performed some acrobatic moves, but Baylor invented that style of play. He was an 11-time All-Star and once scored 71 points in one game. When he retired, he was the number-three scorer in NBA history. You hear a lot about the combos of Pippen and Jordan or Stockton and Malone. I'd take Baylor and Jerry West any day.

Larry Bird

This three-time MVP led the Celtics to three NBA championships and was a ten-time All-NBA player. If you watched Larry Bird practice, you may have thought, "This guy isn't fast, and he doesn't have great jumping ability, but somehow he gets it done better than just about anyone else." Like Magic Johnson, Bird was outstanding in all phases of the game and was one of the smartest players ever to lace up sneakers. He could hit a three-pointer to beat you or make a steal to beat you — whatever needed to be done.

Wilt Chamberlain

While Bill Russell was the greatest defensive force in NBA history, Wilt "the Stilt" Chamberlain must have been the greatest offensive force. The beauty is that Russell and Chamberlain played in the same era. Those were some battles!

Wilt's stats are mind-boggling: He scored over 4,000 points in one season, and 100 points in one game in 1962. Nobody has come within 28 points of the latter record. He averaged 50.4 points per game for the entire 1961–62 season and once had 55 rebounds in one game. Six years later, Wilt decided to show everyone that he was a great passer and led the league in assists. His durability was unmatched; he actually averaged over 48 minutes per game in 1962, and he never fouled out in 1,045 career games.

At a chiseled 7'1", Wilt was the most physically dominant force the game has ever seen. And yes, I know who Shaquille O'Neal is.

Bob Cousy

Bob Cousy was all-world, the original wizard with a basketball. The Celtics won nine NBA championships in a row from 1958 to 1966, but Boston never would have started that run of championships without Cousy. He was by far the most exciting player in the NBA in his early years; his over-the-head and behind-the-back passes set the standard for future guards. He was a ten-time All-NBA player and 13-time All-Star. He also won the NBA MVP award.

Julius Erving

Julius Erving is the only member of my Greatest NBA Players list whom I coached against in college . . . and defeated. In my only year at Fordham, we beat Erving and UMass — but that doesn't keep him off my team. "Dr. J" had as much influence on the game as anyone with his gravity-defying moves that graced the ABA and NBA for 16 years. After becoming one of only six players in NCAA history to average over 20 points and 20 rebounds per game for a college career, Erving became an 11-time NBA All-Star. In 1983, he led the Philadelphia 76ers to the NBA championship. Three times, he led the NBA in scoring, and he remains one of just four players in professional history to score over 30,000 points. Whereas kids growing up today have Vince Carter to hold in high esteem, the players currently in the NBA owe much of their love of the game to Dr. J.

Magic Johnson

Earvin "Magic" Johnson was the game's greatest all-around player in the 1980s. Magic carved out an identity for his Lakers team, if not the entire city of Los Angeles, for an entire decade. LA in the '80s was Showtime — exciting, fast-paced, and glitzy — and Magic was the ringmaster. Magic had 138 career triple doubles, the most on record. He led the league in assists five times. He was the league MVP three times, was a nine-time first-team All-NBA player, and played on five NBA championship teams.

Magic was also first-team All-Charisma for 12 straight years. His smile and personality did as much to promote the game as anything. Along with Larry Bird of the Celtics, Magic returned two things to the league that had been missing for nearly a decade: a love of passing the ball, and a fierce desire to win that only Michael Jordan has since emulated.

Michael Jordan

With a 31.5 points-per-game figure, Michael Jordan is the league's career scoring average leader; his playoff scoring average was even higher. Jordan has revolutionized the game, as Bill Russell did in his era, by playing above the rim. That is to say, he perfected the art of dunking and seemed to be immune to gravity. Ask yourself this: Before Michael came along, how many players in the NBA wore long shorts and black sneakers and shaved their heads? How many do now? Everyone, even NBA millionaires, wants to be like Mike.

DIGGER SAYS Is Jordan the best player of all time? Arguing against him would be hard. I say this: He's the fiercest competitor of all time, and the one guy you want on your team when you're down by a few points with less than a minute remaining. The Bulls have played in six NBA Finals, all with Jordan; they are 6–0 in those series, none of which have not extended past a sixth game. And Jordan has six NBA Finals MVP awards somewhere in his overstuffed trophy case.

No sequence of Jordan's larger-than-life career (which in the summer of 2000 was captured in a movie made for IMAX screens entitled *Michael Jordan to the MAX*) is more fitting than his final minute. Trailing the Utah Jazz in Game Six of the 1998 NBA Finals, Chicago needed to force a turnover and score a bucket. Jordan, sneaking up behind fellow future Hall of Famer Karl Malone, slapped the ball out of the Jazz forward's hands. Having gotten the key steal, Jordan then dribbled down court, put an ankle-buckling move on Utah guard Bryon Russell, and drained the game-winning jumper from the top of the key. His shooting form on that play, which he held for an extra second as if sensing that this was his last shot of his career, should be shown to every aspiring basketball player.

Nobody does it better. Or, as sportswriter John Feinstein said on television one day in June 1997, "There is no next Michael Jordan."

Oscar Robertson

Oscar Robertson's legend benefited from the statisticians who invented the *triple double* (hitting double figures in three statistical categories — for example, 14 points, 12 rebounds, and 11 assists). Because Magic Johnson was never known for his scoring as much as he was for his all-around sublime play, the public relations people at the Los Angeles Lakers (Magic's team) sought an innovative way to quantify his contributions. They arrived at the triple double, but in doing so stumbled onto the fact that Oscar Robertson — like Magic, an oversized guard — had actually averaged a triple double over the course of a season more than 20 years earlier (1961).

"The Big O" played 14 years in the NBA and was a three-time MVP of the All-Star game. He averaged 26 points a game and dealt out almost 10,000 assists in his career, which included a championship with the Milwaukee Bucks in 1972.

Bill Russell

Folks talk with amazement about Michael Jordan winning six NBA titles in eight years. How about 11 titles in 13 years, including 8 years in a row (the final two seasons of which Russell was a player/coach)? This five-time NBA MVP revolutionized the game of basketball with his defense and rebounding; he's still the prototype center when it comes to defense. If you have a young center, show him films of Bill Russell and his ability to block shots and keep the ball in play.

Jerry West

Jerry West of the LA Lakers was Mr. Clutch; I'll never forget that three-quarter-court shot he made against the Knicks in the 1970 NBA Finals in Los Angeles. West had perfect form on his jumpshot — his form was used as the model for the NBA logo. He scored over 25,000 points and made the All-Star game every year he played. Only Michael Jordan, who has said that West is the one player from another era he'd like to face, had a higher playoff scoring average.

Chapter 20

Ten Important Dates in Basketball History

In This Chapter

▶ Playing the first game

▶ Shooting the first one-handed shot

▶ Winning 88 games in a row

*J*ames Naismith never intended to launch a revolution. In 1891, Naismith was an instructor at the Springfield (Massachusetts) Young Men's Christian Academy Training College. He was simply searching for an indoor physical fitness activity for his students that they would not find tedious.

The dean of the physical education department, Dr. Luther Gulick, charged his young teacher, Naismith, with developing a new recreational activity that would both inspire the students and maintain a level of fitness during the long, frigid New England winters.

"There is nothing new under the sun," a thoroughly frustrated Gulick told Naismith one day.

"If that is so, we can invent a new game that will meet our needs," Naismith, then 30 years old, replied.

Naismith drew upon a game that he had played as a youth in Canada called "Duck on the Rock," in which one boy guarded his "duck" while other boys tossed stones at it. Tossing in a few elements of soccer and perhaps even football, Naismith nailed a pair of half-bushel peach baskets to the walls at the opposite ends of the gym, rounded up a soccer ball, and set about instructing his students about the 13 rules he had drawn up to govern the game.

A short 100 years later, Michael Jordan was named the NBA's Most Valuable Player.

December 29, 1891: First Basketball Game

On this date Naismith oversaw the first basketball game ever played at the Armory Street court in Springfield, Mass. Introducing his students to the nine rules he had devised (for example, "A player cannot run with the ball. The player must throw it from the spot on which he catches it, allowance to be made for a man who catches the ball when running at a good speed if he tries to stop."), Naismith divided his class into two nine-man teams. Using a soccer ball and peach baskets, the class played a game that was divided into two 15-minute halves.

Only one basket was scored, a 25-foot toss by William Chase. A basket was worth one point at the time, so the final score was 1–0.

Someone suggested naming the fledgling game after its inventor, but Naismith humbly demurred. "We have a ball and a basket," Naismit said. "Why don't we call it basket ball?"

December 30, 1936: Hank Luisetti's One-Handed Shot

Stanford's Hank Luisetti is often and inaccurately credited with introducing the jump shot to basketball. In fact, he developed a running one-handed shot, but Luisetti's innovation was a paradigm-shifting moment in terms of shooting. Before Luisetti's arrival, every player shot the ball via the two-handed set shot.

During the holidays Stanford and Luisetti traveled across the country to meet Long Island University (LIU) at Madison Square Garden. A crowd of 17,623 filled the Garden to see LIU, which boasted a 43-game winning streak, face the Indians (Stanford is now known as the Cardinals), the defending Pacific Coast Conference champions, and their six-foot-two sophomore forward, Luisetti.

Although Luisetti scored just 15 points in the game, his unique shooting style mesmerized observers in the media capital of the country. That Luisetti was the best player on the court and that Stanford easily defeated LIU 45–31 only added to his aura. Soon the running one-handed shot, and then the jump shot, would render the two-handed set shot obsolete.

March 27, 1939: Oregon 46, Ohio State 33

The inaugural NCAA tournament, staged in 1939, was a far cry from March Madness (although, unlike the current incarnation of the tournament, it did take place entirely in the month of March). It was not even the most prestigious tournament at the time: the National Invitational Tournament was.

The NCAA tournament began on March 17 with eight schools divided into two regions, East and West. The East regional was played in Philadelphia and the West in San Francisco.

Ten days later the champions from each region, Ohio State and Oregon, met inside Patten Gym on the campus of Northwestern University in Evanston, Illinois (Northwestern, ironically, has never played in the NCAAs). Oregon, nicknamed the Tall Firs because the average height of its starting five was six feet, prevailed 46–33 before an audience of 5,500. The game was not televised and even a few of the participants were uninterested.

"We had just won (the Big Ten) title, which was the most important thing in our minds" said the Buckeyes' Jimmy Hull, who was named the Most Outstanding Player of the tournament despite his team's runner-up finish. "The (Ohio) state high school tournament was being played. We wanted to watch that."

November 1, 1946: New York Knicks 68, Toronto Huskies 66

You can say that the NBA was officially conceived on June 6, 1946, when a group of owners met in a New York City hotel room and laid the groundwork for what would be known as the Basketball Association of America (BAA). The league was born on this night, however, and somewhat fittingly in Canada because the game's inventor was a native of that country.

The New York Knicks, whose training camp took place on an outdoor court at a resort in the Catskill mountains, traveled north by train for the inaugural contest. The Huskies, who had just one player on their roster, did their best to promote the game to a city of hockey-crazed fans. Toronto offered free admission (tickets ranged from 75 cents to $2.50) to anyone who was taller than 6'8" Huskies center George Nostrand.

The Knicks led 33–18 at halftime but a Nostrand basket late in the third quarter put Toronto ahead, 44–43, for the first time. New York rallied from a four-point deficit in the fourth quarter and, behind Leo Gottlieb's 14 points, earned the victory. Toronto player-coach Ed Sadowski, who fouled out (five fouls at the time merited disqualification) just three minutes into the second half, led all scorers with 18 points.

March 2, 1962: Wilt Chamberlain's 100-Point Game

The most dominant game in the career of the NBA's most dominant player ever is enveloped in both mystery and myth.

The contest took place in Hershey, Pennsylvania, where Chamberlain's team, the Philadelphia Warriors, occasionally played home games. Only 4,124 people attended and the game was not televised. There is no video of the event. The starting center for the last-place Knicks, Phil Jordan, was sidelined by the flu. The 7'2" Chamberlain, a larger-than-life figure with a lifestyle to match, had been out the evening before in New York City and never slept.

Nearing the end of a season in which he would average more than 50 points per game, Chamberlain had 23 points after one quarter and 41 at halftime. After a 28-point third quarter put him at 69, fans began to chant, "Give it to Wilt!" When he scored his 100th point, there were 46 seconds remaining, but fans rushed the court. The game was stopped for good. The score: Philadelphia 169, New York 147.

January 20, 1968: UCLA, Houston Play "Game of the Century"

It was only a midseason college basketball game. It was much more than that.

Before UCLA agreed to meet the Cougars in the Houston Astrodome, no college basketball game had ever been broadcast nationwide in prime time.

The scene was surreal. The court was placed in the middle of the Astrodome so that the closest of the 52,693 fans were at least 100 feet from the action. It was the largest crowd in basketball history, and yet All-Americans such as UCLA's Lew Alcindor and Houston's Elvin Hayes felt as if they were playing in a vacant arena.

The Bruins, defending champs and ranked Number 1, arrive sporting a 47-game win streak. The Cougars were ranked Number 2. Houston, led by Hayes' herculean effort and game-winning free throws, prevailed 71–69.

More important, each school received $125,000 for the game, four times the payout of an NCAA tournament appearance at the time. This game marks the moment when college basketball became a viable commercial commodity.

September 10, 1972: U.S.S.R Defeats U.S.A.

No championship game perhaps in any sport ever featured a more controversial finish than the gold-medal game of the 1972 Munich Olympics.

Since basketball had been introduced as an Olympic medal sport in Berlin at the 1936 Summer Olympics, the United States had never lost. The Americans had won 63 straight games and seven gold medals heading into their gold-medal game against their arch-rivals, both athletically and politically, the U.S.S.R.

This, however, was the youngest American squad ever to compete for an Olympic gold. The Soviets led throughout, once by as many as 10 points. With seconds remaining and the U.S.A trailing 48–47, Doug Collins stole a pass near mid court and drove toward the bucket. Collins was fouled hard — the Soviet defender undercut the Illinois State guard and he went sprawling into the basket support — but he made both free throws to put the U.S. up 49–48 with three seconds remaining.

What happened next will forever be a source of controversy.

First, the Soviets inbounded the ball and dribbled up court, but a referee stopped play because of a dispute at the scorer's table. The Soviet coaches were arguing that they had called for a timeout before Collins stepped to the line to shoot his free throws (the rules at the time prohibited a team from calling a timeout after a second free throw).

The referees agreed and awarded the Soviets a second inbound pass from beneath their basket with :03 on the clock. The Red team did inbound the ball into its back court, but the horn sounded prematurely, after only about one second had elapsed.

The Americans celebrated, believing they had won. Instead, they were ordered back onto the court for a third Soviet inbounds pass. This time the U.S.S.R. got it right, as Ivan Edeshko threw a full-court pass to center Aleksandr Belov, who outdueled two Americans for the ball. Both of them stumbled, and Belov converted an uncontested layup to give the Soviets the gold as the horn sounded.

January 19, 1974: Notre Dame ends UCLA's 88-Game Winning Streak

For a decade or so, UCLA basketball was invincible. John Wooden led the Bruins to ten NCAA championships in a dozen years and recruited two of the greatest big men ever to play college basketball, Lew Alcindor and Bill Walton. His teams put together both a 47-game and an 88-game win streak.

My team broke that latter streak.

On the eve of our game with the Bruins in South Bend (I was then 32 years old and in my third season as coach of the Fighting Irish), I had my players cut down the nets at the end of our practice. It was a pure psychological ploy to let them know that I believed that we could defeat the mighty Bruins.

For a long time, the gesture appeared futile. UCLA led by 17 in the first half and by 11, 70–59, with 3:30 remaining. All but those of us who clutch four-leaf clovers considered the lead insurmountable.

Instead, the Irish mounted an incredible comeback. The Bruins did commit four turnovers in those final 210 seconds, but the Irish also hit six shots while holding UCLA scoreless. Dwight Clay's long jumper from the left corner with 29 second remaining was the final stroke of a 12–0 run as the Irish prevailed, 71–70.

The longest win streak in the history of men's basketball, college or pro, came to an end at Notre Dame. No men's team has ever come close to approaching it.

April 4, 1983: N.C. State Beats Houston

Between 1979 and 1985, the NCAA basketball tournament exploded. March Madness was born via a string of memorable championship contests, beginning with the 1979 matchup between Larry Bird of Indiana State and Magic Johnson of Michigan State.

That contest was anti-climactic (the Spartans won by 11) but the following years would see North Carolina freshman Michael Jordan bury a game-winning jumper versus Georgetown in 1982 and Villanova, three years later, shock that same heavily favored Georgetown team in 1985.

However, no game played a greater role in the evolution from NCAA tournament to March Madness than North Carolina State's cataclysmic upset of Houston in 1983. The Cougars, with future Hall of Famers Clyde Drexler and Akeem Olajuwon, were known as Phi Slamma Jamma.

The Wolfpack barely qualified for the tournament with a 17–10 record, but their big weapon was an irrepressible young coach, Jim Valvano, with a great sense of humor and an indefatigable spirit. No one thought the Wolfpack would remain within a dozen points of Houston, but Valvano's crew slowed down the game and kept it close. With seconds remaining and the score tied 52–52, North Carolina State found itself with the ball and a chance to win.

Guard Derek Whittenburg held onto the ball too long and heaved a desperation 30-footer from beyond the top of the key with four seconds remaining. The ball sailed short and wide to the right, but as the Houston defender's watched the arc of its flight, Wolfpack forward Lorenzo Charles leaped, caught the ball in mid air and dunked it all in one motion.

The buzzer sounded. North Carolina State, which had pulled off several unlikely wins throughout the course of the tournament, had become the most unlikely national champion ever. Whenever anyone mentions the term Cinderella in regards to March Madness, the 1983 Wolfpack is the first team that should come to mind.

The image of Valvano in the moments after Charles' basket, running around the court in Albuquerque and searching for someone to hug, is one of the most indelible in the history of the tournament.

January 16, 1995: UCONN Meets Tennessee

Women's college basketball had been holding championships since 1972, first in the AIAW (Association for Intercollegiate Athletics for Women) and then, from 1982 onward, as part of the NCAA.

However, the sport never truly arrived in the national consciousness until Tennessee visited Connecticut on a frigid Monday afternoon in 1995. At the time, the Lady Vols and their imposing coach, Pat Summitt, were as dominant as any program, having won three of the previous eight national titles.

Connecticut, however, was a program on the rise. Led by a charismatic young coach, Geno Auriemma, the Huskies were undefeated and entertaining. Also, they were the closest major program to the ESPN headquarters, many of whose staffers were UCONN alums.

An ESPN official approached Summitt with the notion of a nationally televised match-up on the afternoon of the Martin Luther King, Jr., holiday. Nationally televised women's basketball, to that point, was a rarity. Summitt had everything to lose — the game would be played at UCONN's Gampel Pavilion — but agreed to do it "for the good of the (women's) game."

And thus the fiercest rivalry in women's athletics was born. Undefeated Connecticut, which was ranked second (Tennessee was Number 1 and also unbeaten), felled the Lady Vols, 77–66. The excitement was palpable.

"The atmosphere was amazing," Connecticut's All-American center Rebecca Lobo would later recall. "The arena was sold out and the crowd stayed for about 15 minutes after just dancing and celebrating in the seats. It was the best college atmosphere I've ever experienced."

Between them, the two schools would win eight of the next ten national championships. To this day Auriemma and Summitt are still coaching at UCONN and Tennessee, respectively, but the annual rivalry game, alas, was discontinued after 2007.

Part VI
Appendixes

The 5th Wave   By Rich Tennant

"What did I tell you?! You want to be like Dennis Rodman?! Then expect to get your nose ring caught in the net!"

In this part . . .

These two chapters put a cherry and whipped cream on top of this book. Here, you can learn how to talk like a basketball pro as well as get the basics of drills. By the time you're done with this part, you'll be talkin' the talk and walkin' the walk.

Appendix A

Glossary of Basketball Terms

Airball: A shot that completely misses the basket, hitting only air.

Alley-oop: A designed play in which a player lobs the ball toward the basket and a teammate jumps up, catches the ball in midair, and usually dunks it.

Alternating possession: The "we get the ball this time, you get it next time" rule in college and high school basketball only. In a held-ball situation, the lighted arrow on the scorer's table at midcourt points toward the team who gets possession of the ball.

Assist: A statistic for which a player receives credit when he passes the ball to a teammate and the teammate then scores immediately. Thus the player who throws the pass "assists" in the scoring play.

Backboard: A frame, made of plexiglass or hardwood, that supports the basket. Regulation size is 6' x 4'.

Back court: A team's *back court* consists of the defensive half of the court, including the opponent's basket, the inbounds part of the backboard, and the entire timeline. After the offensive team enters its front court, it cannot return to the back court with the ball.

Backdoor: A type of cut to the basket. Offensive player moves to the perimeter, then darts to toward the basket, and looks to take a lead pass from a teammate, resulting in an easy basket. Used by Princeton to perfection in an NCAA tournament win over UCLA in 1996.

Ball reversal: Form of passing the ball from one side of the court to the other, usually with two passes. Used by an offense against a zone defense.

Ball screen: Screen set by a teammate for a player who has possession of the ball.

Bank shot: A shot attempt that uses the backboard.

Baseball pass: A one-handed overhead pass, used to make long passes.

Baseline (or endline): The line on each end of the court that separates inbounds from out of bounds.

Basket: The goal, composed of an iron rim and net, at which shots are attempted.

Basket interference: Occurs when a player touches the ball when it's within an imaginary cylinder that extends from the basket ring all the way to the ceiling, or any part of the basket. An illegal act at all levels except international. See also *goaltending*.

Block: Illegal personal contact by a defender that impedes an opponent's progress.

Block out (or box out): Using the body to block or shield an opponent in order to gain better position to grab a rebound.

Blocked shot: When a defensive player bats away an opponent's shot attempt.

Board: Slang for rebound.

Bonus: A situation in high school and college games in which a team is awarded free throws after non-shooting fouls when the opposing team is over the foul limit.

Bonus free throw: A second free throw that's awarded after a successful first free throw. In college ball, bonus free throws are awarded only after the team has committed seven fouls (any combination of personal, unsporting, and contact technical fouls) in a half.

Boundary lines: End lines and side lines of the court. The inside edges of these lines define the inbounds and out-of-bounds areas.

Box and one: Type of defense where one player guards an opponent one-on-one and the other four defensive players are in a zone.

Box out: See *block out.*

Breakaway: A situation in which a defensive player steals the ball and races toward his basket to score ahead of the defenders behind him. In the NBA, breakaways often produce spectacular, high-flying dunks.

Brick: An especially ugly, misfired shot that clanks off the rim or backboard.

Bucket: Slang for basket.

Buzzer beater: Last-second shot that wins the game. Joined the basketball lexicon in the 1980s when many NCAA tournament games were decided at the buzzer.

Cager: Slang for a basketball player.

Center: One of the player positions. Usually, but not always, the tallest player on the team. Scores from in close, blocks shots, and does the bulk of the team's rebounding.

Charge: Illegal personal contact by an offensive player that involves pushing or moving into an opponent's torso. Charging is the single hardest call for a referee to make because the defensive player must be stationary or the call is a block.

Charity stripe: Slang for free throw line.

Combo guard: Guard who is capable of playing point guard or shooting guard. Michael Jordan and Kobe Bryant are examples.

Crossover dribble: When a player in a stationary position dribbles the ball from one side of his body to the other, then reverses the dribble back to the original side to fool the defender.

Cut: To quickly move from one spot on the floor to another in an effort to elude a defender and try to score.

Dead ball: Any time that the referee has whistled for play to cease.

Defense: The team without the ball, who tries to prevent the offensive team from scoring.

Double-double: Statistical line in which a player records double figures in two areas from the statistics for points, rebounds, assists, blocked shots or steals. Most common is achieved with points and rebounds.

Double down: Defensive strategy where a defensive player on the wing, will leave his man, and join another defender in guarding a post player who has received the ball. Designed to force the post player to give up the ball and force more difficult shots from the outside.

Double dribble: A violation in which a player dribbles with both hands simultaneously or picks up (stops) his dribble and then begins dribbling again.

Downtown: A shot attempted from far away from the basket or outside the shooter's normal range.

Dribble: To bat, push, or tap the basketball to the floor. A player holding the ball must remain stationary on her *pivot foot;* in order to move or advance with the ball, she must dribble. The dribble ends when the dribbler causes the ball to come to rest in one or both hands, the dribbler touches the ball with both hands simultaneously, or an opponent bats the ball away. Dribbling with both hands simultaneously is a violation (see *double dribble*).

Dribble penetration: Offensive strategy in which ballhandler dribbles into the lane in order to draw an extra defender or two. Dribbler then kicks out a pass to an open teammate usually positioned beyond the three-point arc.

Dunk: To drive, force, or stuff the ball through the basket. One of the more exciting and athletic plays in the game.

Elbow: Area on the court that inside the key at the foul line extended. Popular place for players to shoot mid-range jump shots after coming off a screen.

End line: See *baseline.*

Fake: A move in which an offensive player, not necessarily the one with the ball, pretends to go one way and then goes another in order to fool his defender.

Fast break: A play in which a defensive team rebounds the ball and quickly tries to advance the ball down the court ahead of its opponent — ideally, to score an easy basket.

Field goal: A shot made from inside or outside the three-point arc with the clock running, worth two or three points, respectively.

Flagrant foul: A personal foul that involves violent contact with an opponent, such as striking with the elbow, kicking, kneeing, and moving under a player who's in the air.

Forward: One of the player positions. A team usually has two forwards. Forwards rebound, aid the center inside, and shoot the ball.

Foul: See *personal foul* and *technical foul.*

Foul out: To be disqualified by reaching the maximum number of fouls allowed per game: five in college and high school, or six in international play and the NBA.

Foul trouble: A player who is close to fouling out (for example, a player who has four fouls in a college game) is said to be in *foul trouble.*

Four-point play: Offensive score when a player hits a three-point goal and is fouled in the process. He then completes the four-point play by making the free throw.

Free throw: An unhindered attempt to score one point by shooting a basket from behind the free throw line and within the free throw semicircle. Also known as a foul shot. The initial free throw is awarded when a player on the opposing team commits a foul.

Front court: The half of the court where the offensive team attempts to score. One team's front court is the other's back court, and vice versa. A team must cross the mid court line and enter its front court within ten seconds after possession begins.

Game clock: The clock that counts down the time remaining in the game. The clock runs down only while the ball is in play.

Goaltending: A violation that involves touching the ball during a field goal attempt while the ball is in its downward flight and the entire ball is above the level of the hoop. Basically, this violation prevents defensive players from leaping up to swat away shots right before they go into the basket.

Guard: One of the player positions. A team usually has two guards. Guards usually are the primary ball handlers and are often (but not always) the smallest players on the court. *Guard* also means to defend an offensive player.

Hack: Slang for a foul.

Held ball (or jump ball): Occurs when a defender places her hands so firmly on the ball that both the offensive and defensive player can claim possession of it. A held ball results in a jump ball or alternating possession situation. Also, when a defensive player ties up a player in midair.

Hole: Slang for basket, as in "take it to the hole."

Hoop: Slang for basket.

Hoops: Slang for basketball.

Hops: Slang for jumping ability.

H-O-R-S-E: A popular game in which one player makes a shot and his opponent must make the identical shot. Failure to do so results in gaining a letter (starting with "h").

Inbounds pass: A method of putting the ball in play from out of bounds. The player with the ball has five seconds in which to inbound it. The count starts when the official gives the player the ball and ends when the player releases the ball. On sideline inbounds plays and baseline inbounds plays after an opponent's violation, the in-bounder is subject to the laws of traveling. On inbounds plays following a basket, the thrower may run — without bouncing the ball — along the length of the baseline.

Intentional foul: A personal foul that's not a legitimate attempt to directly play the ball or a player. The fouled player shoots two free throws, and his team gets the ball.

Jump ball: A method of putting the ball into play by having an official toss it up between two opponents at midcourt. In pro hoops, jump balls are used to determine the outcome of all held-ball situations. At other levels, a jump ball is used only to start a game.

Jump shot: An aptly named shot where a player jumps in the air and shoots.

Lane: The rectangular area, usually painted, directly in front of each basket, extending out to the free throw line. Also known as "the paint."

Lay-up: A shot that occurs when a player dribbles toward the basket and shoots the ball from (or very near) the lane so that it caroms off the backboard and into the basket.

Man-to-man: A type of defense in which each player is responsible for guarding one player on the opposing team.

Motion offense: An offense in which all five players move at the same time in order to create scoring opportunities. Cynics might say that this is extinct in the NBA.

No-look pass: A pass attempted in which the passer deliberately does not make eye contact with, or looks in the opposite direction of, the intended receiver.

Offense: The team in possession of the ball. Also refers to the plays a team executes while in possession of the ball.

Officials: The referees, although the term may also be expanded to describe the scorer, shot-clock operator, and timekeeper.

One-and-one: A free throw situation in high school and college ball (not NBA) where a player shoots one free throw and is awarded another if the first is made. See also *bonus free throw*.

Outlet pass: The first pass made after a defensive rebound, usually designed to trigger a fast break.

Overtime: A five-minute session that is played when a game ends in a tie.

Paint: See *lane*.

Pass: Movement of the ball caused by a player throwing, batting, or deflecting the ball to another player.

Personal foul: A violation, committed by an active player, that involves illegal contact with an opponent while the ball is live.

Pick: A screen for the player with the ball. See also *screen*.

Pivot foot: A player who is holding, and not dribbling, the basketball must keep one foot anchored to the ground. This foot is known as the *pivot foot*.

Player control foul: In the men's game, a foul committed by the player who's in control of the ball. In the women's game, a foul committed by the player who is in control of the ball *or* by an airborne shooter. Often called an offensive foul or a charge.

Point guard: The primary ball-handling guard. This player usually directs the offense. See also *guard*.

Post: The general area on the outside border of the free throw lane. Low post is nearer to the basket; high post is nearer to the free throw line.

Rebound: Retrieval of a missed shot, which may hit the court first.

Rock: Slang for ball, as in "shoot the rock" or "pass the rock."

Run: Slang for game. On the street, "Wanna run?" means "Would you like to play a game?"

Screen: A legal action by an offensive player who, without initiating excessive contact or moving, delays or prevents an opponent from reaching the desired position.

Shot: An attempt to throw the ball into the basket to score.

Shot clock: A clock, separate from the game clock, that limits the amount of time the offense has to attempt a shot. For example, in men's college basketball, a team has 35 seconds to attempt a shot. If a shot is not taken in that time span, the ball is turned over to the opposing team. When the ball hits the basket rim or changes possession, the shot clock is reset.

Sideline: The lengthwise boundary of the court.

Slam dunk: A particularly emphatic dunk.

Strong side: The side of the court (right or left) where the ball is currently located. Not to be confused with frontcourt.

Substitute: To send in one player for another during a stoppage of play.

T: Slang for a technical foul.

Technical foul: A foul by any active or non-active player, coach, or team attendant that does not necessarily involve contact with an opponent. Technical fouls include unsportsmanlike conduct, acts of deceit, vulgarity, profanity, calling excessive time-outs, and hanging on the rim.

Three-pointer: A shot made from outside the three-point arc, worth three points.

Timeline: The line that splits the court in half; called the timeline because the offensive team must get the ball past half-court in ten seconds or less — failure to do so results in a violation (except in women's college basketball). Also known as the midcourt line or half court.

Timeout: Stoppage of play of a designated length. Either team may signal for a time-out when in possession of the ball. Time-outs are usually used to stop the clock or to discuss strategy.

Tipoff: To start a game, the ball is thrown in the air a referee, and a player from each team tries to bat the ball to a teammate.

Travel: A violation that occurs when the player with the basketball moves his feet illegally. Common examples include running without dribbling (taking more than two steps), dragging the pivot foot from its original spot, or jumping in the air and landing without shooting or passing the ball.

Trey: A slang term for a three-pointer.

Triangle offense: Type of offense made famous by professional coach Phil Jackson. The goal of the offense is to create good spacing between players and allows each one to pass to four teammates. Every pass and cut has a purpose, and everything is dictated by the defense.

Turnover: On offense, to lose the ball to the defense without taking a shot. Examples include losing the ball out of bounds, violations such as traveling or double dribbling, or the defense intercepting an errant pass.

21: A game in which any number of players can play. The player who has the ball attempts to score while all other players defend. A made shot results in two points, plus you are given up to three consecutive free throws, each worth one point.

Violation: An action that causes a team to lose possession of the ball, such as:

- **Traveling violations:** See *travel.*

- **Double dribbling violations:** See *double dribble.*

- **Three-second rule violation:** Remaining in your own team's free throw lane for three (or more) seconds.

- **Ten-second rule violation:** Taking ten (or more) seconds to advance the ball from the backcourt into the frontcourt.

- **Shot-clock violation:** Taking 35 (or more) seconds in men's college basketball, 30 seconds in women's college basketball, or 24 seconds in the NBA to attempt a shot.

- **Backcourt violation:** Bringing the ball into the backcourt after it enters the frontcourt.

- **Goaltending violation:** See *goaltending.*

- **Five-second rule violation:** Holding the ball in a closely guarded situation for five or more seconds.

Walk: A synonym for *travel,* a violation that NBA referees seem to think no longer exists.

Weakside: The area of the court (right or left) opposite the side the ball is currently on.

Wing: The area of the court on either side of the free throw line, outside the three-point arc.

Appendix B

Drilling the Basics

Offensive Drills

1-on-1 dribble, full court

Divide your team into two groups and line them up on the baseline. Have one player from each group dribble the ball the full length of the court and back, then pass the ball to the next player in line. Each time across the court, players should focus on something different. Have them practice the crossover dribble and the stop-go. Have them cross the court for speed, and then ask them to dribble with their weak hands (left hand for righties and vice versa).

Passing drill

Pair players off in center court. Have each pair practice the two-hand chest pass, the two-hand bounce pass, and the two-hand overhead pass. Then have players practice faking right and left with any two-hand pass.

Defend and recover drill

Defender 1 is guarding player 1. Player 1 passes to Player 2. Defender 1 turns around and defends Player 2. Player 2 then returns the pass to Player 1. In this drill, players do not simply pass the ball over Defender 1's head. On the contrary, Defender 1 must engage each player before the player makes a pass. Three sets of players can do this drill simultaneously. (See Figure B-1.)

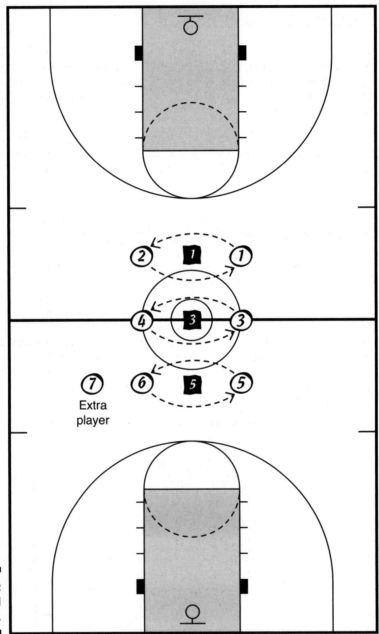

Figure B-1:
Defend and
recover drill.

3-man weave to layup

Divide your entire team into three groups and line them up on the baseline. The drill starts with Player 1 in the middle passing the ball to a streaking player on the right wing (Player 2). Player 1 follows her pass and runs to the right wing. Player 2 then hits Player 3, who started on the left wing and is now streaking down court.

Continue this weave — with each player running (not dribbling) — for the entire length of the court with the last player shooting a lay-up, simulating a fast-break. Make sure the kids shoot a left-hand lay-up from the left side and a right-hand lay-up from the right side.

Secondary break shooting drill

Divide your team into four groups, with two sets of players in each half-court. Create two lines on each half, one at center circle, one on the left wing.

The drill starts with a player dribbling from half-court to the top of the key (see Figure B-2). He makes a quick stop and passes to the player running in from the wing. That player takes a jump shot. The shooter follows in for the rebound and then passes the ball back to half-court. The first two players return to the back of the line. Continue the drill simultaneously at each end of the court for five minutes. Move the wing lines from side to side of the floor.

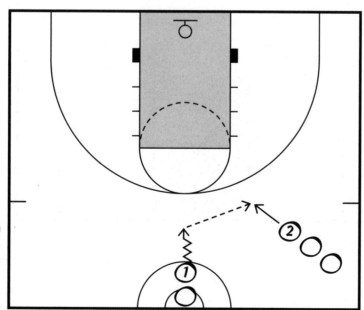

Figure B-2:
Secondary break shooting drill.

30-second shooting drill

This rapid-fire drill features two balls in motion at the same time. The drill starts with the passer, five feet behind the top of the key, passing to the shooter on the right or left wing (see Figure B-3). The shooter gives a ball fake and takes a jump shot. The rebounder blocks out, gets the rebound, and throws the ball back to the passer.

Run this drill simultaneously at each end of the court. Keep the players in one spot for 30 seconds and then move them to another spot on the floor.

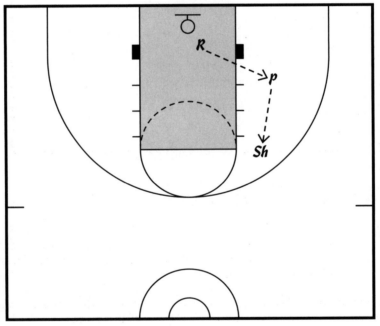

Figure B-3:
30-second
shooting
drill.

50-shot drill

Use three balls and three lines of players for this straight shooting drill. Each line takes 50 12-foot jump shots. Each player takes a shot, gets her own rebound, passes to the next player in line, and returns to the back of her line. (See Figure B-4.)

You need three coaches to monitor the number of shots attempted and made. Each line takes 50 shots. Give the group a goal to shoot for — say, 25 made shots out of the 50 attempted.

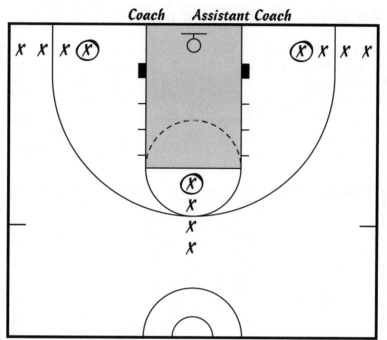

Two line shooting drill

Make two lines of offensive players on the wings. One at a time, the players drive to a spot on the wing and pull up for a jump shot over a defensive player. One player stays on defense until each person in the offensive line has taken a turn.

Have the two lines compete against each other — first team to make 10 shots wins. The losers have to sprint the length of the court.

Down screen, away screen drills

Screening is one of the basics to a successful offense. The sooner a child learns that basketball is not a game of one-on-one moves the better. The two screening drills shown are first executed without any defenders, then with defenders. (See Figure B-5.)

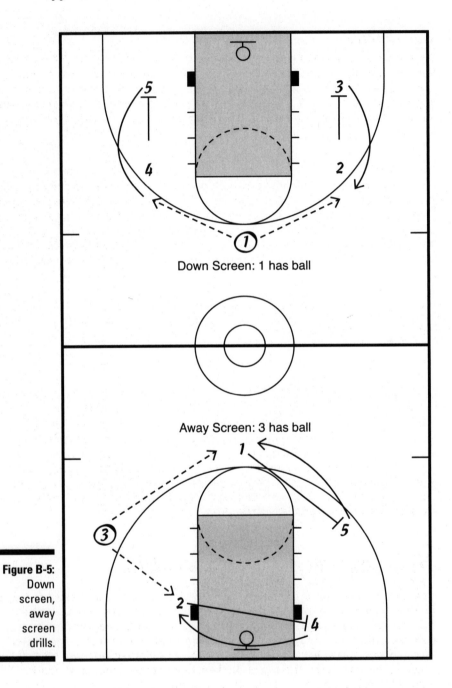

Down Screen: 1 has ball

Away Screen: 3 has ball

Figure B-5:
Down
screen,
away
screen
drills.

Down screens

The down screen drill begins with the point guard (1) handling the ball. She moves from side to side on the perimeter. When she moves right, 2 runs toward 3 and sets an imaginary pick. The 3 player runs off the screen and receives the ball from 1. She passes it back to 1, who moves to the other side of the court. Player 4 executes a down screen for 5, who comes up to meet the pass.

Away screens

In the second option, the players work on screening away from the ball. In this situation, 3 has the ball on the wing. The 2 player, on the baseline, moves away from 3, running across the lane to set a screen for 4, who comes across the lane to meet the ball from 3. In the next set, the point guard, 1, moves away from the ball to set a screen for 5, who comes to the top of the key to receive a pass. The process is repeated with defenders, as is the case in the down screen drill.

Defensive Drills

Defensive slide

This drill cuts to the very basics of man-to-man defense. To start, have all your players line up in two rows facing the coach. At a whistle or verbal command, the coach points back, left, right, or forward (in no particular order), and the players must move their feet in the direction that the coach points. Change the direction in rapid-fire succession to simulate how a player must react when guarding an offensive player. Run this drill for a total of five minutes in 30-second intervals.

Help and recover defense drill

This drill reviews another concept of team defense. When an offensive player beats one of your defensive teammates, you must do what you can to help out, or that offensive player will drive for a score. In the help and recover defense drill the four players, two on offense and two on defense, position themselves on the perimeter, approximately equidistant from the basket. Player 1 drives toward the top of the key, beating his defender. Defender 2, who is guarding Player 2, leaves his man temporarily to pick up Player 1. He must cut him off, then retreat to his original offensive player. Two sets of players, one on either side of the center court, perform this drill simultaneously (see Figure B-6).

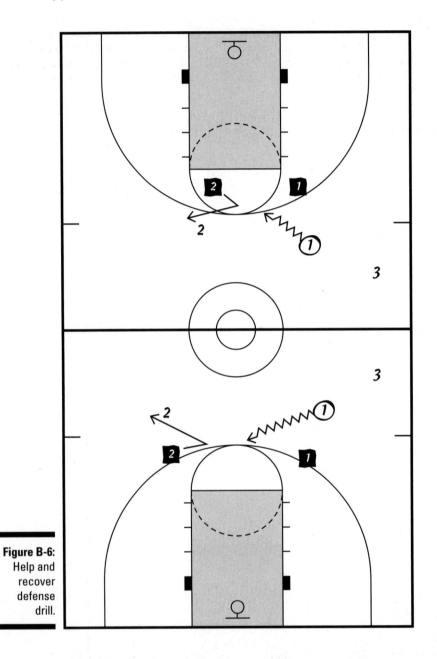

Figure B-6:
Help and
recover
defense
drill.

Backdoor drills — offense and defense

The backdoor play makes up one of the basic plays of basketball. A player is never too young to learn and execute it, offensively and defensively.

This drill requires a coach and four players, two on offense and two on defense (see Figure B-7). In Option 1, the coach fakes a backdoor pass to Player 2 and attempts to throw the ball to Player 3, who has come across from the weakside to receive a pass. Defender 3 must come to the foul line to try to cut off the pass for Player 3.

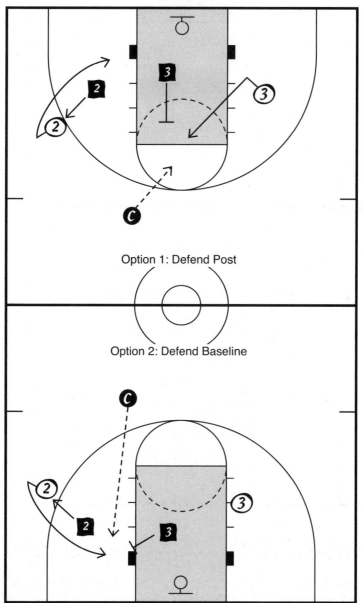

Figure B-7:
Backdoor
drills.

In Option 2, the coach has the ball on the left wing. Player 2 fakes toward the wing and then runs toward the basket, beating her defender. Defender 3 must now leave the middle of the lane and attempt to cut off the backdoor pass from the coach. Defender 3 must guard 2 until Defender 2 has a chance to recover. Defender 3 must yell "rotate" when she picks up Player 2 at the baseline. This drill also teaches the basics of defensive rotation.

Team defense drill

This drill teaches another concept of team defense by using eight players and a perimeter passing game. At the beginning, have your offensive players make at least six passes — slowly, so that you have time to show the defenders the proper position and floor balance. Tell all the defenders to get in proper position after each pass (see Figures B-8 and B-9).

The drill starts with the point guard (1) on the right wing. He passes to 2 (pass A). Offensive player 2 then passes to 4 in the corner (pass B). Meanwhile, the defenders are sliding and staying with their man. Player 4 then returns the pass to 2 (pass C), and 2 returns the ball to 1 on the perimeter (pass D). Player 1 then throws the ball on the right wing to offensive player 3 (pass E), and E returns the ball to 1 (pass F). The offense repeats this process at increasing speeds as the defensive players become more comfortable with their assignments.

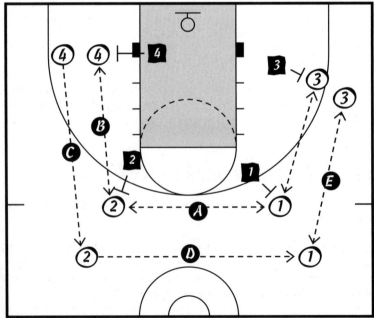

Figure B-8:
Team
defense
drill.

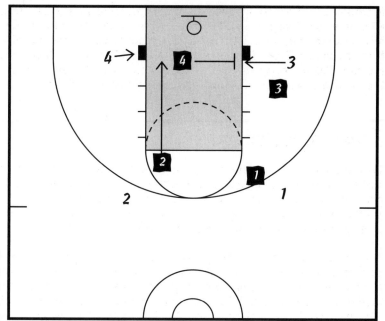

Figure B-9:
Defensive
rotation drill.

Defensive rotation drill

This four-on-four half-court drill teaches a basic tenet of team man-to-man defense. Start the ball on the right wing with offensive Player 1 in possession. Player 3 starts on the right baseline and beats his man, Defender 3, to the baseline. With the ball still on the right perimeter, Defender 4 leaves his man to pick up Player 3 to prevent him from making a lay-up.

When Defender 4 leaves his man, he yells "rotate," which signals Defender 2 to leave his man on the perimeter and pick up Player 4. All players should hold the new rotation until Defender 3 recovers.

Defending the screen drill

This drill, which uses just four players, works on defending the screen as well as setting screens offensively.

Start the drill with a coach holding the ball. After he blows the whistle, Player 2 sets a down screen on Defender 3. Defender 3 goes over the top (between the coach and Player 3) to deflect the coach's perimeter pass for Player 3. Defender 2 stays with Player 2 (see Figure B-10).

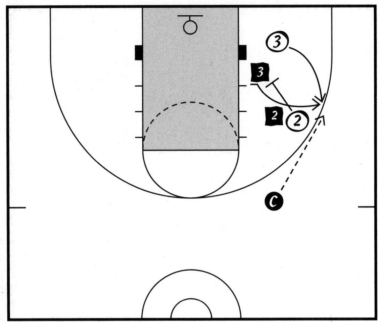

Figure B-10:
Defending
the screen
drill.

8-player rebounding drill

The 8-player rebound has two different drill options (see Figure B-11). Each drill focuses on strengthening different parts of the team.

Option 1: This rebounding drill requires two coaches and eight players, four on offense and four on defense. The drill begins with the two coaches passing the ball back and forth at the perimeter, which creates a live situation and makes the drill more interesting. One coach takes a shot, and the players practice boxing out and rebounding.

Option 2: This drill involves one coach and eight players. The drill starts with the coach taking a shot from the perimeter. When the ball is in the air, each defensive player makes immediate contact with his man (boxes him out), then chases the ball for the rebound. This drill strengthens individual- and team-rebounding concepts.

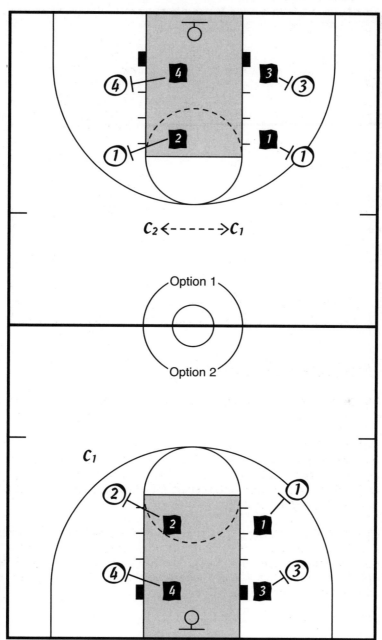

Perimeter shooting drill

The offensive team passes the ball around the perimeter against a man-to-man defense. Before the offensive players can take a shot, they must first make five passes with each player touching the ball. Have the offense take shots from the perimeter against the man-to-man defense and play live, complete with rebounds. Have players slide through all screens. You can also use this drill after you have taught zone defense, but I like to stress man-to-man principles when teaching the game to kids.

Fast-break drill

Eight players line up in a defensive set at one end of the court (see Figure B-12). A coach gives the ball to Defender 3 or Defender 4. The interior defensive players then become offensive players, and Defender 3 or 4 throws an outlet pass to Defender 2 or Defender 1, starting the fast break.

This drill accustoms players to changing from offense to defense. Coaches should keep score on each team's conversion of the fast breaks. Losers of the drill should run a touch-and-go drill. That is, the players start at the baseline, run to the foul line, and then run back again. Next, they run to half-court and back. Then they run to the opposite foul line and back. Finally, they run the full court and back.

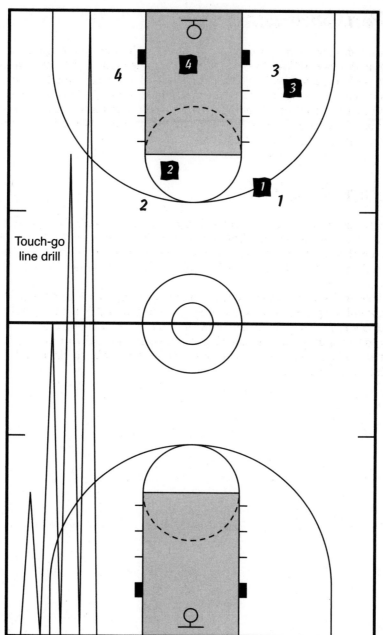

Touch-go
line drill

Figure B-12:
Fast-break
drill.

Index

• C •

• *K* •

Apple & Macs

iPad For Dummies
978-0-470-58027-1

iPhone For Dummies,
4th Edition
978-0-470-87870-5

MacBook For Dummies, 3rd
Edition
978-0-470-76918-8

Mac OS X Snow Leopard For
Dummies
978-0-470-43543-4

Business

Bookkeeping For Dummies
978-0-7645-9848-7

Job Interviews
For Dummies,
3rd Edition
978-0-470-17748-8

Resumes For Dummies,
5th Edition
978-0-470-08037-5

Starting an
Online Business
For Dummies,
6th Edition
978-0-470-60210-2

Stock Investing
For Dummies,
3rd Edition
978-0-470-40114-9

Successful
Time Management
For Dummies
978-0-470-29034-7

Computer Hardware

BlackBerry
For Dummies,
4th Edition
978-0-470-60700-8

Computers For Seniors
For Dummies,
2nd Edition
978-0-470-53483-0

PCs For Dummies,
Windows
7 Edition
978-0-470-46542-4

Laptops For Dummies,
4th Edition
978-0-470-57829-2

Cooking & Entertaining

Cooking Basics
For Dummies,
3rd Edition
978-0-7645-7206-7

Wine For Dummies,
4th Edition
978-0-470-04579-4

Diet & Nutrition

Dieting For Dummies,
2nd Edition
978-0-7645-4149-0

Nutrition For Dummies,
4th Edition
978-0-471-79868-2

Weight Training
For Dummies,
3rd Edition
978-0-471-76845-6

Digital Photography

Digital SLR Cameras &
Photography For Dummies,
3rd Edition
978-0-470-46606-3

Photoshop Elements 8
For Dummies
978-0-470-52967-6

Gardening

Gardening Basics
For Dummies
978-0-470-03749-2

Organic Gardening
For Dummies,
2nd Edition
978-0-470-43067-5

Green/Sustainable

Raising Chickens
For Dummies
978-0-470-46544-8

Green Cleaning
For Dummies
978-0-470-39106-8

Health

Diabetes For Dummies,
3rd Edition
978-0-470-27086-8

Food Allergies
For Dummies
978-0-470-09584-3

Living Gluten-Free
For Dummies,
2nd Edition
978-0-470-58589-4

Hobbies/General

Chess For Dummies,
2nd Edition
978-0-7645-8404-6

Drawing
Cartoons & Comics
For Dummies
978-0-470-42683-8

Knitting For Dummies,
2nd Edition
978-0-470-28747-7

Organizing
For Dummies
978-0-7645-5300-4

Su Doku For Dummies
978-0-470-01892-7

Home Improvement

Home Maintenance
For Dummies,
2nd Edition
978-0-470-43063-7

Home Theater
For Dummies,
3rd Edition
978-0-470-41189-6

Living the
Country Lifestyle
All-in-One
For Dummies
978-0-470-43061-3

Solar Power Your Home
For Dummies,
2nd Edition
978-0-470-59678-4

Internet

Blogging For Dummies,
3rd Edition
978-0-470-61996-4

eBay For Dummies,
6th Edition
978-0-470-49741-8

Facebook For Dummies,
3rd Edition
978-0-470-87804-0

Web Marketing
For Dummies,
2nd Edition
978-0-470-37181-7

WordPress
For Dummies,
3rd Edition
978-0-470-59274-8

Language & Foreign Language

French For Dummies
978-0-7645-5193-2

Italian Phrases
For Dummies
978-0-7645-7203-6

Spanish For Dummies,
2nd Edition
978-0-470-87855-2

Spanish
For Dummies,
Audio Set
978-0-470-09585-0

Math & Science

Algebra I
For Dummies,
2nd Edition
978-0-470-55964-2

Biology For Dummies,
2nd Edition
978-0-470-59875-7

Calculus For Dummies
978-0-7645-2498-1

Chemistry For Dummies
978-0-7645-5430-8

Microsoft Office

Excel 2010 For Dummies
978-0-470-48953-6

Office 2010 All-in-One
For Dummies
978-0-470-49748-7

Office 2010 For Dummies,
Book + DVD Bundle
978-0-470-62698-6

Word 2010 For Dummies
978-0-470-48772-3

Music

Guitar For Dummies,
2nd Edition
978-0-7645-9904-0

iPod & iTunes For
Dummies, 8th Edition
978-0-470-87871-2

Piano Exercises
For Dummies
978-0-470-38765-8

Parenting & Education

Parenting For Dummies,
2nd Edition
978-0-7645-5418-6

Type 1 Diabetes
For Dummies
978-0-470-17811-9

Pets

Cats For Dummies,
2nd Edition
978-0-7645-5275-5

Dog Training For Dummies,
3rd Edition
978-0-470-60029-0

Puppies For Dummies,
2nd Edition
978-0-470-03717-1

Religion & Inspiration

The Bible For Dummies
978-0-7645-5296-0

Catholicism For Dummies
978-0-7645-5391-2

Women in the Bible
For Dummies
978-0-7645-8475-6

Self-Help & Relationship

Anger Management
For Dummies
978-0-470-03715-7

Overcoming Anxiety
For Dummies,
2nd Edition
978-0-470-57441-6

Sports

Baseball
For Dummies,
3rd Edition
978-0-7645-7537-2

Basketball
For Dummies,
2nd Edition
978-0-7645-5248-9

Golf For Dummies,
3rd Edition
978-0-471-76871-5

Web Development

Web Design
All-in-One
For Dummies
978-0-470-41796-6

Web Sites
Do-It-Yourself
For Dummies,
2nd Edition
978-0-470-56520-9

Windows 7

Windows 7
For Dummies
978-0-470-49743-2

Windows 7
For Dummies,
Book + DVD Bundle
978-0-470-52398-8

Windows 7 All-in-One
For Dummies
978-0-470-48763-1

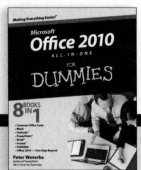

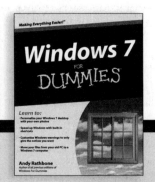

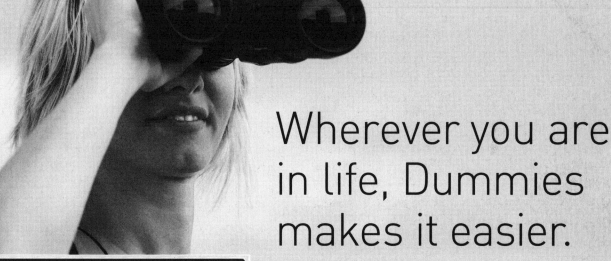

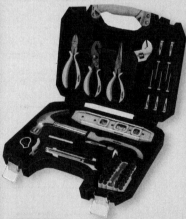

Notes

Notes